Management and Managing: Leadership in the NHS

Second Edition

Michael Walton

Ph.D., C. Psychol.

Stanley Thornes (Publishers) Ltd

First published in 1984 by Harper & Row

Second edition published in 1997 by:
Stanley Thornes (Publishers) Ltd
Ellenborough House
Wellington Street
CHELTENHAM
GL50 1YW
UK

97 98 99 00 01 / 10 9 8 7 6 5 4 3 2 1

A catalogue record for this book is available from the British Library.

ISBN 0 7487 3324 8

Typeset by Columns Design Ltd, Reading
Printed and bound in Great Britain by Scotprint, Musselburgh

Contents

Dedication

This book is dedicated to the following important people in my life, each of whom gave me something vital, something different – all of it needed:

- Dinky Payne, there right at the very start when I needed it most;
- Brenda and Alec Pollard, picking up the pieces and helping me;
- Dr Hornstein, a giant of a mentor and a believer in me; and
- Frances, who made all the difference, and still does.

Introduction

This book will support you in your work as a professional carer and help you to cope with the many varied and stressful pressures that you encounter through working in health care settings. The health care sector is a changing and challenging place to be and has its own dramatic pleasures and pains. All too often, however, these are insufficiently explored or, in some cases, not allowed to be mentioned, let alone discussed and the only acceptable focus for consideration may be the next task to be completed or the need to attend to some currently outstanding request. It can happen – and frequently does – that both patients and carers are somehow moved to the periphery of attention because centre stage is taken up by the process of getting the job done.

This book focuses on the non-clinical aspects of the professional role of the nurse. It combines insights from management studies, historical perspectives on the origins of the NHS, the dynamics of working in a health care setting, and some of the core ideas involved in managing a business.

Above all else this book aims to build on and extend the ideas presented in the first edition without seeking to cover everything or to overcomplicate. One of the prompts for the second edition is the need for a book which alerts and informs the practising nurse about the sorts of non-clinical issues and dilemmas likely to be encountered in the late 1990s.

Specifically this book seeks to:

- provide knowledge and information about 'management' ideas
- encourage readers to draw upon personal experience and to integrate that experience into the contents of the book
- stimulate readers to make use of the ideas presented here, by combining them with personal experience to develop one's personal theories of management and of managing
- help readers become clearer about what managing and management in the NHS means and to become clearer about their own personal styles in order to become stronger and more prepared to face up to the challenge of management and leadership in the NHS.

What we know about the NHS in the 1990s is that:

- the pressure is on to perform to more visible performance criteria
- the scope for mis-information has increased
- the time and speed of response has heightened
- there is more information available and hence scope for confusion
- health organizations have become more 'defensive'
- there is more intrusive media attention and overt press criticism

- many professional 'closed doors' have been removed
- the sanctity of professional carers has diminished
- there is greater awareness of patients' rights
- the fallibility of professionals has been exposed
- the incidence of litigation has increased
- there has been a de-mystification of health care
- patients are more informed and likely to be more demanding.

The impact of such changes has made health professionals more vulnerable to external scrutiny of their personal and professional practice. Health professionals are now more exposed to methods of inquiry and public reporting that may be inappropriate to the investigation of health care performance. There is potential for a double shock: firstly, an erosion of the privileged status of health workers in the eyes of the general public; secondly, the application of business performance criteria from the non-health sector which may sit uneasily with working practices and norms in health care.

In the light of these changes there are a number of issues currently not covered by conventional training which health professionals now need to consider, for example:

- how organizations operate in practice rather than how management theory says they do
- how we manage ourselves at work
- the nature of management and business practice in health care organizations.

This book is intended to be practical, user-friendly and enjoyable to read. It provides managers and carers with the opportunity to relate the ideas presented to their own personal situations and to think about their job, and what goes on at work, in a more dynamic way.

Many elegant management theories have been proposed over the years but they are often difficult to apply in the real world as they rarely describe accurately the chaotic and untidy world of work as encountered by managers. What they seem to lack is the reality, for example, of being on a ward, attending a case review, trying to get the bloods back on time, or trying politely to tell senior colleagues when their judgement is wrong. There is a lack of simple, robust and practical ideas that carers and managers can apply to the work situations they encounter day in and day out. The aim of this book is to offer practical ideas and perspectives which managers and carers can apply in practice to help them in their work.

DIFFERENT MANAGERS, DIFFERENT STYLES

There is no one way to be an effective manager. However, all managers can benefit by thinking about how they function and by identifying other options and ways of managing which are different from those habitually used. Decisions about changing particular ways of working should be personal ones. They are influenced by seeing how other people do things more effectively, by reading about ideas which seem to have relevance and by reviewing and reflecting on recent events or situations to elicit clues about the need to change current ways of working.

It is all too easy to become frustrated and angered by others because they see and do things differently and much time can be spent in trying to make others see and do things the 'right' (i.e. 'my') way. It is however far more productive to acknowledge that different ways of behaving and working exist and to use such differences to create more caring, productive and mutually beneficial outcomes.

THE WORK–HOME SPLIT

One of the most significant benefits which can emerge from considering one's managing style is its relevance to one's total life behaviour. Professional roles influence work behaviour and the difference between a person's behaviour at home and at work can be very different. Even so there is generally enough of the whole individual showing through at work for others to get a reasonably accurate sense of who that individual might be outside the work setting.

There is a difficult balance to be struck between merging too fully with the job and only viewing it instrumentally as something to be done without any personal investment in it whatsoever.

One of the aims of this book is to help you to relate more fully – as yourself – to the job and to reach a comfortable balance between you-at-work and you-outside-work. Most of the ideas and exercises presented are also relevant to your home life activities, and can be shared with relatives, family and friends.

At various points in the book you might get more out of the material by talking the ideas through with colleagues or by seeing how your views are similar to or different from those of others around you. Do please remember to respect the views and information which others give you in the course of using this book: remember that others have as much right to their opinion as you have to your own. If you do pick up differences, you might like to clarify why this might be so since doing so will give you with even more data to use.

A key responsibility of management is that of diagnosing the presenting situation, identifying the nature of the differences which exist between people and then responding in ways which allow the issues diagnosed to be fruitfully addressed. A key to doing this is through enhancing your ability to learn from your experiences so that you can be better informed and better prepared for the future. This book provides you with many opportunities to track back to what you have done in the past and to review it so that you can learn even more about why some things worked well for you and why other things did not.

WHAT DO YOU LEARN FROM OTHERS?

We are constantly faced with opportunities for learning yet it seems that we choose not to make use of these opportunities as often as we might. This may be because of the effort involved, the fear of what might then emerge about ourselves, a lack of personal insight, or a mixture of all of these. Many of us too frequently turn off the 'learning going on' switch. It is not surprising therefore that we find ourselves repeatedly in situations we would rather avoid or which we wish somehow would turn out differently this time.

Unsatisfactory experiences are often repeated if we do not take care. But we can choose to make more use of the many learning opportunities that surround us at work and then implement the additional insights we have gained.

Learning and change are accelerated by pulling together our actual experiences and the processes that we use to think about them. Kolb (1974) suggests that we learn through a sequence of activities which are related and complementary. His learning style and problem-solving model has become well known over the past 20 years and it provides a valuable framework for learning from everyday experience. The model comprises four stages:

1. an experience
2. observations and reflections about that experience
3. a theoretical proposition about the event
4. active experimentation and testing – by further action – of the accuracy of the theoretical view of what has happened; in turn this further action sets off the cycle (or spiral) of learning once again.

In the UK these ideas have been extended and popularized by Peter Honey and Alan Mumford (1986) amongst others. The successful learner in life needs to be able to attend well enough to each of the four steps identified above. Unfortunately we tend not to pay enough attention to developing each of the different skills required by each of these four styles.

Kolb's model can be applied to nurse training. For example, nursing is predominantly a practical profession, hence a large part of the training, at least in the early days, is concerned with teaching the nurse learner to carry out practical procedures. As the training progresses it becomes quite clear that the application of nursing procedures alone is inadequate to secure effective health care, and the learner nurse will increasingly pay attention to interpreting the effect her work has on patients, relatives and colleagues. And so the spiral of learning goes on.

This book suggests possible ways of looking again at – and of learning – what goes on at work and in the process enables health care professionals to improve their practice and their care of others. The book provides opportunities for the reader to apply Kolb's ideas about learning from experience.

To gain the most benefit from this book you need to be prepared to:

• consider more closely what you do
• challenge your theories about personal motivation and effectiveness
• examine the unstated assumptions you work by
• consider how others around you operate

- adapt and apply the ideas presented to your continuing professional development.

It is not essential to agree wholeheartedly with all the ideas presented in the book, nor to accept that what is suggested here is 'right' for you: it is for you to make up your own mind about such things. Do, however, use the pointers and perspectives described as a stimulus to reappraise your situation in the widest sense and, from such a review, to come to a more informed appreciation of yourself, of those around you, and of the dynamics of the different settings in which you work.

MANAGEMENT AND HEALTH CARE

The 1990s have been a period of considerable change for the NHS: a period of ever-increasing external scrutiny, continuing pressure for resources and widespread alteration to the fabric of the Service following the 1992 Act.

These are trying times too for the Department of Health who has the statutory responsibility for the NHS, the NHS Executive and those who hold Chief Executive and other senior positions throughout the Service. Transitions are difficult by definition because they demand that we give up something that is known and familiar – even if it wasn't working properly – and allow the introduction of something that is new, different and unfamiliar. This generates tension; it creates anxiety and often causes reactions against whatever changes are being made.

There is a great deal of confusion about management within the Health Service. For example, as soon as professionals start going up the hierarchy and the word 'officer' is attached, it seems suddenly to be expected that they will know the answers to a frighteningly large range of problems. The reality is different, but this impression can cause considerable distress and anxiety to those in managerial posts.

It could be said that the term 'managing', as opposed to 'management', is more appropriate for the work situation. 'Managing' in this sense is concerned with:

- getting along with the resources that you have
- handling anticipated difficulties
- dealing with unexpected difficulties.

This concept of managing also takes account of the fact that we rarely get everything we want from a situation, and that handling it successfully is a question of achieving the most that can be achieved in the circumstances. There is no suggestion here that the individual is not trying, or is incapable of competent, comprehensive action – it is simply a more realistic way of thinking about managerial responsibilities and how they can be handled.

MANAGING AND A NON-STATIC WORLD

Whilst life might be simpler if things always remained the same, this clearly is not the case, nor will it be in the future. The ever-changing pace of life in health care settings raises important issues so far as managing and coping are concerned. In our everyday work we need to consider such questions as:

- Are the decisions, assumptions, etc., that I made yesterday still relevant today?
- Am I dealing with different people today?
- What is my most important task today?
- What has happened since I last reviewed the situation?
- Whose priorities am I now trying to meet?
- How do I feel today, and will this affect my work?
- Has the main purpose of my job changed?
- What expectations do people have of me, and how are they changing in the light of our work together?
- What has happened that I do not know about?

The list can go on and on, but these types of question and, importantly, the responses which they prompt, can be very helpful in considering the relevance and usefulness of the work you do.

 As an example you might like to think of your job and some of the specific tasks you do, and how you do them. Make a note of a few of these and check:

a. whether you think they are still relevant
b. whether the ways they are done are still appropriate.

Consider also the criteria against which you are making these assessments.

The results of this exercise may prompt you to question the relevance of continuing some current practices because, for example, of changing, or changed, priorities and circumstances since they were first introduced. There may be parts of your job as currently undertaken which are no longer necessary: by discarding these you will save time and effort which can be re-allocated to more valuable work. It may also have become clear that there are other aspects of your work which are demanding an increasing amount of your time and that this now needs to be formally acknowledged and recognized.

MANAGING: A LIFE SKILL

Some people have considerable difficulty in deciding how to behave when at work. It can be as if their personality at work has to be different from the way they are outside their place of work. Whilst there are differences in how one needs to behave, how much a person adjusts their behaviour for work will depend on the precise nature of their work role. Too great a contrast between the work and the non-work 'personalities' may cause undue personal stress and result in harm, however, not only to that person, but to those around them.

The point about managing as a 'life skill' is that we are all managers in the sense of managing our own lives. We are all engaged in managerial decision-making (about ourselves) continually. Some of these managerial decisions are to do with work; the remainder concern non-work activities and choices. It is hoped that you will see a wider relevance in the ideas and exercises presented in this edition and that you will find them useful both in the work context and elsewhere.

HOW TO USE THIS BOOK

Overall my advice is to use this book to search for clues and ideas that you can build upon to meet the challenges and issues confronting you. Do not try to find solutions or ideas that will work unfailingly, or that can be applied to every situation confronting you. There are no 'golden rules' of management: you have to develop your ability to assess a situation and then create the most appropriate adaptive response you can to meet the demands of that case at that time.

There are some suggestions which it is possible to make, but each of us has to work out his or her own personal best ways of being effective. It is hoped that this book will help you set out on , or continue, that very personal journey.

It is intended that you will feel able to use the book as your own personal workbook in order to record your views, thoughts, perspectives and biases at particular points in time. One way to do this – rather than writing on the book itself – is to keep a notebook handy in which to note down your thoughts, observations, experiences and intentions as you go through the book. Keep the material you produce, and remember that it is always helpful to date it: few of us stay the same as the years progress, and it can be very interesting to review how you thought three, four or five years ago on any particular matter.

In this way, you will be able to use the book again and again, not only to remind yourself about some of the issues raised, but to extend and develop them further to make them your own.

Remain sceptical! I am rarely prepared to accept everything I read, and I often amend or adapt what is presented to me, on the basis of my experience and self-knowledge. I hope that you will feel free to do the same.

The ideas set out in the following chapters can be used to provide the basis for study days or reviews of current managerial practice, and you can use them to provide the outline framework for discussions on management topics with colleagues. Many of the tasks and activities described are for individual use but can also be used with colleagues.

I have drawn on and referred to ideas which I believe to be valid and useful; many of them are my own. I have not attempted to be comprehensive:

one of my greatest problems has been deciding what to include and what to leave out. I hope you enjoy the book and come to see it as a friend you can turn to for guidance and illumination.

REFERENCES

Kolb, D. (1974) On management and the learning process, in Kolb, Rubin and McIntyre (eds) *Organizational Psychology,* Prentice-Hall, New York.

Honey, P. and Mumford, A. (1986) *Using Your Learning Styles*, Honey, Maidenhead.

Managing within Health Organizations

Part One briefly outlines the inception and development of the NHS and introduces some key concepts about management and leadership in organizations. It sets out the broader context within which you work and introduces several starting points for you to explore and apply to your own practice.

Since the early 1970s the NHS has been in almost continuous flux and has been subject to imposed external structural changes that have:

- substantially altered its managerial infrastructure
- altered the interrelationships between health care professions and staff groups
- introduced a competitive internal market
- put to the test – some would say to breaking point – a philosophy of clinical need rather than resource availability.

All this adds up to institutional, professional and political change on a massive scale, propelled through the Service by the weight of the government departments, the regional structure and pressure on public expenditure.

The objective rationality of, for example, 'Care in the Community' and the introduction of a general management ethos (NHS Management Inquiry, 1983) are understandable in themselves and make 'sense'. Yet they were resisted, reinterpreted, resented and repelled by many. In response to such challenges the changes were reiterated, imposed and forced onto a largely unwilling Service.

In spite of the good intentions – not to mention the 'man-years' of planning and working things through – not all the imposed changes have gone according to plan. The position is further complicated because the architects of change are rarely the implementors of the plans and ideas proposed. There often appears to be quite a gap between the neat and tidy way change is explained in the abstract from often messy, confusing and problematic experience in practice. Problems sometimes arise because change is discussed 'as if' the organization (i.e. department, team, function, hospital, etc.) was a passive entity ready and willing to embrace the new changes 'just like that'.

There may be a misplaced optimism, an arrogance at times, by the instigators of change in organizations who 'know' what the problems are and who 'know' therefore what needs to be done without engaging the wisdom and experience of those in the field.

One of the potential traps of strategic change planning is underplaying the significance of the emotional reactions generated by the threat of organization change. There is no emotional neutrality so far as change is concerned. As soon as it is realized that one's personal position and role could become affected there will be an emotional reaction generated.

What is also apparent is that processes of change in individuals and organizations are *not* solely rational or logical processes; other influential emotionally-based processes come into play.

In summary:

- Logical rational initiatives will often be resisted if they mean change to the current arrangements.
- True views and feelings are not always expressed.
- In collective settings collective wisdom can result in collective foolishness.
- After the event we are not always clear about why we acted as we did.
- Change means disruption to many and implies a criticism of past performance.

No matter how careful, thoughtful, bright, genuine and far-sighted the instigators of change may be, unless they tap into such non-logically oriented facets of change their best efforts are likely to be frustrated, misconstrued and resisted. Bringing about change is a mixed up and complicated affair because of the implications for personal security, personal competence and personal meaning, and because of the anxiety it raises for those affected.

It is in the careful and free-ranging discussions about implementation of the proposed changes that success or frustration, and possibly failure rest. Good ideas will not of themselves be destined to succeed without a very thorough and far reaching working through of what the changes will 'mean' to those affected. Often this is inadequately done.

What is clear is that change, however it may be resented, is with us. One of the challenges which carers and managers face is how to enhance their abilities to cope with change at a personal level, departmentally, for the profession and for the NHS as a whole.

Adapting to change and changing our views on things we have come to feel definite about can be very difficult. We have to be prepared to listen and consider what others are telling us. Putting one's head in the sand, is not a viable option: the opportunity exists for exploring, contesting, developing and building on the changes under consideration.

This book offers perspectives and ideas for you to use in doing just this. It is with such thoughts in mind that we now move into Chapter 1 and an overview of the evolving NHS.

Historical perspectives on the NHS

1

On seeing new patients for the first time there is relatively little information to hand. You will notice – and have been trained to see and categorize – a range of external phenomena which you use as a guide to your next steps. One of the breakthroughs to a closer understanding and appreciation of the patient – and consequently to arriving at a more informed assessment and diagnosis – arises when you begin to piece together their history and how they have reached you.

The patient's history and unique symptomatology will:

- alert you to the particular significance of the symptoms
- prepare you for the type of expectations the patient may have
- alert you to the patient's likely reactions to proposed treatment plans because of past treatments
- set you thinking about future needs because of health patterns in the patient's extended family.

Too much of an emphasis on what has gone before can over-burden, confuse and blind you to the current needs of the patient. However, knowledge of these antecedent conditions will add to your understanding of the patient. How you 'take' a patient's history is likely to be interpreted by that patient as an early indicator of how she or he may come to believe you will care for them.

As with patients so it is with organizations too. An understanding of how the organization has arrived at its current position can help you to tune in more closely to what is going on today, organizationally speaking. An understanding of the origins, influential local figures and pressures provides a historical basis for looking at how situations have arisen over time. This awareness may give clues about options for managing the present more successfully and about changing things for the future.

'Taking the history' of an organization is not the same, of course, as taking the history of a patient but what you can do is to take a little time to find out how your part of the organization has evolved to its current position. You can then look at the wider organization within which your ward or clinic, for example, is based and get an overall sense of how it all fits together. Of course, different versions of 'history' are likely to be given depending on whom you ask. Your job though is to piece them all together and see how it turns out. Collecting this information about your organization – as with patients – can bring insight, surprise and confusion. Overall you will probably find that in doing this you will have a far better idea than previously about your organization and of where you fit in.

The NHS has an interesting history and an overview of this can put into perspective the current changes and explain what is going on, and how that affects you at work.

INCEPTION OF THE NHS

Following the passing of the National Health Service Act of 1946 the NHS came into being on 5 July 1948. The legislation required the Minister of Health 'to promote the establishment of a comprehensive health service designed to secure improvement in the physical and mental health of the people and the prevention, diagnosis and treatment of illness, and for that purpose to provide or secure the effective provision of resources'.

It remains a huge organization – one of the largest in the world. It is difficult to manage, increasingly costly to fund, and one where there will inevitably be variations in the range of services available between places. One of the difficulties facing the Management Executive is that of how to influence the changing shape of local services in order to achieve a good enough measure of provision uniformly across the country.

Providing a comprehensive health service for all was an enormous commitment and undertaking. The arrangements set up were not fully integrated as part of a cohesive whole. The new National Health Service was split between the three service sectors of:

- hospital services
- primary care
- local authority services.

It was the hospital sector that held the highest profile in the attention of many, received most attention, was able to mobilize clinical opinion in debates, and – not surprisingly – had by far the largest budget.

In contrast to the concentration of services within a physically bounded hospital site, the GP network was by comparison diffuse, fragmented and inhabited largely by sole medical practitioners focusing primarily on the delivery of their services and care to those on their list out in the community.

Local authority medical services were directed by the local authority's Medical Officer of Health focusing primarily on matters of public and environmental health and hygiene. Their emphasis was on sickness prevention rather than the hospitals and GPs who were primarily concerned with treating and curing the sick.

It was not until the 1974 reorganization – over 25 years after the inception of the Service – that moves were formally initiated to integrate more fully these three strands of nation-wide health care provision.

The structure set up by the 1948 Act is shown in Figure 1.1.

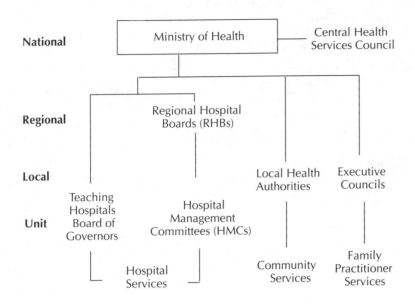

Figure 1.1 The NHS structure, 1948–74

The 1974 reorganization outlined a more integrated and streamlined NHS. It involved pushing together hospital and community-based services, but those in General Practice remained outside the new Health Authorities. Legislation made provision for them to be members of the new management teams, however. At the time this seemed to generate interest and tension within the hospital sector: they were an unknown factor and this caused anxiety.

The 1974 legislation created Area Health Authorities, each having jurisdiction over one or more Health Districts. The District General Hospital was the centrepiece for the integration of local health services. Each Health District was managed by a District Management Team, which for the first time included two elected medical representatives – a hospital consultant and a GP – in addition to a formally appointed District Medical Officer. The former local authority Medical Officer of Health services were disbanded and integrated within the new Health Authorities.

In the primary care sector however GPs remained separately funded and were serviced under a local Family Practitioner Committee which generally served the same patient catchment area as the Health Authority. An elected GP member was appointed to each District Management Team.

Figure 1.2 shows how the new structure looked.

The Area Health Authorities (AHAs) reported into Regional Health Authorities (RHAs) which in turn reported into the Department of Health and Social Security (DHSS) and an elaborate system of planning committees was introduced.

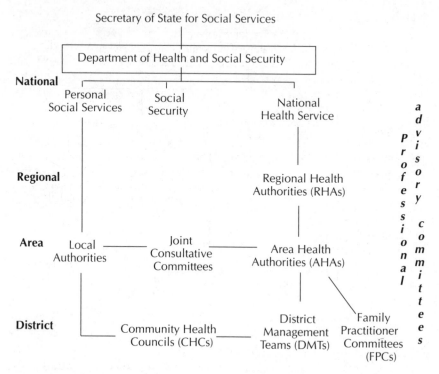

Figure 1.2 The reorganized NHS in 1974 (simplified)

The Area Health Authorities were replaced in 1982 by approximately 200 District Health Authorities (DHAs) which were given more autonomy in planning services for their patient catchment area. Annual Performance Reviews were introduced which imposed centrally-determined targets and outputs. This constrained the relative autonomy of DHAs.

Increasing pressures on the central budget led to a more determined assault on the financial management of the Service and a Government wish to apply approaches, experience and insights from outside the public sector to the organization and management of the NHS.

THE GRIFFITHS REPORT

Roy Griffiths was invited 'to give advice on the effective use and management of manpower and related resources' in the Service. His team saw the need for a greater integration of health care services and priorities at all levels towards the achievement of defined targets and goals. They described what they saw as the lack of a general management process (NHS Management Inquiry, 1983).

The recommendations of the Griffiths Report aimed to remedy this through the introduction of a general management structure and philosophy throughout the NHS. There would be an NHS Management Board to take overall managerial responsibility for the service. Effectively a performance management culture was to be introduced: the NHS would be run, and its performance assessed, as a business.

General Managers were appointed at Regional, District and Unit level and were responsible for the leadership and management of their organizations and the introduction of a general management process and philosophy throughout the Service.

Consensus decision-making – one of the cornerstones of 1974 – would go: competitive tendering was introduced. The cost efficiency and effectiveness of in-house services such as catering, laundry, cleaning and the automatic dependence by hospitals on these internal 'hotel' services would be thrown open to competition to non-NHS providers of such services. These were major changes and they marked a watershed in how the NHS was viewed and how it was to be managed.

THE INTERNAL MARKET: PURCHASERS AND PROVIDERS

The late 1980s saw an even more radical review in the thinking about the NHS and its workings. An internal market (i.e. competition for the provision of clinical services and health care provision overall) was created to stimulate the efficiency and effectiveness of health care services at their point of delivery. This change profoundly shook the NHS. The method selected to do this was to separate out those who:

• were responsible for ensuring that the health needs of their population were properly provided for, i.e. the *purchasers*

from those who:

• were responsible for providing the care services to patients and clients at the point of care delivery, i.e. the *providers*.

'Purchasing' decisions would be made by the District Health Authorities and by GPs who had successfully applied to manage their own budgets (GP fund-holders or GPFHs). Providers – the hospitals, clinics and community-based services – would then contract with Purchasers to provide the levels of services required as formalized in the service level contract. Purchasers (DHAs and GPFHs) would be able to choose where to put their business. The Providers chosen were not required to be in the same geographical area although clearly they would need to guarantee to provide any services that had been contracted.

The management of clinical budgets and doctors-in-management were seen as critical dimensions of the overall package of changes introduced. Clinical Directorates were set up to integrate the work within medical departments and to encourage collective medical responsibility for providing the range of medical services agreed and budgeted for with the Trust Board.

The outline structure of the current NHS structure is shown in Figure 1.3.

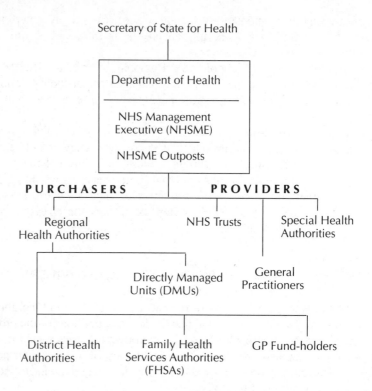

Figure 1.3 The structure of the NHS, 1993

THE NEW MANAGEMENT ARRANGEMENTS

Significant changes were made in April 1996 to the structure of the NHS. The main changes were:

- the abolition of Regional Health Authorities
- the replacement of RHAs by eight regional offices of the NHS Executive (no longer called the NHSME)
- the creation of larger health 'commissioning agencies' charged with integrating the work of the former DHAs and FHSAs.

Figure 1.4 shows the current structure.

One of the changes now in place is the formation of larger purchasing agencies through the merging of District Health Authorities (DHAs) and Family Health Services Authorities (FHSAs) to form unified Health Agencies or Health Commissions. These new supra-purchasers, of which there are to be about 100, have three primary roles of:

- strategy
- monitoring
- support.

In addition they are required to work more closely with GP Fund-holding Practices in carrying out their purchasing functions.

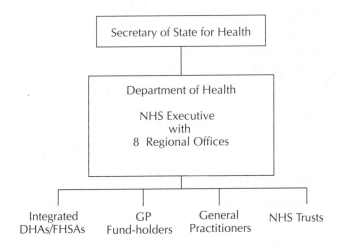

Figure 1.4 The current structure of the NHS (wef 1996)

THE AUDIT COMMISSION

Formed as a result of the 1982 Local Government Finance Act, the Commission's responsibilities were extended through the NHS and Community Care Act of 1990 to include the NHS. Its main responsibilities are the appointment of external auditors and the promotion of economy, efficiency and effectiveness in local government and the NHS.

In addition to its statutory audit responsibilities, the Audit Commission impacts on the service by focusing on selected topics deemed to be in need of attention or where, perhaps through its continuing audit work, significant variations in performance and expenditure between Trusts, etc. have been identified. It then undertakes a more detailed review of these areas and tests its ideas and research within the NHS.

Too little attention was given to the anxiety-provoking impact that such actions can have on health care professional staff if they see themselves disadvantageously positioned in league tables.

MANAGEMENT WITHIN THE NURSING PROFESSION

The organization of nursing management has also had its fair share of changes over the years. In 1966 the Salmon Report was set up to inquire into 'the senior nursing staff structure in the hospital service, the administrative functions of the respective grades and the methods of preparing staff to occupy them'.

It proposed a management structure of Nursing Officers and did away with the familiar 'matron' title although this title persisted in some places.

'Salmon' was primarily an administrative and structurally-oriented change and it emphasized an increasing focus on the managerial and administrative responsibilities of senior nurses.

Nursing management in the 1990s

With the advent of local pay flexibility there is no longer a nation-wide pay structure to follow. Each Trust now has considerable flexibility in setting up its own nursing management and pay structures.

Figure 1.5 shows an indicative nursing management structure.

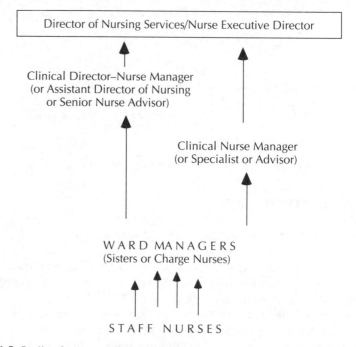

Figure 1.5 Outline framework for nursing posts

Whilst the structure of the NHS will no doubt continue to alter over time, it is likely that the most significant shifts – for the remainder of this century at least – are now in place.

Whereas the Griffiths Report made it possible for nurses to become General Managers and reach very senior positions in Trusts and within the Purchasing Authorities, the full effects of:

- Project 2000
- the impact of Nurse Practitioners
- nurse prescribing

have yet to be seen.

Perhaps the next major shifts within the NHS will be led by the medical profession as they become increasingly effective and proficient in picking up the challenging role of Clinical Director and working with their colleagues – both medical and non-medical – in managing NHS services. The pressure on clinicians to accept even closer responsibility for the day-to-day management of their clinical resources and within a tighter corporate resource framework will continue.

Project 2000

The Project 2000 report recommended fundamental changes to the education and training of nurses and resulted in nurse training being based in colleges of higher education along with other students.

Project 2000 nurse training is more academically focused and leads to a degree in nursing studies and professional nurse registration. The pattern of the three-year training differs from other nurse training programmes in so far as, for the majority of the training period, the trainee is supernumerary and is not counted as part of the ward staff allocation when on clinical attachment.

Development of practice nurse professionals

Nurse Practitioners are qualified nurses who have undergone a programme of further training and who are licensed to diagnose, refer patients and prescribe treatment independently of medical staff.

The term 'Nurse Practitioner' refers to a small but expanding body of nurses who have completed their further education and training at the Royal College of Nursing. The focus is likely to be in support of GPs and where longer term community- or locality-based support is needed rather than as alternatives to hospital-based medical staff.

Nurse prescribing

A further development in the evolution of the role of the nurse towards a more independent practitioner role is the right to prescribe, as legislated through the Medicinal Products: Prescriptions by Nurse Act 1992. This allows certain categories of community nurses to prescribe dressings and medicines from a limited list. This right will only be extended to nurses with appropriate training in pharmacology and related subjects. The additional training will form part of District Nurse and Health Visitor training.

Health care and its organization have a weighty heritage. Medicine and nursing are two of the oldest professions and enjoy a high status in society. Professional standards are expected to be correspondingly high, which is as it should be, but the great weight of tradition and slowly evolved practices do exert certain restraining influences, particularly with regard to the organization and management of nursing and clinical services.

The concern to maintain standards may mean that innovation is difficult and the temptation is to repress ideas for constructive change rather than face a barrage of defensive reactions.

REFERENCES AND FURTHER READING

Audit Commission Reports, HMSO, London.
Department of Health (1990) *The NHS and Community Care Act*, HMSO, London.
Ham, C. (1991) *The New National Health Service*, Radcliffe Medical Press Ltd, Oxford.

IHSM (1997) *The Health Services Year Book*, Institute of Health Services Management, London.

NHS Management Inquiry (1983) *The Griffiths Report*, DHSS, London.

NAHAT (1997) *Yearbook*, National Association of Health Authorities and Trusts, JMH Publishing, Tunbridge Wells.

Stewart, R. (1989) *Leading in the NHS*, Macmillan, London.

Teasdale, K. (1992) *Managing the Changes in Health Care*, Wolfe Publishing Co., London.

UKCC (1986) *Project 2000 – A New Preparation for Practice*, UKCC, London.

Management and leadership $\boxed{2}$

This chapter outlines some influential ideas about people at work. They help to account for what we do in the clinic, on the ward or in the office. You may well have come across some of the following material in years gone by, perhaps as part of your initial management training. My aim is to set out how these ideas are applied in practice rather than in theory. Keep in mind the ideas you use to help explain your own behaviour and that of others.

Organizations are political places in which to work and consequently it is very likely that – whether you enjoy it or not – at some stage you *will* become enmeshed in the 'politics' where you work. This could show itself in discussions about who got the job and who should have been given the job. The politics of your organization could also intrude in to how decisions are made about all sorts of things at work, for example duty rotas, time off, ward allocations, etc. Politics will also be evident in how the Trust Board are working together – or not, as the case may be. At all levels and within all disciplines the political dimensions of people behaviour will be evident in some way: it is part of human nature.

Your ability to carry out your professional work will be made easier if you are sufficiently aware of what is going on around you as this will allow you to tune into the politics and dynamics at play in the organization. This, in turn, will help you avoid unnecessary problems and *faux pas*.

WHAT ARE MANAGEMENT AND LEADERSHIP?

The material presented here will help you to build up and reinforce your understandings about management and leadership and help you to expand your appreciation of the internal politics of work organizations. This is an essential skill; awareness of these matters will help you throughout your career. Be aware, look around you and try to keep in mind the ideas about people at work. Make use of them to enhance patient care and ease some of the stress of the work that you do.

Effective *leadership* is critically important in any organization. Having the resources, for example, whilst being fully staffed, etc. is of course vital. The key to effective management is how the staff are focused towards achieving the desired objectives. The cornerstone of dynamic effective organizational performance is leadership, and the trust others come to have in that leadership.

Much of what goes on in the NHS seems to be more about the efficient management and administration of the service than effective and dynamic leadership. The DoH and the NHS Executive seem to be concerned predominantly with administration and management rather than leadership. Whilst official statements may promote the effective leadership of Trusts, much of that which is valued and rewarded still seems to be more about the careful management and administration of resources and the achievement of measures of performance.

 There is quite a difference between management and leadership and, unless this is clearly set out, considerable confusion will result.

1. Make a note about what you see Management as being about.
2. Now do the same for Leadership.

The concepts of management and leadership are both important and necessary but there is often considerable confusion surrounding discussions about them. They are in fact quite different notions. The critical difference is that management is more about doing things appropriately and properly (making things happen) whereas leadership is more about mobilizing those around you to create a realistic and desired future (creating a momentum for desired change).

Figure 2.1 shows the major differences between these two concepts.

Management is about:	**Leadership** is about:
• monitoring performance to goals	• providing a vision
• doing things right	• doing 'right' things
• ensuring detailed accomplishments	• 'broad picture' driven
• providing professional direction	• inspiring others
• following the procedures.	• major 'sea change' advances.

Figure 2.1 Management and leadership

Another way of thinking about the two is to:

• relate management to the role and position of a person in that organization
• relate the notion of leadership more to the power and influence of the person themselves.

You can have the two together of course so you may be in a management role and be able to accomplish the types of things shown under leadership – a powerful and influential combination. Equally, you can exercise leadership irrespective of any formal role you occupy in an organization. And again you may hold a management position yet be unable to enthuse and engage with others – it may well be that others do what you ask because of the positional power you hold and not because of your leadership qualities as described above.

Here then are two very important but quite different concepts that need to be considered with care. Each needs to be present if the organization is to function most effectively. Figure 2.2 sets out some of the differences between people power and position power.

The leader is more of an enthusiast, a cheerleader, a coach or a facilitator: the manager is more of a monitor, planner, director and reviewer. Bear these thoughts in mind whilst considering some of the more influential ideas about leadership and management that have emerged over recent times. Some of these will be familiar to you, others may be new.

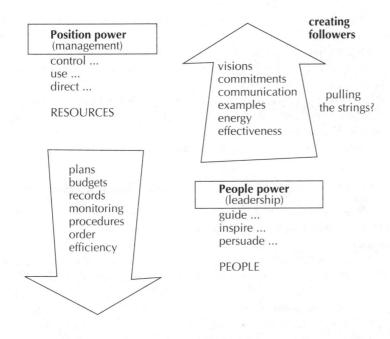

Figure 2.2 People power and position power

THE CLASSICAL APPROACH TO MANAGEMENT

During the latter part of the nineteenth and early part of the twentieth century great strides were being made in the physical sciences through the application of positivistic, 'scientific' bases of study and exploration. The progress made within the pure sciences was seen to offer scope for comparable progress to be achieved through the application of similar approaches to the business world and the management of organizations.

The resultant search for 'scientific laws' of organizational behaviour contributed to the development of an idealized view about the nature of organizations with regard to how they can most productively be organized and how they should function.

An organization which is influenced by this approach tends to view as dysfunctional or deliberately counter-cultural the exercise of individuality at work, or behaviour which does not meet the standards required. There remains in general an expectation in business that individuals should work as if the organization's aims and imperatives were their own.

In many respects organizations are still construed, and designed, as if they were mechanical or as if they functioned according to scientific laws; they are not generally designed for innovation, nor are their employees generally rewarded for taking the initiative or responding flexibly to unexpected circumstances. Efficiency in the performance of expected tasks is often preferred to flexible responses to unexpected situations.

Classical management theory operates from a premise that if organizations are structured on a clearly defined rational-logical basis the tasks prescribed will be accomplished through the workforce doing exactly what is expected of them by following a logical-rational approach. The organization is viewed primarily as a production system with a constrained and pre-determined role for the majority of its members.

Little attention, other than the recognition that people need to work together to achieve outcomes, was given to considering the human factors and forces at play within organizations. Leadership – effectively directive management – was seen as a top-down directive activity.

Scientific management: The work of Frederick Winslow Taylor

Frederick Winslow Taylor developed a body of ideas that came to be called 'scientific management' the principles of which 'have fundamentally influenced the thinking about how organizations work'. In his view it was 'the natural instinct and tendency of men to take it easy' and thus he held that an instrumental relationship was needed to motivate people at work. Taylor emphasized the efficiency of task achievement and reward for performance. He recommended specialization between management and workers and advocated a detailed analysis of jobs and division of labour as a means of optimizing organizational performance (Sofer, 1972).

These principles of scientific management have remained a cornerstone for work design and thinking about the nature of work to the present day. Taylor advocated five simple rules which Morgan (1997) summarizes as follows:

(i) shift all responsibility for the organization of work from the worker to the manager
(ii) use scientific methods to determine precisely the most efficient

way of doing work and structure the worker's tasks accordingly,

(iii) select the best person to perform the job precisely as designed and defined

(iv) train the worker to do that work efficiently

(v) monitor worker performance to ensure that appropriate work procedures are followed, appropriate work results are achieved and necessary 'scientific' adjustments are made.

Taylor's theories were employer-centred: they gave precedence to optimum performance and asserted a right of management to direct, employ, control and manage workers. This means that workers are expected to suppress facets of their individuality and undertake their work responsibilities 'as if' the dynamics of working in an organization and their own feelings have no effect on their organizational performance (Putnam and Mumby, 1993).

The notion of bureaucracy

'Bureaucracy' is often talked about in negative terms but the original ideas embodied in the word are very sound. It's bad reputation has grown from the ways in which it can be used to slow things down and impede performance. The introduction of bureaucracy is linked to the work of Max Weber who coined it to describe ways of working where decisions and control were rationally made on the basis of knowledge, expertise and technical competence in the tasks to be accomplished, where activities were attached to specific roles – not to particular persons – with the appropriate responsibilities necessary to carry out the designated duties duly allocated.

Key characteristics of a bureaucratic form of organization are:

- All tasks to accomplish organizational goals must be divided into highly specialized jobs.
- Each task must be performed according to a 'consistent system of abstract rules' which allows the manager to eliminate uncertainty due to individual differences in task performance.
- Offices or roles must be organized into a hierarchical structure in which the scope of authority of superordinates over subordinates is defined.
- Superiors must assume an impersonal attitude in dealing with each other and subordinates – this psychological and social distance enabling the superior to make decisions without being influenced by prejudices and preferences.
- Employment in a bureaucracy must be based on qualifications with promotion decided on the basis of merit; because of this careful and firm system of employment and promotion, it is assumed that employment will involve a life-long career and loyalty from employees.

These points reveal an underlying emphasis on control and order as a basis for the accomplishment of the prescribed organizational goals. Whilst in practice all of the above are rarely found together, they nevertheless remain an influential 'ideal' in shaping the thinking of managers about the design and management of organizations.

Logical-rational thinking has exerted a strong influence on management thinking and managerial behaviour. The prescriptions and the precision derived from Taylor's 'scientific management' combined with the 'ideal-type' descriptions of a bureaucratic organization describe for many managers the classical approach to the management of organizations. These views continue to underpin a great deal of day-to-day business practice.

 Do any of these ideas and views relate to your experiences of work both within health care and elsewhere? You may find it helpful to take a few moments and set down your thoughts under the following headings:

- My experience of working in an organization
- The related theory/concept.

As a general rule relate the material in this book to your own situation. This will enable you to get a clearer understanding of what type of managerial philosophy or 'regime' you are working within. More importantly, it will help you to become more aware and effective in your work.

Partly as a reaction to the classic – and somewhat mechanistic – scientific management approaches, a more person-focused, humanistic, school of thought developed as described below.

HUMANISTIC APPROACHES TO ORGANIZATIONAL LIFE

Innovative work by Elton Mayo, a Harvard Business School Professor, drew attention to performance motivators which are very different from those described by 'scientific management'. Mayo's studies in the Hawthorne Plant of the Western Electric Company in Chicago – from the 1920s and 1930s – began as investigations into efficient work practices and yielded some startling outcomes. He found that, almost irrespective of the work he and his colleagues did to alter the conditions under which people worked, output increased. This led Mayo (1945) to emphasize the importance of (a) the social organization of the work group and (b) of the informal standards in governing the behaviour of work group members.

As de Board (1978) notes, 'Most surprisingly, output continued to increase even when the working conditions reverted to the original situation of a long working day without rest pauses. Mayo explained it thus, "What actually happened was that six individuals became a team and the team gave itself wholeheartedly and spontaneously to co-operation in the experiment. The consequence was that they felt themselves to be participating freely and without afterthought, and were happy in the knowledge that they were working without coercion from above or limitation from below" (Mayo, 1945)'.

The conclusions of Mayo and his co-workers completely upset the commonly held notions of how workers react to authority and how production can be stimulated. Instead, a social model of the worker was put forward to oppose the mechanistic, economic and even psychological models then current. A new theory of organization began to emerge based on the idea that individuals and groups will operate more effectively only when their social needs are addressed. This social model installed the logic of human emotions side by side with the logic of costs or efficiency. After the Hawthorn studies it had to be granted that an informal structure of social relations did exist behind the formal organizational structure and that numerous phenomena could not be explained on any other grounds. (Sofer, 1972)

This work in the 1920s and 1930s identified the importance of the *social needs* in the workplace and the ways in which work groups can satisfy such needs by informally restricting output and engaging in a range of unplanned but mutually rewarding activities. In identifying that an *informal* organization existed alongside the formalized planned one, these studies challenged the primacy of the classical management approaches of the time and set the scene for more attention to be given to the social and the informal determinants of group and organizational behaviour.

These findings signalled a need for managers to understand group processes, group relations and personality. It was no longer feasible to look for explanations of employee turnover simply in terms of a person wanting just to maximize their earnings. The incentive to work was no longer seen as simple and unitary, but infinitely varied, complex and changing. Going to work was more than turning up, doing the work and getting paid.

The literature of the time however, whilst acknowledging the complex social determinants of organizational behaviour did not – with the exception of the Tavistock Institute of Human Relations – seem publicly to consider unconscious psycho-dynamic phenomena in the workplace. The emphasis appeared to coalesce around more explicitly explainable needs for social relations and the development of normative work behaviours. A more widespread interest in the group dynamics of groups and organizations was to come later.

Motivation

The motivation of people at work is of continuing interest to organization theorists. Maslow's 'Hierarchy of Needs' (1954) and Hertzberg *et al.*'s (1966) two-factor theory of motivation are two often quoted models of personal motivation, yet it has been through the work of Douglas McGregor that the contrast between opposing views about the nature of people in organizations has been most starkly portrayed. His principle contribution to the debate came in his book *The Human Side of Enterprise* (1960) in which he contrasts two very different philosophies, each of which had implications for the management of people in organized settings.

Firstly he proposed a view that workers have to be directed and controlled (the notion of Theory X) and contrasted that with a view that workers were intrinsically self-motivating and self-directed (the notion of Theory Y). These ways of describing people at work have become widely used ways of thinking about management practice. The contrasting characteristics of the two styles are:

- *Assumptions of Theory X:*
  - The average human being has an inherent dislike of work and will avoid it if he can.
  - Because of this dislike of work most people must be coerced, directed and threatened with punishment to get them to work.
  - The average human being prefers to be directed, avoids responsibility and has little ambition.

- *Assumptions of Theory Y:*
  - The expenditure of physical and mental effort in work is as natural as play or rest.
  - Each person can exercise self-direction and self-control to achieve objectives to which they are committed.
  - Under proper conditions each person can learn to accept and to seek responsibility.
  - The intellectual potentialities of people at work are only partially utilized.

The assumptions of Theory Y are dynamic rather than static and they implicitly stress the common potential for personal growth. The assumptions of Theory X are quite different: theory X describes a more restrictive and essentially pessimistic picture of the capabilities, capacity and potential contributions of people at work. As McGregor comments 'Theory X offers management an easy rationalization for ineffective organization performance: [that] it is due to the nature of the human resources with which we must work. Theory Y, on the other hand, places the problems [for poor organization performance, etc.] squarely in the lap of management' (McGregor, 1960).

A major insight from McGregor's study of people at work was his recognition that behind every managerial decision lay assumptions about human nature and human behaviour. Highlighting these assumptions can help to illuminate the styles of individual managers and the overall philosophy about the management of staff within the organization.

1. Take a few moments to reflect on your own work experiences and make a note of where you have experienced approaches to management which match the more humanistic and person-focused ideas set out above. Use these headings:

   - Reflections on my experience in groups and organizations
   - Relevant theory/notion.

2. Where are you in terms of this approach? Do you tend to ascribe to the views set out in Theory **X** or in Theory **Y** – or do your have other views? It might be helpful to talk this through with colleagues and see if any differences exist. If you find you do have a strong preference look to see what evidence there is to support your view and look also to see what evidence there is to challenge the view

you have. Try to reconcile the two and make a note of your philosophy of people behaviour at work, as follows:

'On the basis of my observations and my experience my theory of people behaviour at work is ...'

Keep this in mind as you progress further through this book. Update and expand it as a result of your readings and your practical work over the weeks ahead.

Maslow's Hierarchy of Needs

Maslow's Hierarchy of Needs is usually presented in the form shown in Figure 2.3. He proposed five levels of need (Maslow, 1954). He suggested that only when the lower level needs have been substantially satisfied can an individual begin to consider the higher level needs. There is no suggestion that any of the needs are superior to others, only that some have greater importance for basic survival.

An unsatisfied need will create tension, and will have the effect of energizing and spurring the individual to action. Maslow suggested that it is only when behaviour results in the securing of the first need level that the other needs will begin to manifest themselves. The five levels are:

1. *Basic (survival) needs* (for example, air, water, food, shelter and warmth)
2. *Safety needs* (knowing that one's survival is not endangered)
3. *'Belongingness' (social) needs* (being accepted by others and being part of one's social environment)
4. *Ego (status) needs* (feeling significant, competent and having self-esteem)
5. *Self-actualization needs* (growing, expanding one's horizons, becoming all that one would hope to, and – in the process – challenging oneself).

Figure 2.3 Maslow's Hierarchy of Needs

More recently, the notion that the individual can only move up the hierarchy if lower needs have been satisfied has been questioned. It may be better to think of Maslow's contribution as a model which recognizes the different types of needs we each have and which demand attention, the prominence of each level varying with our own personal situation and aspirations.

Developing a capacity to appreciate the different types of need with which individuals – patients especially – seem to be preoccupied at any one time is be very important in determining how well you are able to relate to them appropriately and with meaning. Beyond a basic level too each of us will redefine what constitute for us the minimum criteria at each of Maslow's levels as we age and progress through life. Beyond the need to secure basic physiological needs for life support, how we choose to define our 'Physiological' and 'Security' needs is likely to alter over time and be influenced by what we have become accustomed to expect.

If each of us strives to meet all our needs, we may limit the potential of colleagues who have similar goals and whose progress we may be blocking. This could clearly be counterproductive, and it would probably be unwise to think of the idea of need fulfilment as a model of behaviour to be rigidly adhered to; instead we could use the notion of self-actualization in a more general way to help us analyse what our personal aims are and whether we are achieving them.

We could begin by recognizing that we do have a requirement to be active in each of the five areas, but that we need to secure our activities at the basic levels first before we are able to pay attention to the higher order needs such as autonomy, independence and exploiting our capabilities to the full.

Maslow's model incorporates a picture of each of us as capable of mature and realistic behaviour with a certain degree of autonomy and inter-dependence. It also recognizes our ability to adapt to different circum-stances as they arise, as well as our potential for creativity, innovation and self-direction.

The role for the manager here is to adopt a strategy similar to that for the social-man concept but designed to enable the individual members of staff to work through issues for themselves, with support, and to allow them to set their own targets in line with agreed standards and professional practice. This means that standards can be negotiated with staff, rather than set for them without consultation.

Hertzberg's two-factor theory

The 'Hygiene-Motivators' theory of motivation (Hertzberg, 1966) suggests that we each have two types of needs that are essentially different, each of which influences our behaviour in different ways.

Hertzberg's 'Hygiene' or maintenance factors are those factors and condi-tions a person looks for in order to do their job of work, such as an appropri-ate level of pay, money, mutual support, pension rights, status. A lack of these factors will cause dissatisfaction but their presence will not, by them-selves, create a sense of satisfaction or dynamic motivation. So these hygiene factors should be seen as pre-conditions, features of the employment package which need to be in place, if that work group is to become motivated in their work.

Given that such hygiene factors are in place the 'Motivators' are those factors which will motivate and energize people to achieve superior performance. These would include an opportunity for achievement, job satisfaction, recognition and self development. These motivating factors are similar to those proposed by Maslow.

Hertzberg's approach can reveal a great deal about the organization where you work and how you 'feel' about working there. For example you may realize that all the necessary pre-conditions that you expect are there (the 'hygiene' side of the equation) but that the conditions that would make you want to do your very best (the 'motivators') are lacking. Becoming aware of this you may be able to influence others to help you get more inspiration and satisfaction from your work.

Figure 2.4 gives some examples of 'hygiene factors' and 'motivators'.

Make your own copy of Figure 2.4 and include in it some of the hygiene factors you would expect to find at work in order for you to do a good job: things that you would look for to feel reassured that this is an appropriate place for you to work. Then make a note of those motivators which would enable you to do even better, to feel engaged with and pleased to be working in your organization.

Hygiene or maintenance factors		Motivators	
Generally	**For me**	**Generally**	**For me**
Good working conditions		Responsibility	
Stable ward team		The chance to achieve	
Clear pay policy		Challenge	
Good pension plan			

Figure 2.4 Hertzberg's two-factor theory of motivation

Assumptions about people: Four styles

One way of using these ideas about motivation and performance is to combine them and try to predict how people may behave in the workplace. Based on your experiences you will have ideas and hypotheses about how people behave at work. Whether you realize it or not you use these personal ideas about motivation to guide you in what you do at work and elsewhere.

Our assumptions about people's behaviour will often show themselves when 'people problems' are discussed, and through the remedies put forward to resolved the problems identified.

Figure 2.5 shows four different ways of describing people at work. Each of them highlights particular dimensions of human behaviour. It is likely that there will be a bit of each of these four styles in how you think about the way people work.

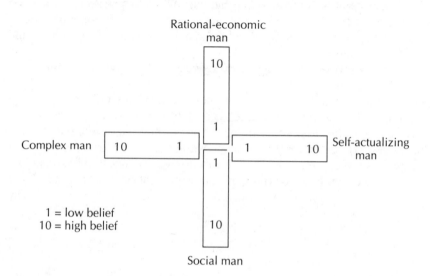

Figure 2.5 Four 'styles' of people at work

Rational-economic man

The basic idea here is that we all work for what we perceive to be our own good almost irrespective of others. Our predominant self-interest means that we act in order to improve our own importance and strength, and our ability to do just that reinforces our own sense of importance and right to recognition. There is little place for personal sensitivity regarding the welfare or concerns of others here, and the theory suggests that we are primarily motivated by economic incentives and by those actions which will give us the greatest rewards.

This view casts the manager as an instrumental user of others, controlling and manoeuvring them to get the work accomplished. For example, the manager will not consider the well-being of staff in allocating them difficult, anti-social or unrealistic tasks and duties: it may just be possible that the manager is acting with the intention of showing senior officers that his or her department is the best and hence allocating tasks with this end in mind.

This notion also emphasizes the logical or rational way in which organizations and people should operate. The assumption will be that if the pay is good enough or if the reasons why certain actions should take place are explained clearly enough, the staff will, of course, comply. Feelings, however, have no part in this theory of working.

This view implies that the manager will adopt a calculating approach to staff; authority is invested in the particular managerial post rather than arising out of the qualities of leadership or understanding which individual officers may possess. In other words, if the chief nursing officer orders all the drugs in the cupboard destroyed, they are duly destroyed. Compliance is rewarded and the burden for responsible work direction and review falls entirely on the managers: other staff are assumed to be motivated only by the economic gain afforded by their work rather than by any sense of responsibility.

Social man

The view of man as social man assumes that behaviour at work is dramatically affected by the quality of the relationships made with colleagues. Work patterns and the quality of the work done are affected by the individual's acceptability within the team and this is as important – perhaps more so – than the economic incentives offered by management. In other words, social needs are a major motivation, and individuals obtain their basic sense of identity through relationships with others.

In an organization where this approach predominates it is likely that there will be some resistance to a competitive work culture. The work group may well handle this by instituting informal work norms or by selecting other methods to counteract management's attempt to introduce competition. The effective manager has to contend with the feelings of the staff, particularly their sense of belonging and group identity.

Group recognition and acceptance can become more important than individual work and behaviour. Especially important is the development – and conformity to – group norms about work behaviour and achievement levels.

Self-actualizing man

The central notion here is that each person has a range of capacities and skills that will be used given the right opportunities and support. The assumption is that each person has a great deal to offer and wants to achieve their potential to the full.

It is likely that there is a huge loss of human potential at work because of the way in which most contemporary work organizations are run. Many jobs have become so specialized that they neither enable employees to use their skills to the full, nor help them to see how the specific tasks they do contribute to the overall purpose of the organization.

Complex man

The three views presented so far may be too simple a representation of what motivates people. The complex man view attempts to take more account of the complex reality of human behaviour. Not only do different individuals have different sorts of motivations, but each individual will have also have varying types of motivations in different situations. This view also acknowledges that people change with the passing of time and as a result of their life experiences.

A difficult nurse learner, for example, may blossom when the state finals are passed and recognition as a professional nurse is achieved; another nurse learner, having been protected by the training status, may become unable to cope with the pressures of the job and leave the profession soon after achieving professional status. Little is straightforward or simple in thinking about – and in trying to predict – human behaviour.

The most important implication here for managers is the need to look at what is going on around them try to identify the important issues and concerns for each individual member of staff. Managers need to take note of the situational differences which arise, the complexity of the issues to be handled, and the impact of the pressure and trauma on staff. They must consider how differences can be recognized and handled rather than denied or brushed away and keep in mind that motivation is a very personal phenomena.

 Use Figure 2.5 to assess to what extent you agree, on a scale of 1–10, with the four views outlined. What does this show you about the way in which you:

a. go about your work
b. think about your own and the behaviour of others
c. seek to influence and work with colleagues, patients and relatives?

STYLES OF LEADERSHIP

Several different ideas about the nature of management and leadership have been introduced, together with some thoughts about what motivates us. The remainder of this chapter switches the focus from what management and leadership is all about to how they are exercised.

Kurt Lewin's behavioural styles of leadership

The behavioural style approach to leadership is best known through the work of Kurt Lewin whose work in this area explored the impact on work behaviour of different behavioural styles of leadership. Three styles in particular were explored: autocratic, democratic and *laissez-faire* (Lippitt and White, 1968).

Autocratic leadership style

This is basically leader-centred rather than staff-centred and works on the basis that 'as the manager I know best!' It sees the principal influence on behaviour at work as being the manager who has control of all important factors, for example, the allocation of resources, reviewing the action taken, distribution of rewards and penalties. The manager also has control of the communication channels, which are probably organized in the form of a straight chain (see Figure 2.6).

Figure 2.6 A straight line leadership style

It is a very restrictive way of working, and allows relatively little autonomy to the staff, who are expected to follow the directions and standards imposed on them from above. This does not mean that there will be no involvement by staff in what happens since they may be asked for their ideas or suggestions, particularly in response to new or unexpected developments. Staff are unlikely, however, to get recognition for their ideas if used, or to be kept in the picture about what is going on in the department as a whole.

The results of this are fairly predictable in that staff are likely to become resentful about the way they are being handled. The extent to which this shows itself openly may depend on the level of absolute power held by managers and whether they can damage the career development and professional standing of their staff. If staff dissent and disagreement cannot be overtly vented, organizational sabotage may occur and evidence of this can be seen in many organizations. It ranges from subtle strategies, such as staff 'forgetting' to do certain things, to outright vocal and physical abuse. The costs – whatever form they take – are significant to the productive running of that group.

There is likely to be little sense of personal responsibility or initiative-taking by staff. If problems arise, staff are unlikely to respond flexibly; they are more likely to let situations develop into a crisis, which can then be blamed on poor leadership. (This is one way of covertly 'getting back at' the boss.) Autocratic styles do have their place and value but, as with so many things in life, the key to their use lies in striking the most appropriate balance. Too much autocracy risks alienation of staff; too little autocracy in situations when it is needed – in a crisis perhaps – and risks chaos and collapse.

Democratic style of leadership

This is very much a staff-centred style and links well with McGregor's Theory Y. It recognizes that the manager, whilst competent, cannot know everything nor necessarily have the best ideas in every situation, and that it makes good sense to work in ways which build the staff group together in a collaborative framework. It also allows staff to become involved and take part in decisions which affect them and their work.

A climate is created in which members can openly express themselves, share their differences without fear of rejection, and explore the different types of contribution they can each make. This work climate demands a much more equal manager whose role is to guide and collaborate rather than to direct. The consequences are that each member of the group takes on appropriate responsibilities, and morale and involvement are usually high (though it has to be said that there is a danger that the group can become too intimate and collusive).

Laissez-faire *style of leadership*

This is neither member-centred nor leader-centred: the essence here is of letting things run their course. In this respect it is rather unsatisfactory for all concerned, with the leader neither taking a very active role nor making clear to staff exactly what is expected of them and where they stand.

Whilst there may well be situations where it is appropriate to sit back and let things sort themselves out, this tends not to be a useful style as far as nurse managers are concerned. It can add to the already high levels of anxiety and uncertainty in nursing activities, and so work in a destructive way. It is unlikely that clear goals for the ward would ever be formulated, decisions would be *ad hoc* and there would be no evaluation of ward performance against targets. There would be confusion and a general low level of responsibility and action, and staff would show apathy and a minimal interest in both the tasks set and the group itself. Productivity is likely to be low and a generally unhappy and unfocused style of working would probably characterize the ward.

Action-centred leadership

From his work in the military John Adair (1988) recognized the need to pay attention not only to the task that needs to be done but also to the individual and group needs associated with doing that particular task. He represented these three vital needs by showing them as three interlocking circles (see Figure 2.7).

Adair makes the very valid point that too much concern for any one of these three areas will interfere with the most productive working of the task group. For example, if too much attention is paid to the needs of individual group members this may result in too little attention being given to the details of the task itself and too little group cohesion being established. Similarly, an over-concern for getting the task done can actually result in it not being successfully achieved, because too little attention is being paid to how the group is working and how individual members are coping.

This action-centred leadership (ACL) approach is a very straightforward and practical model for thinking about your everyday work activities. For example, when you go about your work, what proportion of your time do you give to the task, to the need to ensure that you and your colleagues are working well enough together, and to your own individual needs as part of that group?

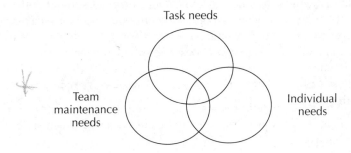

Figure 2.7 Action-centred leadership

You may realize that you generally give very little attention to one or more of these three sets of needs. Adair suggests that if you do not maintain a sufficient level of attention to each of these in relation to the others then there will be consequences for the quality of the outcomes delivered, the morale of the group and your own sense of positive motivation and accomplishment.

Leadership behaviour: A continuum

If you apply the ideas covered you will have a clearer and more informed view of what is going on around you. It will mean that you have more of an opportunity to decide what to do and how to go about it. There will a whole range of choices open to you about how you respond in a situation as manager and colleague. It is surprising how many of us prefer to use only a small range of the responses open to us.

Another way of increasing your effectiveness at work is to broaden the range of behavioural responses available to you. Some of these are shown in the very compact continuum first set out many years ago by Tannenbaum and Schmidt (1973) (see Figure 2.8).

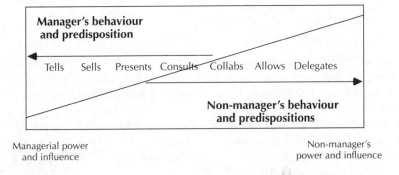

Figure 2.8 Continuum of leadership behaviour (derived from Tannenbaum and Schmidt, 1973)

Figure 2.8 relates the behaviour of a manager to that of another colleague. The range of behaviour is from a more autocratic approach (far left) through various stages to a more democratic stance (far right). The descriptive headings through the middle of the figure describe different ways of relating to a colleague at work.

You can use this framework in a number of ways, for example:

- to review how you function when you are in a directing role (as a manager), noting which styles you most frequently use and which styles you rarely make use of
- to review how those around you work and to consider (a) What do they do most of and least of? and (b) Why that might be?
- as a means of trying to classify the type of organization or department you are working in.

One of the most helpful uses of this continuum is to review the ways in which you most often work with others. For example you may realize that you nearly always *tell* people – even when they are very experienced – what to do. Not only does this take more of your time but it is likely to aggravate and demotivate such colleagues. On the other hand you may realize that you generally allow or delegate responsibilities and actions to more junior staff when you should be directing and telling that what needs to be done.

In both instances it is likely that you can increase your satisfaction – and that of those around you – by working in a more flexible way that is determined by the needs of the case to be tackled rather than automatically reverting to your preferred style of managing.

PATTERNS OF MANAGEMENT

In reflecting on management practices within the NHS there are a number of different patterns which show themselves at all levels of the service. These are:

- management by formality
- a reliance on procedures and rules
- management by committee
- settlement and decisions by negotiation
- team consensus management (this is far less prominent now).

Beneath these formalized ways of working are other less easy to define tensions and dynamics which critically affect what is done in any organization. They contrast sharply with the five patterns shown above and are noted in Figure 2.9.

People tend not to talk about the concerns highlighted in Figure 2.9, perhaps because they are embarrassing to acknowledge, or too close to home, or because good managers are not meant to recognize the importance of such issues as power and politics.

The word 'fear' figures at the centre of Figure 2.9 because at the heart of so much of the tension and anxiety evident in organizations – and in life gen-

Concerns about ....

Figure 2.9 Underlying issues in organizations

erally perhaps – is a fear of something or other. By and large people tend to be unwilling to admit to being afraid – at home as well as when at work – and choose to focus on other considerations such as the business planning cycle, the absence figures or the car parking.

You may find it helpful, therefore, when you are under stress or in pain, to check whether there is some underlying fear contributing to your level of stress. If you do identify some specific concern it is likely that your subsequent actions will be sharper, more informed, better focused and more in-tune with what is really on your mind and guiding your thoughts, emotions and decisions.

Many people find it hard to share their uncertainty or anxiety about how things are going. It is as if owning up to the way we feel is an indication of weakness, or of unsuitability for managerial responsibility. The clearer a manager can be about the widest range of influences which affect how decisions are taken, the more informed and appropriate their actions are likely to be.

PULLING THESE IDEAS TOGETHER

The key message of this chapter is that you need considerable awareness and understanding of what goes on inter-actively between people at work if you want to make the best use of your professional skills and remain in good health. What is required is that you understand and respond flexibly to the environments in which you work and to the mix of people around you.

There is no one best way of responding to situations, nor is there any notably 'good' or 'bad' management style because 'it all depends.' Whilst this can be a frustrating conclusion to reach it also means that as managers and as individuals we are free to try out many different ways of behaving and to learn from the resulting experiences.

You may decide that you value Theory Y ideas but that the circumstances of a particular work situation make it totally appropriate to behave in a very authoritative manner – in a way which corresponds to McGregor's Theory X.

Equally, you may normally prefer to be the clear manager who knows exactly what has to be done, but situations will arise where you need to respond in a less directive, more accommodating manner. It is in your interests not only to be aware of the different styles which match the different demands being placed upon you but also that you can actually behave flexibly too.

In thinking about management styles and patterns of leadership, it would be easy to pretend that any one of the notions considered above is 'the right one'. However, this would be misleading. It is more useful to think about them as different perspectives, different ways of viewing management and leadership roles, some of which will link well with your own experience, and others about which you will continue to have some doubts.

The main point is that you should be able to use them and make them your own. A good theory should help you become clearer about what goes on and should be capable of being applied in a practical way. You also need to remember that a management or leadership style is not just a question of your own personal preference. Those around you are also working according to the assumptions by which they make sense of their life at work, and which are in tune with their own preferred ways of working with others.

REFERENCES AND FURTHER READING

Adair, J. (1988) *Effective Leadership*, Pan Books, London.

Barker, J. (1992) *Paradigms*, HarperCollins, New York.

de Board, R. (1978) *The Psychoanalysis of Organizations,* Tavistock, London.

Clutterbuck, D. and Crainer, S. (1990) *Makers of Management*, Macmillan, London.

Goldratt, E. and Cox, J. (1989) *The Goal*, Gower, Aldershot.

Handy, C. (1990) *Inside Organizations*, BBC Books, London.

Heifetz, R. (1994) *Leadership Without Easy Answers*, Harvard University Press.

Hertzberg, F. (1966) *Work and the Nature of Man*, Staples Press, London.

Hickman, C. (1990) *Mind of a Manager – Soul of a Leader*, Wiley, New York.

Jay, A. (1987) *Management and Machiavelli*, Hutchinson, London.

Kouzes, J. and Posner, B. (1989) *The Leadership Challenge*, Jossey-Bass, San Francisco

Lippit, R. and White, R. (1968) Leader behaviour and member reaction in three social climates, in Cartwright, D. and Zander, A. (eds) *Group Dynamics*, Tavistock, London.

Lombardo, M. and Eichinger, R. (1989) *Preventing Derailment Report*, Center for Creative Leadership, Greensboro, North Carolina.

Maslow, A. (1954) *Motivation and Personality*, Harper & Row, New York.

Mayo, E. (1945) *The Social Problems of an Industrial Civilization*, Harvard University Press.

McGregor, D. (1960) *The Human Side of Enterprise*, McGraw-Hill, New York.

McKenna, E. (1994) *Business Psychology and Organizational Behaviour*, Lawrence Erlbaum Associates Ltd, Hove.

Morgan, G. (1997) *Images of Organization*, Sage, London.

Peters, T. and Waterman, R. (1982) *In Search of Excellence*, Harper & Row, New York.

Putnam, L. and Mumby, D. (1993) Organizations, emotion and the myth of rationality, in Fineman, S. (ed.) *Emotion in Organizations*, Sage, London.

Shackleton, V. (1995) *Business Leaders*, Routledge, London.

Sofer, C. (1972) *Organizations in Theory and Practice*, Heinemann Books, London.

Tannenbaum, R. and Schmidt, W. (1973) *How to Choose a Leadership Pattern*, May–June, Harvard University Press.

3 The market dynamics of the NHS in the 1990s

THE INTERNAL MARKET

This chapter is about the NHS as it evolves following the 1990 legislation and the creation of an internal competitive market for the purchase and provision of health care services across the UK.

The Community Care Act (1990) resulted in a dramatic change to both the structure and the nature of the NHS. It profoundly shocked the system and those within it. It continued the drive for a business culture that had begun in earnest in the early 1980s with the publication of the Griffiths Report and the introduction of a general management philosophy throughout the service.

The impact of the internal market has drastically altered the market conditions within which health care organizations now have to operate. The scene is now populated as follows:

- over 550 independently constituted NHS Trusts
- private hospitals and clinics challenging for NHS business
- NHS/private sector collaborations
- GPFHs
- amalgamated Health Commissions with more buying power
- an inquisitive and inspectoral Audit Commission
- development of NHSE Regional Offices
- dissolution and reformulation of Regional Health Authorities
- quantitative-based performance criteria
- an increasing engagement in 'management' by the medical profession.

The NHS in the late 1990s is an intensely different work environment even from the sweeping changes that were being introduced in the 1980s. Many care professionals and managers have found the changes disconcerting and remain unconvinced about their value. It may not be the high profiled emphasis on internal competition and performance criteria that has caused tension so much as the lack of limits to which these changes will be allowed to extend. In the world of global competition the market is allowed to find its own level through open competition. Through such a mechanism the market self-regulates and after a period of settling down the marketplace (in this case for the provision of health care services) sorts itself out.

Whilst this may be a very appropriate regulatory device for a competitive and price sensitive product market, it may need to be restricted when applied to services such as the provision of health care. One of the fears is that unrestricted provider competition within the NHS could force out of the market very competent health care providers who – perhaps, for example, because of the buildings inherited, or of high cost patient groups – may well find themselves unable to compete with other providers.

The question is not whether the NHS is changing or not, but how and in what ways are the changes being defined and pursued. One of the great difficulties in working to achieve the changes desired with such a diverse and large entity as the NHS is that it all takes time and the interpretation and implementation of changes will vary a great deal from place to place, and from person to person.

One of the major problems for the service at the moment is the high level of stress at work being experienced by staff. Some of this will inevitably have been induced by the type of changes introduced and – importantly – how they have been interpreted and implemented locally.

Figure 3.1 sets out some of the forces speeding up the pace of change within the NHS.

This then is what you are faced with and what you are a part of. To varying degrees, whether directly or indirectly, you will be affected by these changes. Being clearer about such pressures and pulls will help you to cope with them more readily and help you to appreciate some of the pressures on some of your colleagues.

The 'internal market', with the initiation of competition between Providers, has led to increasingly more sophisticated, cost conscious and influential Purchasers who have been able to exercise considerable pressure to secure what they want for the populations they serve.

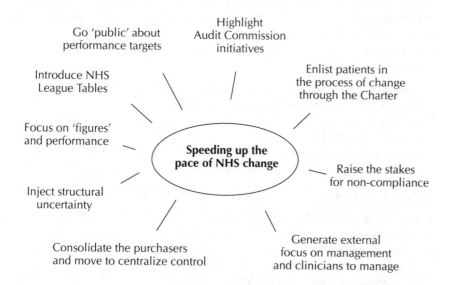

Figure 3.1 Forces for change within the reorganized NHS

Competition between Providers to meet the needs of Purchasers however has the potential for some quite dysfunctional and unexpected consequences for the provision of health care in the UK. Firstly, it creates 'winners' and 'losers' and the possibility that the 'winners' may have agreed to a service contract at a loss in order to win the contract. But why would anyone want to agree to a service contract that will lose them money? Perhaps they see it as part of a longer term strategy where they are able to sustain a loss to begin with – and beat the competition – only in later years to start to increase prices.

Introducing a more competitive 'spirit' into situations is often seen as away of achieving change and movement. Indeed it could be said that one of the 'UK Ltd' legacies from the 1980s is an increasing willingness within the UK to allow 'market forces' to define the shape, course and form of hitherto 'protected' sectors. The notion of competition and 'survival of the fittest' may not be totally appropriate or sustainable in this context.

COMPETITION, COMPETITION AND MORE COMPETITION

Too strong an emphasis on competitive survival may lead to a loss of meaning, purpose, pride or service. For example, if cost reduction or the achievement of higher 'throughput' measures is all that seems to matter at work it is increasingly likely that managers will alter some of their practices just to reach target and avoid the hassle of not doing so.

The publication of league tables of performance measures, of costs for various items or procedures, etc., may *not* act as a spur to improvement but merely alienate, distance or pressurize many who are trying their very best with what has been made available to them. This is not to say that quantitative performance measures are unimportant in health care settings; but they should not be the primary criteria on which 'performance' is based. Figures and statistics are always open to interpretation, depending on which position you want to emphasize 'prove'.

Overall the question is this, 'How competitive should the NHS become?' It needs to be said that:

* unrestricted competition will *not* be universally beneficial
* there will *not* inevitably be an overall beneficial effect
* market forces will *not* always find a level that benefits the consumer (in this case the patient)
* the funding agencies (the DoH, the NHSE and the Providers) will *not* always get the optimum outcomes from encouraging internal competition.

Competition within limits *can* offer benefits to the NHS through:

* a desire to match the performance of other providers
* an incentive to review current practice and change
* external comparative pressure to do better
* a realization that performance to 'public' criteria is required
* the stimulus to look again and try new ideas
* reward for achievement and performance to agreed goals.

On the other hand it can be argued that too much of an emphasis on competition may result in several negative and undesirable outcomes for the NHS, for example:

- a climate where only the results matter
- qualitative care can suffer through emphasis on through-put
- pressure to perform to externally imposed targets without adequate regard to local factors, etc.
- an obsession with systems to control, monitor and direct
- a preoccupation with looking good to external observers
- a climate of self protection (within and between Trusts).

If continued funding, and a Trust's survival, start to be determined primarily on meeting externally imposed performance criteria, it is probable that Trusts will reshape the services they provide which will enable them to 'satisfy' such criteria. In this way they maximize funding opportunities and political approval for the work they do. In the process however the services provided may be less geared to the locally resident populations served.

GOOD INTENTIONS

The need for change within the Service led to creative ideas about:

- how it could be more carefully managed and controlled
- how to get better value for money across the service on a more uniform basis
- how to engender more internal dynamism that would shift the culture to one more open to continuous review and change.

The strategy designed was innovative and viable on paper but appears to have been insufficiently worked through in its implementation *and* in anticipating what the likely dynamic effects and implications of setting up relatively autonomous Purchasers and Providers would be.

By deciding to stimulate a largely unfettered competitive push, the dysfunctional consequences of free competition have not, as yet, been fully guarded against. Consequently there is:

- anxiety throughout the service about security
- over the shoulder management
- a risk-averse climate where mistakes are punished
- increasing fear of failure by those in senior positions
- a culture of external management by meeting publicized targets
- short termism over sustained longer term decision-making
- an over-politicization of health care
- lack of trust, lack of belief
- fragmentation of the service
- culture shock and trauma with inadequate support.

There appear to have been few 'winners' and the general effect on staff morale, belief in the NHS at large, and the attractiveness of the NHS as a career have – so far – generally been negative. It is very likely that many within the Service feel less positively towards it than before and there is little evidence of those in clinical and managerial roles who feel less stress and personal trauma as a result of the changes.

All those working in the NHS will be affected by the implications of the Purchaser–Provider split and the introduction of the internal market. Not everyone will agree with the view presented here of the changes but the purpose of this chapter is to set out some of the consequences of the changes which have been made and which have affected the working climate within the service. My view is that if you have a clear understanding of the changes to the structure of health care contracting and provision that have been introduced, then you are likely to be more able to cope with them. You are also more likely to show more care and understanding of the pressures some of your more senior colleagues may be experiencing as a result of the changes made.

Figure 3.2 records some of the dimensions which have now become a part of what it means to work in the Service for many people. You may not agree with them all and you may want to add further items based on your experience.

If Figure 3.2 presents the wider picture – and of course your experience and your view may be quite different from that presented in Figure 3.2 – then consider what impact all of this may be having on you in the Service. Make a note for yourself of what comes to mind.

Figure 3.2 Impacts of the internal market

ACHIEVING A BENEFICIAL BALANCE

Figure 3.3 contrasts some of the effects of too little competition with what can arise when competition is too prominent.

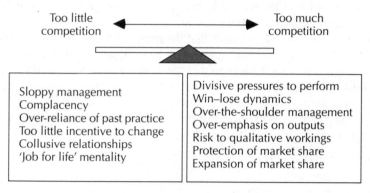

Figure 3.3   Functional limits of market competition

Neither of these extremes is desirable and it is an appropriate balance between the two that is generally the most productive. The challenge for the NHS, at all levels, is to be able to find and maintain such a balance; one that optimizes the dimensions in Figure 3.4.

Figure 3.4 illustrates the balance of care and attention that needs to be achieved between 'people care' and 'resource management'. Each of the four dimensions needs to be well attended to, for if any one of them takes over at the expense of the others, the overall system of care and support will be damaged in some way and will not deliver the desirable results.

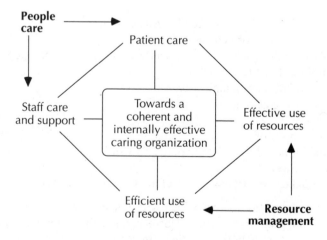

Figure 3.4 Balancing people care with resources

It is easy to see how the system above can very easily be pulled out of balance perhaps because there is just too much emphasis placed on the through-put figures, or the cost per case; or perhaps because there is so much of an emphasis on the administrative procedures that the whole service delivery gets bogged down in the trivial details and misses the wider care objectives which should have remained paramount.

On the 'people' side it could be that the needs of the carers take too much of an emphasis and hence staff cover may be difficult to achieve, or it could be that too much pressure and unrealistic workloads on staff lead to excessive stress.

Make a note of how you would describe each of the four dimensions shown in Figure 3.4:

- *People care dimensions*
  - Patient care
  - Staff care and support

- *Resource management dimensions*
  - Effective use of resources
  - Efficient use of resources

PROFESSIONAL AND INSTITUTIONAL POWER AND INFLUENCE

Another way of thinking about the changes in the organization and structure of the NHS in recent years is to look at the whole thing in terms of power and influence. Looking at an organization from a political perspective can be very revealing and can help to explain what goes on when logic otherwise fails to explain what has happened.

The sources of political influence are varied. The following are just some examples:

- professional bodies (RCN, RCM, GMC, BMA, etc.)
- the do's and don'ts of your organization
- key position holders (Chief Executive, Director of Nursing, Medical Director, the Trust Board, etc.)
- the 'culture' of your organization
- the power of 'past practice'
- local taboos
- groups of top people
- personal influence over the internal career structure
- 'whistle blowers'
- the external career structure (i.e. referees for future posts).

These are a few of the sources which will in some way or other affect what happens within your organization. This is not an exhaustive list so please add others which you have noticed and experienced.

There are three sub-sets to the list above which are:

- institutional power
- personal power
- role and procedural power.

Each of these sub-sets will exert influence where you work and to varying degrees. For example, you may work in an organization which constantly reminds you of its long history and traditions, and where contemporary decisions and actions seem often to be resolved through comparing them with past history and traditions (institutional power). This influence could be so strong that to suggest actions which go against past practice – even though they may be necessary – is so difficult to contemplate that it rarely happens.

Perhaps you work in a place where there are some very forceful and dynamic senior directors and managers; where it matters less what happened yesterday but more what can be done today and tomorrow; where the influence and drive comes more from the people and the energy and enthusiasm they create than from past practice (personal power).

Or you could work in a health care organization where doing things by the book is what counts; where appropriately graded individuals make the decisions expected of them given the limits of responsibility allowed them by their job title. Power here comes through the job description, the rule book, through what the care protocol says and through following procedures as specified (role and procedure power).

If you now use these notions to reconsider the changes within the NHS following the 1990 legislation you are confronted with a very different scenario. The changes introduced were about increasing the effective and efficient use of resources but they also affected the distribution of power and influence within the service.

BUSINESS STRATEGY AND PLANNING

Health Commissions (combined Purchasing Authorities) are allocated monies to provide health care services for the population in their catchment area. In turn they translate the services they require into a series of contracts or 'service agreements' which they put out to tender.

Bids are then submitted by interested Providers (Trusts, private hospitals and other service agencies) some of whom will then be invited to enter into a negotiation with the purchaser. Those invited to present their proposals are then interviewed and, in accordance with formal standing orders, a decision is made to award a contract and a formal 'service agreement' is entered into between the commissioning Purchaser (Health Commission) and the successful Provider(s). Service contracts are then put into force on the terms agreed and are often on a three-year rolling basis with built-in monitoring and performance measures.

Health Purchasers, including GPFHs, are not obligated to buy their services either from the Providers they have traditionally used or from the hospitals and clinics nearest to hand. They will put their money where they believe they will get the best service given the criteria and type of service they have specified.

This flexibility changes the power base of Purchasers considerably and puts strong pressure on Providers to do all they can to meet the requirements as set out by Purchasers. In a competitive environment it is easy to anticipate that one of the dangers to be guarded against is that a Purchasing body, which also has to work within budget constraints, may drive the price down below the point considered by the Providers to be safely manageable and financially viable – a point which, however, for the sake of securing the contract, may nevertheless be agreed by a Provider.

This is a dangerous and inappropriate course of action but it may, in some instances, be the only viable way in which a Trust (or a department within it) can remain in operation in the short term. There are cases where the base line service agreements that have been made are now felt to be too low given the services being provided and where this has placed the Provider in a precarious financial predicament. One consequence of this may be that the service contract is honoured, but at a loss. This can contribute to driving the Trust into a financial overspend – with the potential for all sorts of unexpected pressures and problems which that brings!

Decisions are made by taking a variety of matters into consideration such as price, quality of past services provided, special expertise of the provider, patient feedback and peer assessment where available. Caution will be exercised if a Provider promises too much for an unrealistic price.

It is the responsibility of the Purchaser to ensure that it has accurately assessed the service needs of the community it serves and to convert these into realistic contracts with reputable, focused and competent providers.

Types of contract

'Rolling' contracts are reviewed on an annual basis and fall into different types, the three most common being:

- *Block Contracts:* covering a range of health care services for a patient population. Depending on the variability of the demand levels, maximum patient usage limits beyond which the price is renegotiated may be included in the Service Agreement.
- *Cost and Volume Contracts:* the contractual base is defined for specific treatments, for example, within one specialty. They provide for a specified number of patients with agreements for the cost of additional treatments once the base level of treatments has been reached.
- *Cost per Case Contracts:* the Purchaser pays an agreed price for the treatment of each patient. It involves no pre-allocation of purchaser monies and allows the Purchaser to 'shop around' as and when the need for the particular treatment arises. Providers are likely to charge a premium price for this type of service because it provides them with no secured income, makes them vulnerable to changing Purchaser behaviour and is difficult for them to plan for.

The implications of these moves are far reaching because they establish a very different relationship between, for example, a hospital and what – in the majority of instances – was once their Health Authority. There is now a 'bite' and an 'edge' in this relationship. Hospitals (clinics, community-based services, etc.) *have* to secure financially viable contracts if they want to stay in business. Purchasers on the other hand have a duty to provide the range of care services which their population require and at a price that can be afforded but which will allow Providers to undertake viably the services needed .

Strategy development and planning

Before the creation of the internal market the main considerations affecting the development of locally-based business plans were:

- the Regional Health Authority
- Government priorities
- NHS–ME initiatives and Directives
- statutory instruments
- local custom and practice
- the opinion of the Chairman on the initiatives in view
- the wishes and wants of the local Health Authority
- the priorities and 'weight' of the Regional General Manager
- how the hospital/General Manager was viewed within the Region.

Generally these were the principal *external* influencing forces. In addition there were a number of important *internal* factors that shaped and focused decision-making about future plans, for example:

- the views of the consultant body
- the standing and power of individual senior consultants
- Chairman's wants and wishes
- the Chief Executive's priorities
- the budget history and current financial position
- the cohesion, focus and standing of the Board
- internal climate of the Trust, etc.
- local pressure groups and issues.

What may not have been taken into account sufficiently were the workloads and patient care development strategies of neighbouring hospitals and health authorities. Whilst GPs were also clearly of importance here, their needs and wishes were not necessarily acted upon nor taken into account fully in the setting of hospital-based decisions. All this has now radically changed. With the advent of GP fund-holding, suddenly being 'on-side' with local GPFHs has become critically important for Trusts because GPs now exert influence on patient flows *and* are able to buy the care services they want for their patients. They are obligated to secure the professional services they diagnose as necessary for their patients and now have considerable choice as to who provides them; they do not have to make use of their local hospital. For you as a member of a NHS it means that there have been some fundamental changes that have taken place in how each health care organization sits within the wider NHS and in relation to other providers of health care services around you.

Whilst the services and ward routine may not seem to be very different from a few years ago, behind the scenes much has altered. To begin with there may be a different case mix now (reflecting the mix of the service contract) and some of the 'routine' checks and procedures may have changed as a result of the change in the type of care and the contents of the Service Agreements affecting your ward or clinic. There should now be more awareness of the costs of care (on the cost of disposables, for example), and more emphasis on efficient practice and use of time. At the heart of it all there should be more effective contributions from staff at all levels.

Better use of theatre time, better use of the beds available, better run clinics and patient follow-up procedures, etc. are all part of the drive for a more effective and efficient service for patients and staff. All of this should lead to a more focused and cost effective approach to patient care. One of the keys to this should be through the constructive impact of Service Agreements which will have clarified the work to be done, a sensible time allocation within which to provide the care required, and attention to effective working procedures and work practices.

Many more managers now have all or a portion of their budget devolved and are expected to provide the appropriate professional care needed – in line with the contracted Service Agreements – within the financial allocation given to them. A great deal now rests on the effective people management capabilities and skills of staff at all levels.

Assessing the present and looking to the future

The practical impact of all this is that to survive and prosper from now on health care organizations need to look much more carefully at:

- how they are performing
- what they are actually providing
- what their customers require
- where they want to be in the future as a Provider
- what needs to be maintained
- what needs to change to keep themselves effective
- who are their competitors and their strategic allies
- defining their market strategy
- managing their public image and profile.

The result of the changes is to push Providers and Purchasers to be as efficient and as effective as they can be, and to be very responsive to patient feedback and to the changing requirements of their Purchasers.

One way of doing this in an ordered manner would be for each NHS organization to review its market position viably and undertake an analysis covering the following main areas:

- a review of financial performance

- an environmental mapping survey
- an investigation into what stakeholders want
- a SWOT analysis
- a GAP analysis.

For the purposes of 'checking out' how things are going these not need be particularly elaborate nor require a mountain of work to be satisfactorily accomplished. They are 'sensing' surveys intended to trigger emerging difficulties or identify potential problem areas. Once this has been done then a more detailed and extensive follow-through can be set in motion when necessary.

Each of these five perspectives provides a different and complementary perspective on the organization's current situation and in combination can give quite a comprehensive overview of how the organization is performing, and what needs attention.

A review of the financial performance

This would cover the performance of the organization against the financial criteria it has set up for managing its affairs.

A mapping of your organization's environment

This is where you 'map' out what your competitors are doing, who seems to be exercising influence on whom, and what you believe – or expect – others are saying about the performance of your organization; you are trying to build up a picture of what is going on around you and where you fit in it all.

Finding out what stakeholders want

There will be several key individuals or groups whose views will affect how you are perceived by others and what you are allowed to do; here you clarify who these stakeholders are and what they want.

A SWOT analysis

One straightforward means of checking out how your organization is performing is to set out its Strengths, Weaknesses, Opportunities and Threats (SWOT). This can be done to whatever level of detail you decide but it is surprising how quickly this simple model highlights some of the key things that need looking at.

A GAP analysis

With some information about how the organization *is* performing you are able to compare that with how you *want* the organization to be performing. There will be a 'gap' between these two positions – this way of looking at your situation highlights what these gaps are, and will lead you to consider what needs to change to close the gaps you have highlighted.

Assessing the current position in these terms will give you a great deal of information, not only about how the organization is performing but also about how those outside the organization (whether it be a ward, a hospital, a clinic or the Trust as a whole) may view how you and your colleagues are doing. This type of information is essential to enable the Board to conduct discussions about the current performance, future direction and any changes that need to be made, both within the Board itself and, importantly, with the many key and influential people who, whilst not on the Board, exercise significant influence within the organization.

I have emphasized the value to the Trust Board of such information, but it is equally valuable information for any manager to have because it goes beyond a financial or an output assessment of performance.

Figure 3.5 suggests that these five sets of data can be used to help construct a business and development plan.

Figure 3.5 Developing the business plan

This is an approach (FESSG) which pulls together dimensions often seen as separate and consequently rarely integrated together in the way suggested. However, undertaking this type of integrated review on a regular basis will enable the Board (ward, department, clinic) to become clearer about its market position and it can be used (a) to help assess the viability of plans for the future, and (b) set out a 'bite-sized' action programme.

Constructing a business plan

Constructing a business plan does not have to be a daunting task so long as some very simple points are kept in mind and a clear and uncomplicated format is followed. One Trust uses the following structure:

1. Introduction
2. Achievements since 1997/8
3. Key service developments since 1997/8

4. Directorate objectives for 1998/9
5. Planning and contracts
6. Financial strategy
7. Human resource management
8. Estates and assets.

It also uses the following *appendices* to give the necessary back-up information and statistics:

• Service developments pending investment
• Planned activity profile
• Quality standards
• Financial plan
• Staff profile.

Clarity about key priorities and the work that needs to be done are at the heart of every successful organization and health organizations are no exception. However, it is not enough for the top few to be in agreement on what they are seeking to achieve; there has to be a shared understanding and a good enough shared commitment by the majority of the staff if the organization's priorities are to be successful accomplished. To do this means that time and effort has to be given to contact by senior managers with staff groups up and down the organization in order to get their message across and to defuse any misperceptions, worries and fears.

One of the difficulties that can arise from too much analysis is that it becomes unclear precisely what is to be done, or what the critical information actually is. The process can become far removed from the practicalities of what at the start seemed to be very straightforward and logical 'on paper'. Planners and top level managers can even experience a type of *analysis paralysis* where they get stuck because they have so much data to work from that they lose sight of their objectives and end up not knowing what to do.

One way out of this is make a note of all the options that you are trying to decide between and then assess each of the options in terms of:

• how much additional resources will be needed to opt for that path of action
• who else – other than yourself – will be involved in taking that action forward.

These two parameters have been put together in Figure 3.6 to form four categories into which you can put all the action possibilities you are seeking to prioritize.

By putting these two dimensions together in this way you will get an idea of how much effort is likely to be needed before action could be taken on the priority matters you have identified.

Make a note of how easy or more difficult you would expect it to be to get agreement to proceed with your suggested actions for each of the four categories shown in Figure 3.6.

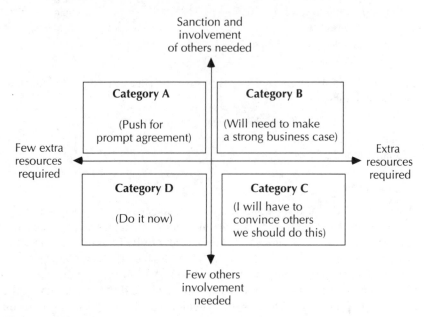

Figure 3.6 Priortizing actions

Generally it is easier to do things – so long as they are relevant – if there are few additional resources needed and if there are only a few of you involved in taking the necessary action.

So it makes sense to take action on those matters which fall into category D. By working to accomplish the priority actions in that category there will probably be some early successes that will help to demonstrate to others that things are on the move. In addition this may encourage them to become more proactive and supportive of making the changes which your business planning analysis had identified.

At the other extreme, if you decide to focus on the big issues alone, those, for example, that require significant additional resources and the further agreement of many others (Category B), then not only will this take time to secure but there may be restrictions on resources which could – for the time being at least – result in no action being taken at all.

Some would say that the art of facilitating change in organizations lies not in tackling the big issue all in one go, but in starting many smaller initiatives and building on the successes and changes which these accomplishments bring.

MARKETING IN HEALTH CARE

One strategy through which Trusts (and Health Commissions) are adopting to build their business service base, keep on the good side of the public and secure their future is through marketing and public relations.

This is an important management activity which until comparatively recently had been neglected within the NHS. Marketing is the business function which is concerned with the creation of the demand for what you have to offer.

Creating an internal NHS market suddenly opened the door for marketing as a function to come alive. When there are suddenly so many Providers out there competing for the Service Contracts you want, it is essential that potential Purchasers (at local, regional and national level) and consumers (patients, patient interest groups *et al.*) know about the work and reputation of your care services, the facilities you provide and that they come to want to be looked after by your Trust.

Having clarified what your business plan and priorities are, an important next step is to clarify what you do *not* want to be involved in providing. From a business perspective – rather than as a provider of all health care services which may be requested – once you are clear about what can be offered and what others are looking for, a decision can be made about the services to be offered to potential Purchasers.

Four steps in the development of a marketing plan are:

1. Decide who your customers and your consumers are.
2. Clarify their needs as carefully as you can.
3. Decide what you will offer and can provide them.
4. Tell customers and consumers what you are doing.

There is now a growing recognition of the need to find out what the 'customers' and 'consumers' of Trusts are looking for. So this means building very good relationships with the Purchasing authorities on the one hand, and with consumers (those who use the services provided) on the other.

Look at Figure 3.7 as if you were the Chief Executive and currently planning your business strategy for the next period of time. Whose needs will you try to meet? How will you handle any shortfall in the expectations of your client population? How will you keep the politicians (local and national) 'happy'?

You need to know who your clients are. Some of them will be within your organization – prominent and influential colleagues perhaps, the Chairman and the Board as a whole. Then there will be a whole range of outside bodies and influences that you need to bear in mind when deciding what you are going to do.

The next step is to be as clear as you can about what they each want and it is likely that some of the needs will be mutually exclusive. When that happens decisions have to be made about how to resolve such situations without offending those who may be very influential.

You need information when deciding where to position yourself in the internal market, which contracts to bid for, which Trusts to collaborate with. Relevant information can be gleaned from undertaking the sorts of analysis outlined earlier in this chapter, from observing the market and from listening to what is going on within the organization too.

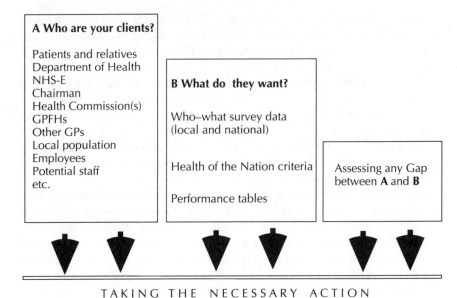

A Who are your clients?

Patients and relatives
Department of Health
NHS-E
Chairman
Health Commission(s)
GPFHs
Other GPs
Local population
Employees
Potential staff
etc.

B What do they want?

Who–what survey data
(local and national)

Health of the Nation criteria

Performance tables

Assessing any Gap
between **A** and **B**

TAKING THE NECESSARY ACTION

Figure 3.7 Deciding what to do and whose needs to meet

Highlighted below are two other major developments now also showing themselves, each of which is likely to change the pattern of health care provision in the UK.

THE INDEPENDENT HEALTH CARE SECTOR

The development of private health care in the UK is big business and it is growing. Until relatively recently private health care was a somewhat privileged service for the few who were either rich, well connected or who had jobs of sufficient status that entitled them to membership of a private health care provider. This position has radically changed in the last five to ten years and there are now several large private health care providers catering for an increasing proportion of the population.

The creation of the internal market and the duty of Purchasers to secure the services they require for the best cost has opened the market for service agreements to be placed with private hospitals as well as with NHS Trusts. So not only are NHS Providers in competition with previous NHS colleagues but they are also in competition for service contracts with the private sector.

JOINT VENTURES: NHS AND PRIVATE

The second major change to the pattern of care provision is that of collaborative ventures between private health care organizations and NHS Providers. More awareness of the external market within which Trusts are competing naturally raises the possibility of mutually beneficial collaboration with other bodies. It is not difficult to appreciate why this has appeal to the Chief Executive, the Chairman and the Board of an NHS Trust:

- more combined resources
- more political weight
- scope for broader range of services on offer
- economies of scale
- strategic alliances to ward off perceived threats
- better utilization of fixed costs (facilities, equipment, people, etc.).

Joint ventures offer a means though which a private health care provider can secure their access to a restricted range of continuing work which the NHS Trust may prefer them to deliver, thus enabling the Trust to concentrate their resources on a different care service. Overall each party benefits from the support of the other.

In conclusion the Purchaser–Provider split has radically and fundamentally altered the tone, shape and relationship between health care providers within the NHS. To understand the profound impact of the changes that have been made means thinking about some of the implications for the way in which NHS Trusts now have to do business within a commercially-oriented business internal market. That is what this chapter has been about.

REFERENCES AND FURTHER READING

Audit Commission (1994) *Reaching the Peak? Getting Value for Money from Management Consultants*, June, HMSO, London.

Department of Health (1989) *Working for Patients*, HMSO, London.

Department of Health (1990) *The NHS and Community Care Act*, HMSO, London.

Department of Health (1991) *The Patient's Charter*, HMSO, London.

Department of Health (1992) *The Health of the Nation: A Strategy for Health in England*, HMSO, London.

Department of Health (1995) *The Patient's Charter & You*, HMSO, London.

Goold, M. and Quinn, J. (1990) *Strategic Control*, Hutchinson Business Books Limited, London.

Karlof, B. (1993) *Key Business Concepts*, Routledge, London.

McDonald, M. and Morris, P. (1987) *The Marketing Plan*, Heinemann, Oxford.

Merry, P. (1975) *NAHAT–NHS Handbook*, 10th edition, JMH Publishing, Tunbridge Wells.

Porter, M. (1985) *Competitive Advantage*, The Free Press, New York.

Porter, M. (1980) *Competitive Strategy*, The Free Press, New York.

Sibley, D. (1995) The hyperthyroid economy, *Journal of the Royal Society of Medicine*, June, **88**(6), pp 305–6.

Spurgeon, P. and Barwell, F. (1991) *Implementing Change in the NHS*, Chapman & Hall, London.

Teasdale, K. (1992) *Managing the Changes in Health Care*, Wolfe Publishing Company, London.

4

Time management and quality performance

This chapter is about creating the conditions to be in a position to deliver 'quality' work even when there is an emphasis on 'throughput'. The more conventional approaches to maintaining quality of work suggest adopting a methodology of working, whereas the approach of this chapter suggests adopting a philosophy of care.

It is, of course, important to be clear about what needs to be done and to assess the competence of the work completed. All too often 'quality' can come to be viewed in a rather mechanistic and procedural way where the overriding aim is to codify tasks and actions so that they can be measured, assessed and ticked off when completed. This chapter emphasizes the importance of doing the very best you can to *secure the time you* need to do what you are in post to do, whether it be direct patient care or the provision of a quality support service.

'Quality' is an important issue in health care: 'quality' is about the well-being of others and appreciating that the consequences of inattentive, inaccurate or otherwise poor performance could lead to a worsening of the patient's condition or even contribute to an untimely death. It involves specifying the precise nature of the tasks to be completed and then defining the standards to which those tasks and service levels are to be performed. However, the concept of 'quality' embraces far more than this alone: it is about a state of mind, a framework within which everything you do receives the attention and rigour it deserves; it is about ensuring that what is done is necessary, timely, and undertaken in an appropriate manner.

THE PATIENT'S CHARTER AND QUALITY MANAGEMENT

Gone are the days when patients are so grateful for any care they receive that they will tolerate anything in the process. Indeed, the communities we serve have become increasingly prepared – encouraged even – to challenge and demand better services. In the internal market this has an added edge: if the level of patient complaints is consistently high this constitutes a high risk strategy for the Provider as there will be competitors (other hospitals and clinics) able and ready to provide the services required.

Meeting Patient's Charter standards and waiting list demands, 'keeping on the good side' of the Department and of the NHSE mean that there is a lot of pressure on care providers at all levels – from the bed on the ward to the Trust Board meeting – to perform to the levels demanded.

Health services remain firmly in the public eye – you have only to note the number of discussion programmes and hospital-based series on the television. Part of the fascination could be that viewers 'see' themselves as part of the dramas and dilemmas being played out on the screen, perhaps as patient or perhaps as one of the clinical team. One consequence at any rate is that patients and visiting relatives will bring with them their view of what hospitals are all about and of what goes on in hospitals.

Health care is one of the core preoccupations of each of us: we know that we shall get ill; we know that we shall die; we need reassurance about the type and level of care we shall receive. Each of us is intensely interested in what goes on because we know it could be us at some time in the future.

The impact of all this is a sustained and highly profiled pressure for high quality care services at the point of need from an increasingly vociferous and informed public. The work of the Audit Commission, the pressure from Purchasers and the NHS Executive all combine to make quality in care provision a matter of central and continuing importance. Figure 4.1 shows some of the sources of comment about NHS services.

Figure 4.1 Who comments about the NHS anyway?

'Quality' emerged as a major business issue in the early 1980s. It was then that a book appeared which in many ways revolutionized the lay person's approach to business life. It presented a credible and very readable account of what it requires to become a successful company. It was not directed at any single market segment, nor was it focused on any particular culture although it was angled towards North America.

The book was called *In Search of Excellence* and it put on the world business map not only its authors (Peters and Waterman, 1982) but also 'quality' and 'customer attentiveness' as core determinants of what it takes to be a successful company. Overnight customer focus and quality became bywords for company success. Quality circles – one of a number of quality and customer service initiatives – were implemented widely across the NHS in several locations.

Combined with the introduction of a general management approach (DHSS, 1983) the notion of 'quality' stimulated considerable debate, interest and action. It has been in the 1990s however that 'quality' as an operational issue has come into prominence, largely because of the internal competition generated through the internal market. Before the internal market was introduced, 'quality' was viewed as something which certain nurse managers were formally designated to deliver and it was generally separated from the responsibility of the line manager. This has now altered because of its importance in sustaining the reputation and viability of the Trust as a competent provider.

Today 'quality' is everyone's business because without it there will be no business. It does not seem, however, that this business reality has as yet hit home to the extent it ought to. Over the next few years the critical importance of what 'quality' means in practice – in terms of the continuation of its service contracts, etc. – is likely to become more profoundly acknowledged.

In 1993 the NHS Management Executive emphasized the importance of developing an organization-wide approach to quality and offered guidance as to how they considered this could best be achieved. The core components of this guidance included:

- a firm commitment to quality and leadership from the Chief Executive
- quality as an integral part of both corporate objectives and individual staff objectives reflecting the organization's business
- an organization-wide quality management programme
- high quality care achieved through an emphasis on teamwork and partnership across the organization
- effective communications both internally and with outside bodies.

There are several significant forces in the background that will influence what you do and how you are asked to do it at local level. To be operationally effective demands more than being professionally proficient and technically competent. To do your job well you need to understand and be able to work with many different work pressures exerted on you in your day-to-day work.

TIME MANAGEMENT AND QUALITY PERFORMANCE

Figure 4.2 highlights the main sources of influence which affect and shape what goes on at the point of care delivery. As a result of the interplay

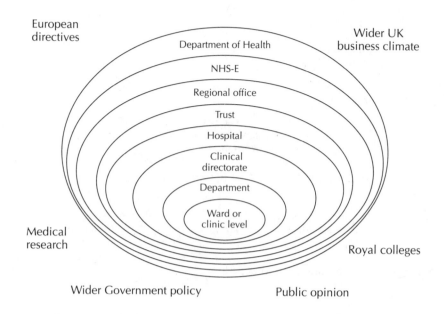

European
directives

Wider UK
business climate

Department of Health

NHS-E

Regional office

Trust

Hospital

Clinical
directorate

Department

Ward or
clinic level

Medical
research

Royal colleges

Wider Government policy   Public opinion

Figure 4.2 Sources of influence on NHS funding and practice

between these forces, decisions are made about care priorities, the levels of service to be provided, the allocation of a service budget, and those procedures to be adopted or resisted. This goes on at the levels of government, NHSE, Health Commission and Trust. The activities and budget at any one level 'fit' into the next highest as the figure illustrates.

Naturally enough we will tend to focus on the changes we see occurring around us, or what we are told is going to happen locally, in our part of the NHS. We will be less aware of the wider pressures for change – those external to the local Trust – even though we will ultimately feel the impact of higher level decisions about the shape and resourcing of the service. We are unlikely to know about all the pressures and the constraints under which local decisions have been made about the care services to be provided.

When decisions are made at a higher level, for example setting out an agenda for the country's health and allocating a budget to that end, there is no guarantee that the desired outcomes will be delivered. It is the same at local level. One way of increasing the likelihood of achieving the outcomes you want is by taking into account as many as you can of the possible factors you think will interfere with the delivery of those plans.

Some of these 'intervening' influences are shown in Figure 4.3. Make your own copy and add in any influences that occur to you.

There is a surprising range of factors that can interfere with your scheduled work programme which either result in tasks not being completed, or perhaps not completed to the level of quality required.

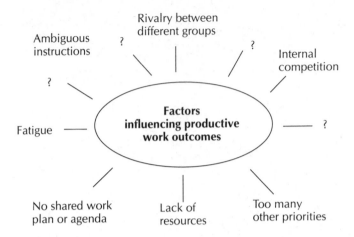

Figure 4.3 Factors influencing work performance

Completing an allocated work schedule (or for example the Trust's Business Plan) is far more difficult to achieve than many would have us believe. Denying how difficult it often is working collaboratively with others is one of the greatest causes of work stress. It is one thing deciding what has to be done and allocating the work but quite another thing to implement success-fully the workload specified.

This 'reality-gap' exists because of the everyday difficulties and obstacles that arise in the course of trying to work with others in an unpredictable world. This is not at all an excuse for lack of co-operation or achievement but more a case for the need to acknowledge that 'things' *do* get in the way and that, in the light of this, more realistic expectations are set.

There are actions you can take, however, to ease the pressure on you and to keep focused on the provision of high quality care. Quality work perfor-mance can be enhanced by:

- clarifying the work to be done (the *task* aspects)
- defining who works with you and on which tasks (the *people* aspects)
- making the best possible use of your *time*.

These three key features in delivering quality work are shown in Figure 4.4.

Looking at your overall work responsibilities in these ways will increase the likelihood of your doing the work that needs to be done, with the most appropriate colleagues, in a time effective and appropriate manner and utiliz-ing the resources available to you in the most efficient way.

Each of these three themes, the tasks, the people, and the time are now considered in turn. When balanced together – in achieving the overall service to be provided – they will lead to enhanced levels of quality performance, and professional and personal satisfaction.

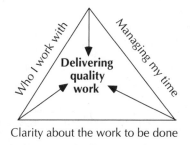

Clarity about the work to be done

Figure 4.4   Three features in delivering quality work

The task aspects: What I am in post to do

At work there are so many things to be done and without prioritizing it is easy to become overwhelmed by the work facing you. Putting the work into different priority categories will enable you to superimpose a hierarchy of importance which will help you to focus on the most critical aspects. The key skill here is that of clarifying what the most important tasks are and then deciding how to prioritize them.

The first step is to identify the *key* tasks that need to be completed and the appropriate performance measures that can be applied to assess how well you are doing. To do this you need to be as clear and as precise as you can about your work responsibilities. Whilst this may sound an unnecessary step, it is very easy to lose sight of key priorities especially when the pressure is put on you to do lots of tasks. Retaining a clear overview of the most critical tasks will help you to see your way through.

Begin by setting out your key tasks and activities, and then arrange them in order of priority. Go through your list and decide whether you are paying adequate attention to the task you have rated highest on the list. It is very easy at work to give priority to those parts of the job which you find most enjoyable – or which you are very good at doing – rather than those parts which are the more important or which you don't enjoy doing.

With the exception of emergency care it is not always necessary to respond immediately to every demand; nor is it appropriate always to delay or push aside demands. There needs to be some balance between the demands confronting you and how and when you respond to them.

To this end a key skill to develop is that of rapidly assessing the *importance and the immediacy* of the response required for each piece of work that comes your way.

Figure 4.5 combines these two dimensions as an aid to helping you decide what should receive top priority attention. When you apply this grid to your work it will become clear that some tasks are higher in importance whereas others can be put to the bottom of the action list.

Cases 1 and 4 are straightforward: Case 1 requires immediate action; Case 4 in your assessment is low in importance and immediacy and you can hold off responding until the other three sets of scenarios have been attended to.

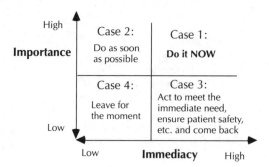

Figure 4.5 Deciding when to act

Case 3 requires that you do what is necessary to ensure safety and care but you hold off being fully diverted by those tasks until all the Case 1 work has been attended to. Case 2 items need attention as soon as possible but not before Case 1 work has been dealt with.

Having decided on the hierarchy of tasks, there are choices about how, when and where to take action. This gives you the opportunity to consider viable alternative care strategies and options given the circumstances and helps you decide on what constitutes the most prudent and effective care possible (see Figure 4.6).

Figure 4.6 What, when, how and why

How you think about what you do is influenced by how you see yourself in your role as a nurse. Set out in Figure 4.7 are four specific roles, each of which describe an aspect of the overall nursing role. The relative predominance you give to each of these roles will lead you to set different priorities and performance criteria and will lead you to seek to establish different types of relationship with colleagues and patients.

 Think about the different roles shown in Figure 4.7. Make your own copy and complete it as fully as you can. Do not try to do this all in one go. Make several attempts because each time you go back to this grid you will see different facets to the four roles noted.

	Nurse as care giver	Nurse as care team member	Nurse as leader	Nurse as business manager
Top priorities				
Success criteria				
Type of relationship with others				
Scope of view needed				

Figure 4.7 Four roles of nurses

The point of this exercise is that each of these four roles will lead to different preoccupations for you as a nurse. The roles are not mutually exclusive but exist side by side. They do, however, vary in prominence for each individual nurse and the challenge lies in being able to integrate and blend them appropriately.

The work priorities alter depending on the particular role of the nurse at a given moment. To cope with this role inter-changeability it is important to have an overview of what you are doing and to keep the overall picture in mind. Not only will this help to resolve conflicting pulls on your time but it will reduce the likelihood of the your becoming too enmeshed in the detail and lose your wider perspective on the care to be provided. Maintaining an overview of your job in this way will also help to keep the stresses and strains of the job in perspective particularly when you are feeling overburdened

One feature of providing a quality service is the ability to see each specific task in the wider context of providing health care for the patient. It is quite easy to become drawn too deeply into the minutiae of 'just another task to be done' and to forget why it is that what you are doing is so important, or how it contributes to overall patient care.

Figure 4.8 presents two contrasting patterns of thinking about work, and about one's competence at work. Several different propositions are posed and you may like to see to what extent any of these describe you.

Neither of these perspectives are inherently good or bad. You will be more effective in your work however if you can see both the detail *and* the big picture, and if you are able to switch between these two perspectives. It is surprising how effective and helpful doing this can be since it can help you to put events, tasks, and behaviours into context and perspective in ways that are just not possible if you are 'stuck' in either of these two extremes.

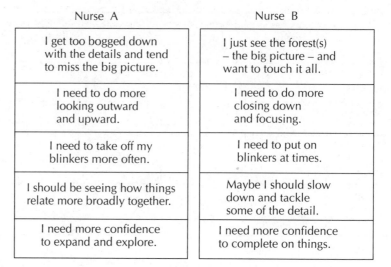

Figure 4.8 Two contrasting approaches to taking action

You can use all these ideas to help build up a hierarchy of tasks to guide your day-to-day work. One method of recording a hierarchy is illustrated in Figure 4.9.

 On your own copy of Figure 4.9 note down all the tasks to be done and rank them in order of their overall importance. You can do this on a scale of 1 (low) to 10 (high) importance, or using a high, medium or low rating as shown in Figure 4.9. Next rate each task in terms of its immediacy and rank them as you did before. Multiply the two figures together and you will end up with a hierarchy of tasks. Check it to make sure it makes sense and then you do the ones with the highest scores first.

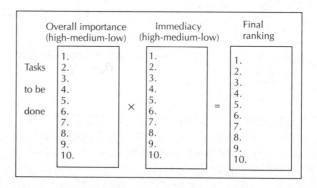

Figure 4.9 Ranking tasks

If your actual behaviour at work does not match the priority gradings you have given, you may need to reorganize your work accordingly. Confronted with lots of things to do it is not always easy to sort out the top priority tasks – this simple procedure will help you do so.

It can be very helpful to ask work colleagues to comment on the above. For example, do they see things as you do. If not, why not? Useful points for comparison are: what are the main purpose and priorities of the job; what are the key tasks to be undertaken; how should tasks be ranked in order of importance.

The people aspects: Those with whom I work

On a busy ward, once the priority tasks have been identified, it is crucial to think about how your time can best be used, and to sort out which tasks you need to do yourself from those which can be delegated.

'People' constitute a key ingredient in the provision of a quality service. The quality of working relationships with colleagues is hugely important for how you operate in your job and this will directly affect the quality of care provided. It pays to think about your colleagues, and reflect on how well you work together. It may sound obvious but much of your success and satisfaction at work will revolve around those with whom you work.

The first step is to compile a list of all those colleagues you work directly with on a regular basis in your day-to-day work. The list could well be a long one. Make a note of how frequently you work with them (daily, every two weeks, hourly, most of the time, etc.). Make a note of how important you consider them to be in enabling you to do your work using the headings in Figure 4.10 as an initial framework to record your notes.

Who	Frequency of contact	Why they are important to me	How they can help me	How they can hinder me	Changes, if any, I need to make

Figure 4.10 People important to me in my job

This information gives you the basis for making some decisions about the current pattern of work relationships. For example, you may find that you are spending too much time with colleagues who may be impeding your work performance in some way, and that you have been neglecting or not spending enough time with the few people with whom you need to collaborate more frequently. You may be able to highlight some of the reasons why certain people are so important to you in your work.

With the above points in mind, the next task is to check:

- if you have clear and appropriate access to those colleagues whom you see as most important in enabling you to get your work done
- if you have the necessary amount of contact with them
- how much of your time – perhaps your energy too – is taken by the other people you work with and whether it is too much or too little given the overall responsibilities of your job.

Figure 4.11 shows a way of displaying this information. It can alert you to the possibility that some of your colleagues may be crowding out those with whom you may need more contact if you are to do your job effectively.

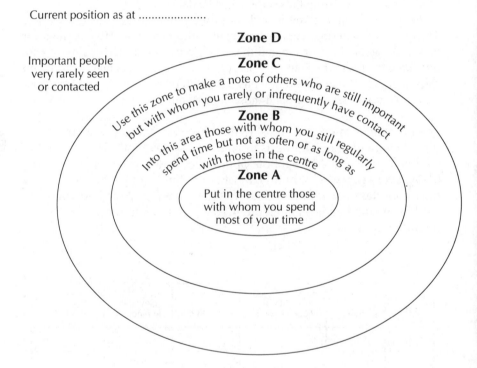

Current position as at ....

Zone D

Important people very rarely seen or contacted

Zone C

Use this zone to make a note of others who are still important but with whom you rarely or infrequently have contact

Zone B

Into this area those with whom you still regularly spend time but not as often or as long as with those in the centre

Zone A

Put in the centre those with whom you spend most of your time

Figure 4.11 Plotting frequency and intensity of current contacts

 Complete a diagram like Figure 4.11 for the current situation as you see it.

You now have a visual summary of those you have contact with at work separated out into different categories depending on how much time you spend with them at work. You also have – by looking at the names in Zone A – a list of those with whom you spend most of your time and who should be those most important in getting the work done.

On the basis of Figure 4.11 you may want to reshape the pattern of contacts you currently have at work. Draw and complete a second diagram like Figure 4.12 to show how the new arrangements should look.

New position as at ....

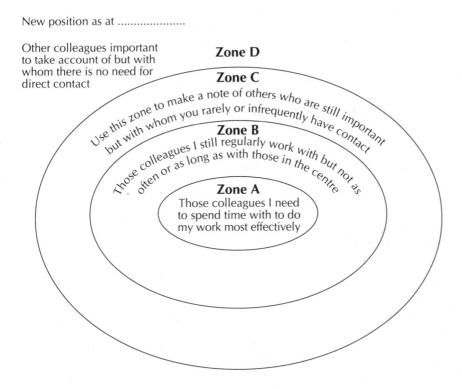

Other colleagues important to take account of but with whom there is no need for direct contact

Zone D

Zone C

Use this zone to make a note of others who are still important but with whom you rarely or infrequently have contact

Zone B

Those colleagues I still regularly work with but not as often or as long as with those in the centre

Zone A

Those colleagues I need to spend time with to do my work most effectively

Figure 4.12 Re-plotting frequency of colleague contacts

Sharpening up the types of contact you have with colleagues does not mean that you forget or shun others, merely that you stay focused on the work you need to accomplish and that you have clarified how best to achieve that.

What Figure 4.12 does *not* show however are the inter-relationships between your colleagues. Figure 4.13 illustrates how you can do this.

For each of your main areas of work, note down those people you collaborate with. At times you will be working alone, at other times you need to collaborate, or perhaps you need resources from others and therefore require open access to them when necessary.

Using Figure 4.13 as a guide, set yourself at the centre with your colleagues around you. In the inner circle enter those with whom you work *very often*, in the middle circle those you *regularly* work with and in the outer circle enter those colleagues you work with *occasionally*.

Go on then to show how they are linked to you by connecting direct lines of communication between them where they exist. You may find

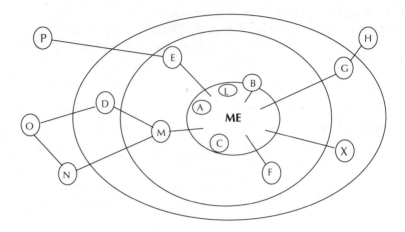

Figure 4.13 Colleague inter-relationships

that there are some colleagues who are important to you in your work but with whom you have no direct link, for example such as N, O, H, and P in Figure 4.13.

Seeing yourself at the centre of a web of contacts in this way can help you to appreciate why, at times, you may feel so hemmed in, or perhaps so much at the beck and call of others that you have too little time for yourself. You may decide that there are just too many people whom you see on a daily basis and that you need to reorganize your work patterns in order to reduce the number, if possible, of those who have a call on your time.

You can also use Figure 4.13 to highlight staff with whom you may want to have more contact but where this can only be achieved through others. For example N, O, P and H might be very senior colleagues and you may well need to work through intermediaries such as G, M, N or D.

Making the best use of your time

To deliver quality results an optimum balance needs to be reached between the demands of the tasks to be completed, the quality of the working relationships with those needed to get the work done, and the use of the resources available. A pivotal resource in delivering quality care is making the best use of the professional carer's *time*.

Achieving this is not easy in a job where the nurse is often juggling different pulls on her time, and where there is an inherently high level of stress and tension. Handling the day-to-day responsibilities, 'getting through the day' and coping with unexpected events means that a rigid and inflexible time schedule is not possible.

It is possible though to clarify how you use your time during the day. Figure 4.14 uses the format from the previous section to assess where your time goes during the working day – and who it is that takes it!

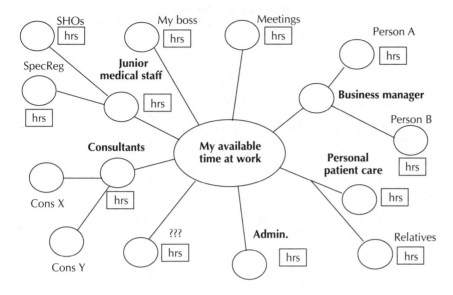

Figure 4.14 Who takes my time?

With this overview you can work out if anything needs to change and then begin to make those needed changes to your working practices happen.

Structuring your working day

Another way you can gain more control over your hours at work is to split up your day – where this is viable – into different sections so that you can concentrate on specific responsibilities which it would be more difficult to attend to otherwise.

For example, the working day can be split into 'operational' and 'restricted' time periods. Operational periods would be when you are freely available whereas restricted periods would be when you are not to be disturbed except for emergencies. Whilst emergencies will throw your plans into disarray over short periods of time, it *is* possible to follow this type of pattern and for your colleagues to learn to respect this way of organizing your time. It will give you more control over your day.

The 'restricted' time periods can be used to work on difficult problems, for planning, for coaching colleagues, for doing the budget, and for thinking about patient care developments and strategies. It is for you to decide how long these periods can feasibly be. These periods give you an opportunity to think, reflect, plan and recover; they allow you to regroup your energy, and refocus on your priorities. All of this contributes to delivering better quality care. All staff can benefit from an opportunity to reflect on and learn from their experiences over the day.

Figure 4.15 suggests a way of structuring the working day to build in periods for recovery and reflection.

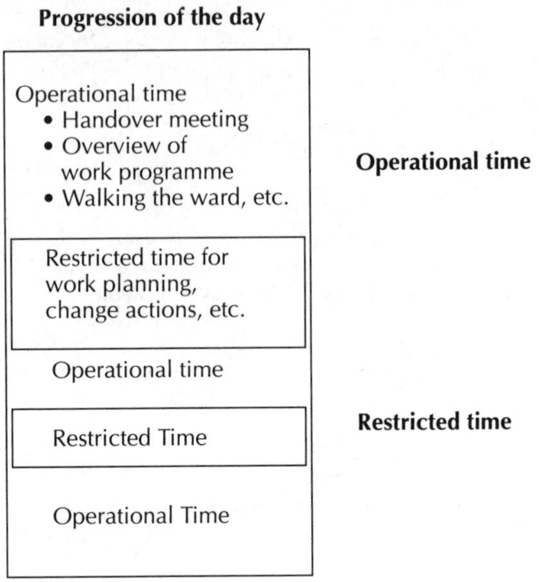

Progression of the day

Operational time
  • Handover meeting
  • Overview of
    work programme
  • Walking the ward, etc.

Restricted time for
work planning,
change actions, etc.

Operational time

Restricted Time

Operational Time

Operational time

Restricted time

Figure 4.15 Structuring your working day

Whilst the ability to think on one's feet, to take the best action in the circumstances and generally 'cope' are highly valued and important skills for managers to possess, the capacity to take a broader view of what is going on and to plan for the future is equally important. In fact, the extent to which you are able to learn from what is going on around you and identify the reasons why difficulties occur will have an impact on how far you are able to avoid unnecessary trauma or an unnecessarily high workload.

Analysing workloads and thinking about why difficulties occur can sometimes enable you to plan them out of the job next time around. The way you choose to organize the ward, or the communication patterns you insist on following, help to create the kind of workload you have and have a bearing on effective ward functioning. It will pay you to look frankly at how matters are organized and to see if you are inadvertently causing difficulties yourself.

Freeing yourself from the 'monkeys on your back'

By attending to the points outlined so far, you stay focused on the work you are in post to do and manage your time with care so that, through not allowing yourself to become overloaded or diverted, you have the best chance of providing quality care.

One of the major obstacles to effective quality performance at work is that of becoming too entangled in work which others should be doing for themselves; where, because of possibly wanting to be helpful, you may take on the work of others.

Each of us might be prepared to take on the problems of colleagues for the following reasons:

- an opportunity to display competence
- a chance to show-off
- a wish to help (even if inconvenient)
- it confirms the supposed vulnerability of the person seeking assistance
- it confirms the position of a senior colleague
- it confers power over the requestee
- being asked for help can be flattering
- people feel validated by being asked for help.

Underlying these possible reasons are a few very pervasive and powerful themes about human nature which play themselves out at work. These may be about:

- a confirmation of personal meaning
- self-worth and validation in the eyes of others
- an opportunity to exercise influence and control
- a chance to exercise personal power and influence
- an opportunity to display competence and reduce feelings of anxiety.

If you can resist taking on the work responsibilities of colleagues then you will save yourself additional work that is not yours to complete. You will, of course, want to step in and help in a crisis or where the system is about to collapse and this should not change. When colleagues invite you to take over their work problems it is more appropriate for you to support them in tackling their issues for themselves so that they become more competent and confident for the future.

REFERENCES AND FURTHER READING

Department of Health (1991) *The Patient's Charter*, HMSO, London.

DHSS (1983) *NHS Management Enquiry, The Griffiths Report*, HMSO, London.

NHS-ME (1993) *Achieving an Organization Wide Approach to Quality*, HMSO, London.

NHS-ME (1994) *Clinical Audit 114/95 and Beyond*, HMSO, London.

Peters, T. and Waterman, R. (1982) *In Search of Excellence*, Harper & Row, New York.

People at Work

This part moves the focus to internal organizational processes and practices. How decisions get made, the sometimes weird and unexpected ways in which groups work, and how organizations create their own internal cultures and systems of belief.

The practical frameworks, ideas and approaches introduced will enable you to gain greater insight and understanding about organization behaviour and alert you to the management ideas which probably guide the thinking of your senior colleagues.

Working effectively and efficiently in an organization is far from straightforward. It is a sad fact but there are many who get damaged by their experiences, feel frustrated and not listened to, and come to dread the daily journey to their place of work. Relatively few staff seem able – or willing – to really give of their best for much of their time at work. The market pressures of the 1990s with de-layering, increased work pressures, higher levels of experienced stress, etc. are likely to increase the sense of personal detachment and disappointment for many individuals.

Organizational life is not – as many would have us believe – just a matter of defining the work to be done and then expecting that those in post to execute that work in an almost automatic and predetermined manner. What is found instead is a complex set of inter-relationships some of which are to do with getting work done and some of which are not. Status, the exercise of influence and power, ambition, fear of failure and of being seen as inadequate all complicate what goes on at work.

Many of us could do well to develop still further our understandings of organizational life and of how we can remain effective and in good spirits at work. Organizations are intensely social entities with a great deal bubbling under the surface; they are challenging places to be in. At any one time there will be several levels of interaction occurring at one and the same time. This complexity is often neglected or forgotten, and generally too much emphasis is placed on the facts and figures of a situation and too little on the social interactions and dynamics which are also having a major influence at work.

In health care organizations this complexity is increased even more because of the tension and anxiety inherent in the provision of care services. The material presented in Part Two will throw more light on some of the complexities noted above and allow the reader to consider the logical, the emotional and the 'hidden' aspects of what goes on in an organization.

Thinking about your organization $\boxed{5}$

This chapter introduces some ways of thinking about the organization you work in. Regardless of what job you do or the professional training you have completed, the way you are able to go about your work will be affected by the organization you work in. Understanding how organizations work will help you to remain effective in your professional work and cope better with the institutional, and personal, pressures of the job.

To make the most of the ideas presented, keep in mind an organization that you can relate the material to. Your choice could be a clinical department, a ward, the Trust, a CMHT, the Patients' Records Department or a health clinic; equally it could be a sports team, the local RCN branch or a constituency party of a political party. What is important is that it should be an organization with which you are familiar.

THE NOTION OF ORGANIZATIONS

The first thing to do is to define what an 'organization' is for the purposes of this book. Most management books on organizations tend to focus on the following characteristics. Organizations:

- are *task focused:* they have been formed for a purpose and are there to get those things accomplished
- are *logical-rational based:* generally they set about their work in an ordered, logical-rational way with procedures, processes and protocols intended to ensure that the desired tasks are completed to the expected standards
- are *exchange based:* there is some exchange made between the people involved in the work of the organization usually involving a mixture of financial, non-financial and psychological benefits in return for the employee's time, effort, skills and commitment
- are *quantitative more than qualitatively focused:* generally what matters are the tangible achievements rather more than the quality of the working relationships involved in getting the tasks done
- develop their own *identity, ethos and culture:* organizations develop their own unique culture, style and tone that affects all who work within that setting – in effect organizations take on an identity and a character of their own.

Chapter 2 set out some of the main 'schools of management' which have influenced the expectations people have about organizations, and what organizational life should be like. The predominant emphasis is on tasks and on internal order and regularity – control, in effect – with the emotional dimensions of working in organizations generally being pushed to one side. Yet organizations are at their heart groups of people who have come together for a predefined work purpose and who cannot avoid bringing with them their emotional make-up and their feelings as well as their specialist skills and knowledge.

Far from being static bureaucratic entities, organizations are intensely interactive and emotional ones. The ebb and flow of the internal dynamics and emotions that arise from people working together exert a dramatic effect on the quality of whatever that organization is seeking to accomplish, and the well-being of those involved.

Just as an individual's personality develops over a period of time so it is with organizations. They come to develop an identity of their own to which staff often attach themselves with great commitment. Such strong emotional attachments can then lead those inside an organization to defend it against any hint of criticism and threat even when they can see that such criticism is relevant and justified!

Organizations though can take on a life of their own and lose sight of their original aims, objectives and ethics to the extent that preserving the integrity (status, name, honour, etc.) of the organization can become more important than all else. A situation might arise where even dubious actions are undertaken to preserve an organization's standing, goodwill, or influence. Examples of this could be not disclosing information, of being 'economical with the truth', or in some other way operating in a disreputable manner.

Organizations too can lose touch with reality and believe themselves to be impervious to the changing world around them. They can come to believe what they want to believe and pretend that external changes will not affect them. There are likely to be examples of this attitude within the NHS either in relation to the changes to the NHS structure, and to developments in clinical practice.

It is easy for the those in organizations to become confused and bemused by all that goes on around them. This confusion and pressure will impair the quality of decision-making yet still relatively little emphasis is given to the emotional, the dynamic and interactional aspects of organizational life.

How staff feel about working in the organization affects what they will do. Each person has a choice about how much effort they will put into their responsibilities at work. If they feel good about how they are treated and the work asked of them they are likely to contribute more. If they feel badly about how they are treated, and if they are uneasy about the work being asked of them they will contribute far less. They may well complete the tasks required but how they do them will reflect in some way their lack of contentment.

How each person fits into their organization and their understanding about how it functions are important determinants of that organization's success and the well-being of staff. Two frameworks for looking at the structure of your organization are now presented followed by several ways of looking at its internal workings.

TWO ORGANIZATION FRAMEWORKS

To be able to discuss your organization you need to have a framework which will help you to describe its core functions and how they need to relate to each other if that organization is to function successfully.

At the heart of any organization should be the rationale for its creation in the first place, that is the *work* that it is there to do. This is the key starting point from which to think about any organization, for example about how it is structured, about the various tasks to be done, about how decisions are to be made, and about what staff it needs, etc.

Galbraith's 'Fit' Model

Galbraith (1977) developed a way of thinking about an organization's structure which emphasizes five key functions of any organization. He suggests that an effective organization is one where each of these five functions is in balance with each of the others. In this way they 'fit' together and can work in harmony rather than, as can happen, against each other. These five functions are:

- *Work*: the work to be done – this is the natural starting point from which other decisions should be made
- *Structure*: the structure required to do that work
- *People*: the people necessary to make it function
- *Rewards*: how staff are rewarded for the work they do
- *Information and decision-making*: the information and decision-making arrangements necessary for the organization to operate effectively and efficiently.

Figure 5.1 shows how each of these five functions connect with each other.

A change to any one of these five functions should be looked at in relation to how that change will impact on the other four. If, for example, a decision is made to change the management structure, some thought also should be given to the effect that will have on work flow, on the reward and pay structures, on the type and flow of management and clinical information, etc.

Before any change decision is finalized and implemented the wider internal effect of that change should be considered. In this way the full internal consequences of any decision are considered before a final decision to change is taken.

A well integrated and effective organization is not dissimilar to a sophisticated and well balanced mechanical system – like a high performance car – with the separate parts linked together and working for each other to create the end result. When a change is made to one part of the system, change is triggered in the other parts in order to compensate and to regain a balance overall.

Figure 5.1 Galbraith's 'Fit' Model

From my experience the three most common organizational changes involve either changing the structure, the people or the reward systems. However, in each of these cases, the other parts of the system need to be readjusted and realigned if that organization is to continue working effectively and efficiently. Often though such readjustments are neglected (sometimes not even anticipated!) and consequently the organization is thrown out of balance with either a new remuneration system, new people or the new structure causing internal difficulties in other parts of the organization. For example, it may be that reporting relationships are altered without the Finance Department or the Patient Information Officer being informed – the end result being confusion as to who should have been given reports, statistics, a different pay grade, etc.

The key message is that:

- the five dimensions are interdependent and if change is made in one then the effect of this on the others needs to be considered
- if a change is made on any one of them on its own without consideration of the organization as a whole, then you can expect problems.

It is an uncomplicated way of thinking about any organization. For example, a clinic, theatres, the CSSD and wards can be looked at using these dimensions and this framework for linking it all together. If you have noticed problems at work, check back to see if any of them are arising because these five dimensions have become out of focus: if they no longer 'fit' together as they need to, if changes to one part of the set-up were made without sufficient thought to the wider impact of that change to the running of that organization.

The organization pyramid

The most common way in which an organization is depicted is in the form of a hierarchy of job levels as illustrated in Figure 5.2. This shows five directors, each responsible for a part of the business. This could be a large hospital or, for example, finance across the Trust. In turn they are supported by senior managers each of whom is responsible for a part of the total responsibility their director carries.

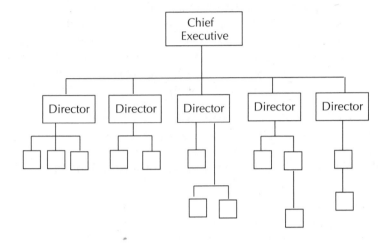

Figure 5.2 An organization hierarchy

Whilst this way of looking at an organization is helpful at clarifying reporting relationships and the formal levels of reporting used, it gives no clue about the inter-relationships between the separate directorates. This way of depicting organizations suggests that it is the responsibility of the person at the top to pull it all together and make sure the organization functions efficiently and effectively.

The top team will meet on a regular basis, as the Board, to make corporate-wide decisions but this way of looking at organizations may encourage each director to look after their own domain – or fiefdom – rather than promoting cross-functional collaboration. It gives no way of indicating how initiatives taken in one part of the business affect the rest of the organization nor any clue about the organization's tone and culture other than its formality and functional separateness.

However with these two frameworks in mind we can now move on to look at what goes on within them.

THE FORMAL ORGANIZATION

As useful as these frameworks are they do not give the full story. If you ask people to describe their organization they will probably begin to describe some of the formal aspects such as its structure, job titles, reporting relationships, grades and levels of staff (rather like the organization hierarchy in Figure 5.2). These are important facets of an organization because they provide the infrastructure which then enables work to be undertaken. But they do not explain or account for much of what actually happens in practice.

Most of the reported difficulties and disputes are also described in terms of the formal 'structural' dimensions such as grading and pay disputes, role confusion and reporting disputes, competition for formal power, and cross-professional competition about who is more senior to whom.

Whilst it may seem that all hospitals, clinics, specialist units, etc. would be very similar in how they are set up, and in how they function, this is not the case even though they may have the same formal terms of reference. The formally set down features of any organization do not tell the whole story by any means. We get no sense about what it is like to work in an organization from these. As soon as we add-in some of the 'people issues' we find out more about the interactions within a unit, on a ward, in the clinic, etc., and we start to find out about some of the tensions and dynamics going on.

What actually happens in practice in an organization will be a mix of:

- the *formally* expected and desired ways of behaviour
- the *informal* patterns of working locally (custom and practice)
- the wishes and influences of the *key people* currently in place
- '*hidden*' influences within the workplace.

THE INFORMAL ORGANIZATION

Whilst it is very convenient to have a nice and neat organization structure that is backed up by carefully worded statements that purport to codify and show how the place works (for example, vision statements and codes of conduct), they do not always accurately reflect what happens in practice.

Organizations develop their own informal patterns of influence, power and authority and new staff usually find out very quickly who to go to for reliable professional guidance and support. They find out who the informal leaders are, i.e. those people who get things done but who, according to the formal structure, may not feature prominently on the formal organization chart.

The emotional dynamics of organizations – the 'emotional organization structure' – are also features which are not usually talked about because they are difficult to describe and pin down with any accuracy, and are uncomfortable matters to openly explore because they highlight the actual power and influence of personal dynamics that are operating in the workplace. It is far easier to talk, for example, about performance figures and plans for the future, and the performance of the Trust against its projected budget spend.

THREE LEVELS OF INTERACTION

One of the difficulties in attending to the non-formal aspects of organizational life is the absence of a common framework for describing such interactions. One way of doing this is simply to differentiate between different levels of an organization's dynamics. Figure 5.3 suggests three levels of interactions each of which are taking place at the same time – the manifest, the covert and the unconscious.

Nearly all of the focus at work is confined to discussions and communications about Level One interactions and behaviours (see Figure 5.3). This is about what are the formal tasks to be done, about the problems and difficulties which are showing themselves, and the various sets of information available to managers and staff to chart the progress of their work. This is what goes down in the case notes, in the reports of the Trust Board, and is the meat of what gets talked about in recruitment interviews and during staff appraisal meetings.

What also goes on are Level Two interactions – the covert side of the organization – which are usually not discussed openly. These are the intentions and agreements which exist but which are not shared with those who are not a party to them. In part these can be an aspect of the informal side of the organization but they are more than that. In effect Level Two interactions represent a closed and secret aspect of an organization's functioning. Generally this side of organizational life may be alluded to but is unlikely to be openly talked about because of the political implications of doing so. In other words it could adversely affect a person's standing and possible career development in that location.

It is though the third level of interaction that is invariably denied, laughed away or pooh-poohed as non-existent. Yet there are a lot of things that go on beneath the surface which seem to be just outside our awareness but which influence what we do, see, feel and experience at work. Because they are out

Level of dynamics	Type of influence	Description of the behaviour
Level One What is there for all to see	Explicit intentions Implicit intentions (access is open to all)	MANIFEST BEHAVIOUR
Level Two What is there for only some to see	Covert intentions (access is hidden, restricted to the selected few)	COVERT BEHAVIOUR
Level Three What is there but not consciously seen by any	Psycho-dynamic and unconscious intentions, drives and tensions	UNCONSCIOUS COMMUNICATIONS

Figure 5.3 Three levels of organizational dynamics

of awareness, the effect of these influences cannot readily be described, defined or captured in any direct way. However just allowing for the possibility of Level Three influences at work opens up a new dimension to thinking about our behaviour at work. Level Three influences could help explain what otherwise can appear as unusual, bizarre or unexpected at work.

One of the most surprising – and disconcerting – facets of organizational life is how work practices which have become embedded can actually start to restrict the effective performance of staff. Some of these are deliberate and can be plain to see (for example, restrictive work agreements) but some may not be consciously initiated. In many instances what is and is not acceptable somehow filters in to one's work behaviour guided more by what colleagues tell you than the particular demands of any particular task on its own.

ORGANIZATION CULTURE

It is generally possible to pick up 'vibes' about an organization almost immediately on entering the hospital or the ward – vibes which lead to assumptions about what it would be like to work there. A great deal of information is taken in from the surroundings: the positioning – or absence perhaps – of notices and directional signs; the feel, smell and state of the place. The way people behave, the types of interactions that go on between them and the way they relate to you personally adds more information to the initial perceptions so that after quite a brief period of time it is possible to build up a rich picture of the organization.

All this information describes the work *culture* of the organization and it is amazing how varied and numerous these cultural messages can be. They reveal much about what it is like to be there, irrespective of what formal information has been passed on beforehand or is proudly displayed in formal organization charts and the PR literature.

Whilst conventionally used to describe the customs and behaviours of different peoples and communities, *culture* is an apt notion for capturing the essence of an organization such as a hospital or a health clinic. These are, after all, separate communities in their own right and each generates its own unique feel and work culture.

'Organization culture' has been described in the following ways:

- 'the collection of traditions, values, policies, beliefs and attitudes that constitute a pervasive context for everything we do and think in an organization' (McLean and Marshall, 1983)
- 'Culture … is a pattern of beliefs and expectations shared by the organization's members. These beliefs and expectations produce norms that powerfully shape the behaviour of individuals and groups in the organization' (Schwartz and Davis, 1981)
- 'how things are done around here' (Ouchi and Johnson, 1978)
- 'Values are the bedrock of any corporate culture. As the essence of a company's philosophy for achieving success, values provide a sense of common direction for all employees and guidelines for their day-to-day

behaviour' (Deal and Kennedy, 1982)
- 'the taken for granted and shared meanings that people assign to their social surroundings' (Wilkins, 1983).

An organization's culture profoundly affects the thoughts and the behaviour of its members yet much of it can be very difficult to describe in detail. An organization's culture will highlight what is seen to be important and what is irrelevant attending to. The culture will often work in subtle ways where what is expected is hard to determine, rather like being assessed but where no one has told you what assessment criteria are being used! You may have direct experience of suddenly being carpeted but you didn't know why, or where you were welcomed and supported because of something you did – but which you had no idea beforehand of its importance.

Roger Harrison (1993), initially with Charles Handy, presented an uncomplicated view of how an organization can become oriented towards one of four basic cultural types (see Figure 5.4).

Harrison's framework offers a way of getting an idea of the relative weighting that an organization gives to these different orientations. It is intended as a way of describing the culture of your organization, rather than as a means of making a good–bad judgement of it. Each of the four cultural types have their positive and negative sides and it is unlikely that any organization will exclusively fit any single type to the extreme. A mix of types can usually be seen and these will vary from organization to organization, and possibly from department to department within the same organization.

You can use these ideas to reflect on what seems to be given most attention where you work. For example:

- Which of these styles is your workplace most similar to?
- Which would be the next most similar type?
- Which do you see it as being least like?

Power culture	**Role culture**
Based on *strength*:	Based on *structure*:
• influence • winning • success	• following the rules • reliability • 'procedure'
Acheivement culture	**Support culture**
Based on *competence*:	Based on *relationships*:
• rigour and logic • task focus • shared purpose	• mutual support • caring • personal expression

Figure 5.4 Harrison's four organizational cultures

Each of these four types can become so prominent that they take over and influence the whole style, nature and tone of the organization in question – possibly with disastrous effects – so far as the effectiveness of the organization is concerned. For example an organization that becomes preoccupied with power is likely to foster a high level of internal competition and rivalry. An organization where a role culture takes precedence may well become so 'rules and procedures' driven that it doesn't matter what you do so long as you go about it in the accepted manner!

Thinking about your organization's culture is important in helping you to become clearer about the type of place where you are working, about what seems to be especially valued and wanted from you in your work, and if this suits you.

The internal culture influences:

- what people's actual preoccupations are in their day-to-day practice
- the styles of management deemed to be acceptable
- how non-members are viewed and dealt with
- what is not valued, not talked about
- what is taboo.

Blake and Mouton (1976) proposed another set of notions which you can apply to thinking about your own job and your work culture. They revolve around the types of issue which people feel are important. They suggest four common core issues which are ever present in some respect in organizations. These are concerns and issues about:

- power or authority
- morale or cohesion
- standards or norms
- goals or objectives.

All four of these link to each other in the sense that a change in one may bring about change in another, but they are separate in terms of how those in your organization view their importance. As with Harrison's framework, any one of these can become too prominant and skew the thinking and the decision-making where you work. For example, if power or authority becomes dominant then this may lead the organization to become less concerned about morale and cohesion, and indeed the standards and ethics to follow.

These ideas can be used to look at what goes on where you work in a more exacting and enquiring way. They can be used to help you build up views about the culture where you work and the extent to which this seems constructive and productive or dysfunctional.

WHEN YOU SAY 'ORGANIZATION', WHICH ONE DO YOU MEAN?

At any one time there are a number of different – and competing – perceptions of what the organization is in the minds of those who work there. When you talk with colleagues about 'the' hospital, ward, clinic, etc., as an organization your colleagues could be responding using a different definition to the one you are using.

Below are some alternative ways of describing an organization:

- as set out on the formal organization chart
- as it actually functions
- as its members would like it to be
- as denied by its members
- as the mythology would have it
- as we pretend it is to ourselves.

Each of these definitions will give a different picture of your place of work. Each of these views is valid, because if a person sees your organization in a particular way that view will be valid for them irrespective of your opinion.

Taken together each of these rather different angles will give you a richer picture of your organization than you would get from relying on the formal organizational chart alone. It is this fuller picture that can help you to understand a little more about the dynamics of the place, and should help you manage the inevitable stresses and strains more successfully.

Remember that *what* you are looking at is still the same, it is merely *how* you look at it that makes the difference – and each different perspective offers insights that are worth considering.

WHAT IS IT LIKE WHERE YOU WORK?

The best way of understanding the ideas in this chapter is to apply them to your own organization. This will help you to decide which ideas work for you and which do not. You can then start to construct your own models to explain and account for what you see going on around you to help you become more effective at work.

Choose a part of your organization you know well and have worked in for at least a month or so because you need to have some history to draw upon. Now ask yourself four simple questions:

1. What is it like where you work?
2. What are the underlying themes?
3. What are the taboos and myths?
4. What gets rewarded?

Record your answers on a diagram like that shown in Figure 5.5.

Your responses to these questions will elicit a deal of information. You can respond to them as briefly or as fully as you wish. They provide you with an initial framework for exploring what goes on in your organization over and above the job descriptions, the publicity material, and the organization charts.

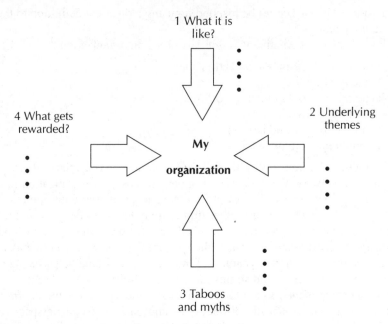

Figure 5.5 Re-looking at my organization

Question 1: What is it like?

The aim here is to build up a picture – make an assessment – of your current situation. So, what comes into your mind when you begin to think about it? For example:

- immediate thoughts and impressions that arise
- what you like about it
- what you dislike
- what seems to matter here
- what is not attended to or pushed aside.

Question 2: What are the underlying themes?

Look at what you have recorded to see if you can identify any underlying themes or patterns – any hidden messages about your organization and how it functions, for example. Are there any issues that you know to be really important which you seem somehow to have missed or just omitted from your notes. Why might that be? It could be that the most obvious things are easily forgotten, or overlooked; or it could be that it is easier at times to pretend that particular issues or concerns don't exist and are therefore best forgotten (particularly if others adopt the same strategy).

Question 3: What are the taboos and myths?

In thinking about where you work, are there any topics or aspects of how the organization functions that people never seem to talk about? Have you been told not to ask about particular matters, or have you noticed that when certain things come up your colleagues go quiet, for example? If so, this could be because there are some areas of business that are taboo. By identifying these you can get invaluable information about the workings of your organization. Conversely, are there any stories or is there mythology that is ritually handed down to newcomers where you work?

Question 4: What gets rewarded?

Are there particular behaviours that seem to be looked for – and then rewarded – and, conversely, are there ways of working or of 'being' that seem not to be encouraged, valued or wanted? If so what are they? What you can pick up here are the subtle shaping and conformity pressures that will, somehow, reflect the nature and character of the organization in a way that an organization chart or a mission statement fails to do.

Developing these observational and diagnostic skills will help you to develop a clearer view of what you look for in your work settings and also what you don't want. If you do not develop these skills in 'sussing-out' organizations you may find yourself inadvertently committed to working in settings where you are at odds with the prevalent organizational tone, experiencing avoidable stress and wishing you weren't there in the first place.

Do try to take note of what is going on around you organizationally because there is much to see and few people take the time to look. The information you put together from these four questions, and any others you might want to use, can also help you to think more fully about your future career and what you want from your work.

Pulling these dimensions together will give you:

- interesting sets of data about where you work
- information as well about how *you* look at your organization and make sense of what goes on there.

Never forget that each of us is biased about some things and sensitive about others so whatever 'picture' you develop will not necessarily be shared totally by others around you.

WHY ALL THIS MATTERS

The models of organizations outlined can be used to diagnose what is going on around you and to build up some idea of just how well your organization is functioning. With so much of your career likely to be spent in one organization or another the ideas covered here may help you to identify the types and styles of organization you prefer and those where you might become very unhappy.

These ideas – together with those in Part Four – will also help you to play your part in facilitating constructive change. The culture of an organization will affect how well you can deliver your professional work, the quality of the relationships you have with your colleagues, and the degree to which you can be yourself in doing your work in a careful and professional manner.

The nature, style and the tone of the organizations we work in profoundly affect our sense of well-being, and the quality of the work we do. Therefore it is surprising that more attention is not routinely given to thinking about:

- how organizations are set up
- what actually happens in practice
- the tensions that often occur between the needs of the person and the needs of the organization, and how these are resolved.

WHY HAVE THESE IDEAS NOT BEEN TAKEN UP MORE FULLY?

More recognition is now being given to exploring how behaviour in organizations can become distorted by unconscious or 'out-of-awareness' processes, and from psychological anxieties generated at work. Employers have a responsibility for a duty of care for their staff which includes a responsibility for the psychological well-being of staff. Understanding more fully how your organization works, and the culture it promotes, can help staff to become more informed and more resilient at work.

So called logical decision-making and scientific management are necessary but they may be influenced by additional, 'other-than-rational' drives and processes that are elusive to define and hard to pin down.

The clinical premise of not taking for granted what is directly observable can also be applied to organization behaviour. Look beyond the obvious behaviours and practices you see around you at work and consider the possibility that some of what you see and experience is in response to an organization's more hidden and deeper motives and needs.

REFERENCES AND FURTHER READING

Blake, R. and Mouton, S. (1976) *Consultation*, Addison-Wesley, Reading, MA.

Deal, T. and Kennedy, A. (1982) *Corporate Cultures*, Addison-Wesley, Reading, MA.

Fineman, S. (1993) *Emotion in Organizations*, Sage, London.

Galbraith, J. (1977) *Organizational Design*, Addison-Wesley, Reading, MA.

Hampden-Turner, C. (1990) *Corporate Culture for Competitive Edge*, Economist Publications, London.

Hampden-Turner, C. (1994) *Corporate Culture*, Hutchinson Books Limited, London.

Handy, C. (1976) *Understanding Organizations*, Penguin Books, Harmondsworth.

Harrison, R. (1993) *Diagnosing Organizational Culture*, Pfeiffer & Co., San Diego.

Kanter, R. (1989) *When Giants Learn to Dance*, Simon & Schuster, New York.

Kets de Vries, M. and Miller, D. (1987) *The Neurotic Organization*, Jossey-Bass, San Francisco.

Kilman, R. (1987) *Beyond the Quick Fix*, Jossey-Bass, San Francisco.

McKenna, E. (1994) *Business Psychology and Organizational Behaviour*, Lawrence Erlbaum Associates Ltd, Hove.

McLean, A. and Marshall, J. (1983) *Intervening in Cultures*, University of Bath.

McLean, A. and Marshall, J. (1988) *Cultures at Work*, Local Government Training Board, Luton.

Morgan, G. (1986) *Images of Organization*, Sage, London.

Ouchi, W. and Johnson, J. (1978) Types of organizational control and their relationship to emotional well-being, *Administrative Science Quarterly*, **23**, 292–317.

Peters, T. and Waterman, R. (1982) *In Search of Excellence*, Harper & Row, New York.

Trompenaars, F. (1993) *Riding the Waves of Culture*, Nicolas Brealey Publishers Ltd, London.

Waterman, R. (1995) *What America Does Right*, Plume/Penguin, New York.

Weisbord, M. (1978) *Organizational Diagnosis*, Addison-Wesley, Reading, MA.

Wilkins, A. (1983) Organizational stories as symbols which control the organization, in Pondy, L. *et al.* (eds) *Organizational Symbolism*, Greenwich, CT.

6 Making decisions and learning from experience

This chapter introduces ideas about decision-making which will help you to become clearer about the bases on which you work. As a result you will be clearer about the approach and the logic you tend to follow and in turn this will help you be more flexible when the situation demands it. Under the spotlight in this chapter is *non-clinical* decision-making and problem-solving: the focus is on the organizational, administrative and managerial decision-making work that you do.

Each of us is a natural decision-maker and problem-solver. We have to be – we have no choice! Much of what we do in life boils down to making decisions about the course of our life. We collect data, and do our best to make sense of it, then we respond in some way which seems valid to us given what we know through making a decision. We are continually solving problems and making decisions. We may not be aware of doing so, perhaps because we no longer 'see' the matters we are sorting out as a problems requiring a decision as such, or maybe it is because we have become so adept at decision-making that doing so has become automatic.

MAKING THE 'RIGHT' DECISION

You do not have to be a manager to be interested in problem-solving and decision-making. Deciding what to do about the many issues that have to be resolved day-in and day-out can be tricky for anyone. Pressure to make the right decisions comes not just from within but to a great extent from others. Pressure to make the right decision all the time can come from the expectations others have of you at work. There may be several reasons for this: perhaps you have more experience; maybe you are more senior; perhaps others at work have not developed their own problem-solving model and hence find it hard to make decisions. For many people, however, reaching a decision – and then having to live with the consequences of that choice – is not an easy task.

An important first step in addressing issues is to ask some basic questions about the situation to be resolved such as:

- what the problem is actually about
- who has the problem

- why it has arisen (and why now)
- the priority of the viable options.

The next thing to bear in mind is that different people see things in different ways and that there will be few 'right' decisions because it depends on (a) the position from which you are looking at the problem and (b) what you want to achieve from the situation. There will be variations in how people define the problem, the urgency and pressure for its resolution and the range of response options they believe are appropriate. Even with unanimity about the nature of the problem, there are likely to be considerable differences in the *what*, *when* and the *how* of the responses suggested.

CLARIFYING AND DEFINING THE PROBLEM

Problems are not necessarily defined in the same way by different individuals. One person may interpret a situation as 'no big deal' whereas others may perceive that same situation as an intractable problem of great proportions. The way in which an individual chooses to identify, define and 'own' problems depends on many factors, such as:

- individual past experience, practice and training
- professional issues
- the work setting
- individual preferences with regards to being in control of a situation
- the desire to understand everything
- tolerance of uncertainty and ambiguity, etc.
- level of personal involvement.

Once a problem has been identified and defined, the steps taken to resolve it depend on:

- the speed of response required
- the perceived importance of the matter
- the characteristics of the people involved
- the setting and context
- external pressures and constraints
- the risks associated with it all.

Whilst there may be agreement that something is not going as it should, one difficulty is that the same facts may be interpreted differently by those responsible for resolving the problems identified. From the same facts several different diagnoses can be reached.

As an example, think about how you would respond if you were told that there was a problem of low morale on a ward. There are several different ways in which you could look at that situation. For example, one manager may see it as a problem of staff not getting on well enough with each other, another as a result of too much work and too few resources, yet another view is that it is because of bed shortages, whereas a fourth may see the problems as emanating from the attitude of the medical consultants towards nursing staff.

Who should be believed? Who is right? Is it perhaps more likely that it is a combination of all of these factors but that each of us will 'see' things slightly differently from our colleagues. Each of these different diagnoses though will lead to different decisions being taken to address the initial problem of low morale on the ward.

To increase the likelihood of reaching a soundly based organizational diagnosis – which then allows you to consider appropriate options – you can use frameworks and guidelines to help clarify what is going on and reduce the chance of a mis-diagnosis.

Problem diagnosis: Some frameworks to consider

Two helpful ways of diagnosing the problem to be resolved are shown in Figures 6.1 and 6.2. They suggest some of the questions that need to be asked to clarify the nature of the problem (i.e. problem-finding), and what to do about it (i.e. problem-solving).

Figure 6.1 notes the different aspects where there is potential for problems and difficulties to arise. You can use Figure 6.1 as a reminder to look at each of these areas to see if there is cause for you to be concerned about problems that may already be surfacing, or which seem imminent, in that part of the job.

You can use this framework as a basis for regularly 'scanning' your work responsibilities in a more strategic manner and this will help you to keep an eye on what is going on and to remain alert to potential difficulties. Picking up problems early, as they begin to appear, will reduce the likelihood of their growing into big issues.

Another approach is to use the problem analysis grid in Figure 6.2. Here you fill in as many boxes as possible, as and when the diagnostic information

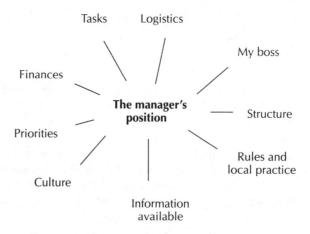

Figure 6.1 Defining the problem

W H A T	What is the problem? • • •	What isn't the problem? • • •	What are the problem's distinctive features? • • •
W H E R E	Where is the problem? • • •	Where isn't the problem? • • •	What is different about this place? • • •
W H E N	When did it occur? • • How often does the problem occur? • •	When do no problems arise? • • When is it generally absent? • •	What is different in the period when problems occur? • • What is distinctive about its frequency of occurrence? • •
W H O M	To whom or what is the problem attached? • • •	Who or what does not get the problem? • • •	What is different about them or it then? • • •
S I Z E	How big is the problem? • • •	In what ways does it not matter? • • •	What is distinctive about its growth ? • • •
	W H Y	**W H Y**	**W H Y**

Figure 6.2 A problem analysis grid

becomes available. You can use this problem analysis grid for any type of issue, stating clearly at the beginning what the problem is about, and using the various boxes to speculate about some of the causes – rather than the symptoms – which might be involved.

Once you have built up as complete a picture of the situation as you can, you are in a better position to make decisions. You can make a more informed choice about whether you react at all and, if so, how. You can decide whether to go for the root causes of the issue or – because it might be more prudent to begin with – to tackle some of the symptoms.

The whole purpose of the problem analysis grid is to prompt you to think more broadly about difficulties and problems that you may encounter. It is very easy to jump to conclusions both about the definition of a problem, and the likely reasons for its emergence. However through doing so you could be very mistaken in your initial views, and this could lead you to respond inappropriately and in ways that will not help to identify the actual reasons for the problem.

Think of a current situation that you could explore using the framework above. You do not need to have a response to each of the boxes in the grid but ask yourself each of the questions posed and make a note of your responses. Look to see what other questions or thoughts come to mind, based on the notes you have made on the analysis grid.

You may be surprised at how much information you have at your disposal about the issues you need to tackle – far more perhaps than you initially thought. The key is to make the fullest use possible of this information to help you decide what needs to be done and what needs to be checked further. By way of example, consider a situation where you and your colleagues seem to have been under almost continuous pressure on the ward; where few tasks seem to have been completed on time and where you seem to have been continually playing 'catch-up'. Perhaps it seemed that there was just too much work for staff to do within the time available. Completing Figure 6.2 may highlight other possibilities as the root of the problem. It is just possible, for example, that what may initially have appeared to be a staffing problem could, on reflection, have been more of a problem created by giving too many issues 'top priority' status – even though the resultant problem could, superficially, have looked the same.

If staff are given too many 'top priority' jobs they will become confused about what to do first and what to postpone. They will worry about what they are not doing and are less likely to concentrate fully on the task in hand. They will be increasingly preoccupied by the pressure of work and they may come to feel they are in an increasingly untenable situation. Much of the work they do is likely to be rushed and they may feel under pressure to work even faster with obvious consequences for the quality of care.

Under these sorts of conditions, what an observer may see is a group of people rushing around under pressure who may not be doing their work as diligently or as effectively as they ought. The observer may conclude that there is a shortage of staff whereas in fact the problem is less about the number of staff and more about poor management practices.

It is only through looking at the situation in an ordered way that the underlying causes of the problems become apparent. Looking at it superficially can give a totally misleading impression as the above example illustrates. The two frameworks suggested here will help you to clarify the core issues that are causing problems and enable you to 'home-in' on their underlying causes.

It is also important to check to see if you are alone in being concerned about particular problems – perhaps because you are being over-sensitive or over-reacting for some reason. One way of checking this out is to let colleagues know when you are feeling uneasy or concerned and check whether they share your concerns. If it turns out that it is more about you in that situation – rather than there being a operational problem – then you have the opportunity to consider what may be causing you to experience some concern.

Categorizing issues and concerns

With more clarity about the types of problem arising, you now need to categorize them into different types of issue and concern. You may find that the sorts of problems you have to deal with fall into several different patterns. If you can work out what these patterns are then you may have more of a chance of sorting them out rather than treating each one as if it were a separate case.

The following are some examples of ways of categorizing issues:

- the same people involved?
- the same department, ward, professional group, etc?
- the same professions, for example nurses, pathologists?
- repeating operational issues, for example budgets, planning, particular theatre, procedures, etc?

If you find that there does seem to be some repetition in the types of issue that are causing problems then you might want to look a little deeper and consider why these problems seem to be cropping up in the way they are.

The classification formulated by Blake and Mouton (1976) is useful in looking beneath the surface to see if there are underlying factors that might be causing problems. They suggest that differences and conflicts can be about:

- power or authority
- morale or cohesion
- standards or norms
- goals or objectives.

These types of concern can often be at the heart of issues, although of course people are generally unlikely, if not prompted, to admit to them and these influences may strongly denied if raised for discussion!

SOLVING PROBLEMS SENSIBLY

When problems arise there is usually quite a lot of pressure put on staff to sort them out and solve them immediately. This can mean that too little attention is given to clarifying the facts or taking sufficient account of all the forces involved. This may be because:

- as professionals we are taught to focus on particular aspects of a problem
- you as a person are particularly competent at certain types of actions
- you do not have a ready method of handling problems that will enable you to take a broader view of what is involved.

The ideas outlined thus far provide ways of helping you to step back, assess and become clearer about the nature of a problem and why it may have arisen. With this in mind the following steps provide a formula for deciding what action should be taken (see Figure 6.3).

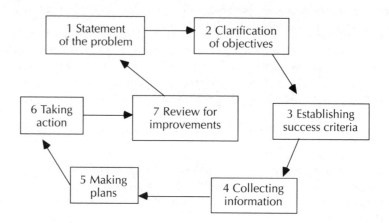

Figure 6.3 Addressing problems

1. *State the problem:* Precisely what is causing difficulties? Be as explicit as you can. Do not aim for one general statement if several would be more informative.
2. *Clarify objectives:* What are you trying to achieve in responding to 1 above? In general terms, what result are you after?
3. *Establish success criteria:* In resolving the immediate problem (and perhaps some of the underlying issues) what measures of success or progress can you realistically establish?
4. *Obtain necessary information:* In order to be in a position to take action, what sort of information do you need, where from, how often, etc?
5. *Make plans:* With a clearer idea of what is involved, what success criteria are you now looking for? Using relevant information, you need to plan your sequence of actions in order to solve the problem.
6. *Take action:* With the necessary preliminary work completed, you are now in a position to take your considered actions.
7. *Review and improve:* Review the success and appropriateness of the actions you have taken in line with steps 1 and 2 above. Compare the outcome of your actions with your success criteria in step 3. If they fit, fine; if not, then define more appropriate ones to replace them and work accordingly.

Your decision-making will become more soundly based if you look at problems in their wider context. If you are under pressure to act quickly and need to be seen to be taking charge, it is very easy make poorly judged decisions and take actions which fail to focus on the critical issues. These pressures can be countered by using a systematic approach to defining those issues, by systematically collecting relevant material, and by deciding what to do from the viable options you have determined.

Following these steps need not be a lengthy or protracted affair. It is more a question of remembering to use this pattern of thinking about problems. Whilst each of us has our own preferred ways of going about things we are likely to be more successful if we take the time to collect the necessary information and plan the most constructive actions available .

DECISION-MAKING STRATEGIES

We expect managers to make decisions. At times though this means making a decision *not* to decide. It all depends on what the issue is, how much background information is available, and the level of urgency – panic perhaps – which exists. But how do *you* make decisions? Do you always go about it in the same way, or do you adopt different strategies at different times?

Make a note of the different decision-making strategies or actions which:

a. you notice in yourself
b. which you see others taking.

Here is a possible list of decision-making strategies. They may or may not be similar to the ones you noted above.

- By rational–logical analysis
- Open debate
- By flattery
- Using the old boy network
- Exerting time pressure
- By quid pro quo
- Via professional loyalties
- By paying back favours
- By intimidation
- Through custom and practice
- Following rules and procedures
- Through challenge
- By data overload
- By appealing to feelings
- By collusion
- Via personal ties
- Through threat
- Through bullying.

Some of the styles listed above may surprise you, but they actually represent a range of bases on which decisions are made. For example, at one end of the spectrum are decisions made through a detailed logical assessment of the situation, whereas at the other extreme would be decisions made on a spur of the moment whim. Some of the time we make decisions on the basis of the work to be done; at other times we make our decisions on the basis of interpersonal relations and who we like or want to work with.

However, underlying it all there will be several themes that we each use, consciously or not, to guide us in making sense of our experiences and in reaching decisions. Figure 6.4 illustrates one decision-making model which contrasts two important decision-making dimensions, rationality and feelings with the professional and personal.

Both of these dimensions exercise considerable sway in how we decide things and often the quality of our decisions will reflect how well we have been able to integrate these two different, but complementary, perspectives.

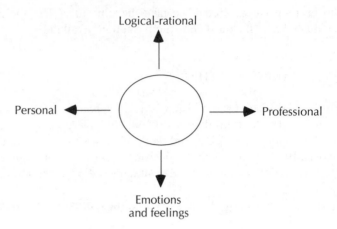

Figure 6.4 A decision-making framework

Decision-making in groups

Whichever decision-making strategies we choose to employ, it is likely that the arena in which we have to operate will be a group of some description. Deciding what needs to be done at work usually means satisfying the needs and wants of several people who will be involved in the working through and implementation of any decisions that are made.

Whilst each of us will have an idea of what we want the decision to be – because it will suit us in some way – we can never really be sure of our colleagues' motives in spite of what they may have said beforehand. This is one of the reasons why watching how decisions are made in meetings is such an interesting – and frustrating – affair. We can never be sure what precisely will happen, and even when a decision is made we can never be sure that it will be implemented in the way intended (or even implemented at all!).

Some decision-making ploys

Set out in Figure 6.5 are some of the common reactions and responses that you will encounter during meetings. It is often only when these occur that it becomes a little clearer who really wants what.

Resigned indifference

Fatigue and frustration may allow one person's idea through at the expense of others offered – often with less than full consideration. There tends to be a lack of commitment to decisions made in this way as most members' ideas have been ignored or bypassed in an arbitrary manner. This can be an expensive and time-consuming way of reaching what is not a very acceptable solution to a problem.

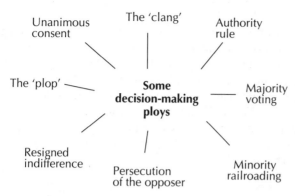

Figure 6.5 Some decision-making ploys

The 'plop'

A common but rather negative way of making decisions. An idea is put forward and before anyone has a chance to comment, someone suggests an alternative idea. The process continues until the group finds an idea that is generally acceptable.

The 'clang'

This happens when a member proposes an idea which, whilst seemingly in line with the current discussion, is totally disregarded or rejected. This response inhibits further contributions. It is more destructive than the 'plop' sequence because the idea is not merely bypassed or obscured by another; it is actually allowed to crash into pieces in an obvious manner, and with it inevitably goes the member's self-confidence.

Authority rule

Most groups meet the need for organization through the election or designation of a chairperson or co-ordinator. In this approach, a suitable person in authority takes the decisions following a free discussion by the members. The comprehensiveness of the discussion and the quality of the final decision-making will depend on the abilities of the person taking that decision. The commitment of the members is often low because they are not directly involved in the making of the final decision and may often see good points being brought up in discussion that do not seem to bear fruit in terms of influencing the final outcome.

Persecution of the opposer

This is where those who disagree with the 'wants' of the main power players in the group are isolated and penalized in some way. The ultimate intention is to pressurize the opposer into backing down and to discourage future opposition.

Minority railroading

A small number of members with high status or with powerful personalities work together in order to bulldoze the discussion, often pushing it along so fast that the rest of the group have no time to think objectively or to influence the discussion. This is wasteful of the group's resources, given that every member is there to make a contribution. Those who are not part of the 'active' group will feel uninvolved, dissatisfied and antagonistic. Commitment to resultant decisions will therefore be low. The ability to protest openly about the bulldozing may be limited because of the status of those in the dominant role.

Majority voting

If, after discussion, no agreement is emerging, a show of hands can often be requested. It is a speedy and clear way of getting an idea of where the various members of the group stand on any particular issue. It can, though, split a group into separate camps and be unreliable as a method when the issues being discussed are more political in their importance than operational. It is quite easy to jump from a voting split into 'them and us' group situations.

Unanimous consent

This is where everybody is in total agreement with the decision. Ideally this would be the outcome of every group decision-making situation but in reality it is virtually unattainable. This is partly because of the time and effort required to persuade people to a particular viewpoint, and partly because there are very few things in life to which any group of people will be unanimously committed: individuals have their own needs and strongly held opinions, some of which will be mutually exclusive.

Apart from being an interesting exercise in its own right, 'group watching' can be especially valuable if you want to function more effectively as a member of any group. The ploys noted above are rarely obvious. It is only by noting what is going on at the time that you start to see some of them being put into action.

Some decision-making gambits

From observing groups you may well have also come across a range of decision-making gambits designed to encourage the other group members to behave in a particular way. Below are just a few examples often associated with the rapid, forceful 'we have got to make a decision now' type of decision-making strategy.

- *Claiming support:* where one person says 'Well it's obvious that the group feeling is … ' or 'We all think that … ' without actually checking with the others that this is so. Individuals who want to object will feel uncomfortable as there is the danger of being labelled the 'odd man out'.

- *Isolating dissidents:* a variation on the above, making those who want further discussion feel that they are going against the group. When the question is asked: 'Does anyone object to that?', it takes a strong individual to object, and a still stronger one to support his or her objections.
- *Time as a fixed commodity:* the ploy of pointing out that further discussion would take the group outside the time allotted (which has, in any case, usually been set arbitrarily). Members who want to continue are made to feel that they are interfering with group achievement and wasting the group's time.
- *Time is money:* a variation of the time-as-a-fixed-commodity ploy. It works from an angle of pseudo efficiency. Those who are not 'toeing the line' or who want to explain their objections fully are made to feel that they are wasting the resources of the group and holding up procedures. In fact the extra bit of time it may take to ensure that a properly considered decision is made tends to be an excellent investment.
- *Referring to outside specialists:* often used when the 'railroading' technique is running into snags because somebody is challenging the assumed technical competence of the 'railroading group'. An attempt is made to neutralize this difficulty by name-dropping (for example, 'The Director of Nursing told me yesterday that she would have no objections on technical grounds to … ') or by reference to supposedly unimpeachable authorities (for example, 'The ENB are quite clear that … ' etc.).
- *Threat of fragmentation:* where one or more of the principal proponents of the idea either threatens to walk out, resign or leave within a short period of time unless the decision he or she supports is made.

Gambits such as those above are so powerful in influencing decision-making that, unless challenged, inappropriate or impractical decisions can be made. By looking out for them, you can at least be aware when they are being used and decide how, if and what you are prepared to do to counter them.

Consider the following:

- How do decisions appear to be made in your meetings?
- Do these ideas fit your experiences elsewhere?
- Which ploys do you utilize to get the decisions you want?
- How do you feel when these strategies affect you personally in meetings?
- How will you use these ideas in group meetings?

Making decisions: Personal differences

As a result of our experiences at work, and contact with people we see as effective managers, we each have developed our own views on how managerial situations should be handled. Figure 6.6 suggests five possible approaches to managerial decision-making, each of which you may notice in use where you work.

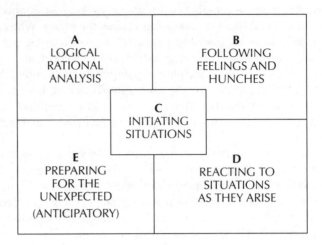

Figure 6.6 Response styles

- *Logical-rational analysis:* The manager makes decisions by carefully collecting all the necessary information and analysing it in a logical manner which, it is believed, will lead to the right answer.
- *Feelings or hunches:* The manager's main criterion is that the decision 'instinctively' feels right. This approach inevitably carries risks because of the lack of a sound fact-based assessment of what needs to be done.
- *Initiating situations:* The manager, having assessed the situation, actively involves other staff members and manages the decision-making/problem-solving dynamics which then emerge. One cautionary note is that stimulating action in this way can provide crisis problems for other managers.
- *Reactive management:* Here the manager prefers to be called in to deal with major problems or impending disasters. The manager adopts a *laissez-faire* style and waits for crises which allow coping skills to be exercised in a reactive and powerfully decisive manner.
- *Anticipatory management:* A style of decision-making focused on ensuring that the current situation is always in 'good shape' and being fully prepared for contingent future developments. It is a relatively low-risk decision-making pattern designed to minimize failure rather than to encourage a developmental work climate.

1. On what bases do you make your decisions? You can use the ideas set out in Figure 6.6 to think through some of your recent decisions in terms of:
   a. how you tackled them
   b. how you may have contributed to the problems themselves through your preferred response style.

2. Consider whether you neglect any of these styles or if you rely too heavily on particular ones. One way of finding out is through

reviewing several recent decisions both at work and outside the workplace to see what type of pattern emerges.

One of the biggest blocks to effective managing is that our background and experiences have channelled us into relying on a relatively narrow field of decision-making and thinking styles.

In the resolution of any problem, the final decision-making processes should ensure that those people most competent to decide on the issue in question are allowed to exert adequate influence. Yet, paradoxically, the contributions of others who are not directly involved in the situation can be invaluable in the decision-making process. Within the professions it is very difficult to allow the intelligent and interested outsider an adequate opportunity to make these sorts of contributions, yet they can prove vital in opening doors for development, resolution or remedy.

> To decide wisely, problems must be looked at from a distance ... We do not get progress in naval disarmament when admirals confer. We do not get legal progress from bar associations. Congresses of teachers seem rarely to provide the means for educational advance. (Laski, 1992)

The above quotation suggests allowing the views of informed non-specialists – who will not be totally bound up in the particular situation or profession – to make a contribution and to have their say

Jumping on clouds in helicopters

It is important to keep at a distance from some problems in order to make a better decision regarding the range of actions that can be taken. Some years ago a major international oil company commissioned research on the key quality which distinguished extremely effective managers from merely good ones.

The research concluded that 'the helicopter's ability' to 'jump on clouds' – by which was meant the effective manager's ability to consider problems from a wide range of angles – was *the* distinguishing feature. Being able to take an overview, to look to the side of and around a situation, rather than merely looking it in the face at ground level (also necessary!), is a valuable asset to have in the making of decisions.

We also make decisions that will be guided by our concerns to be seen as:

- a valuable and needed contributor
- someone who is flexible and able to 'fit in'
- a person who is competent and who gets results
- able to look after ourselves (and others) and guard against loss.

Personal concerns such as these will influence what we do, how we see and interpret what is going on around us, and how we decide to respond to the problems we are confronted with.

A LEARNING PROBLEM-SOLVING CYCLE

How human beings learn has been a subject of considerable interest to researchers. In recent years the question of how managers learn has assumed more and more importance because of the far-reaching impact that managerial decision-making has on the lives of many people. Managers were traditionally taught their 'management' theory in rather didactic ways and were led to believe that the business world was relatively ordered and predictable; that a sound knowledge of management theory would allow the rest to fall into place and that success would follow.

Whilst business knowledge and an understanding of business processes is of course important, on their own they do not equip managers to be effective in the workplace. The effective use of theory learnt at college is tempered through practical work experience. What this suggests is that both theory *and* practical experience are important and necessary if you are to be effective as a manager at work.

Kolb, Rubin and McIntyre (1974) proposed an approach to thinking and problem-solving which integrated practical experience with theoretical knowledge. They proposed a learning and problem-solving cycle which throws light on how we can learn to make better decisions by making use of all that we know, and experience, about the situations which regularly face us.

Kolb *et al.* formalized a learning sequence, each aspect of which is related and complementary to the others. As outlined earlier, in the Introduction, the cycle comprises four main stages each of which leads to the next one:

1. an experience
2. observations and reflections about that experience
3. theorizing about the experience, drawing on relevant ideas and frameworks already available to us
4. planning of further action based on our sense of what has happened. This sets off the learning cycle – I think it is more like a spiral – once again.

Kolb *et al.* describe four styles in their learning cycle as follows:

- *Concrete experience (CE):* An individual with a strong preference for this style prefers to learn through practical experience and action; by doing.
- *Reflective observation (RO):* Here the individual prefers to make sense of experience by thinking and reflecting on it all; through reflecting.
- *Abstract conceptualization (AC):* This person prefers to build models and ideas from presented and observed experience.
- *Active experimentation (AE):* Here the individual tries to work out what would work where, and when.

Kolb *et al.*'s hypothesis is that if we are to be at our most effective – and if we are to make the most of our experiences – we need to attend to each of these four different ways of working together. Honey and Mumford (1986) have built on this model and developed a Learning Styles Inventory with the terms Activist, Reflector, Theorist and Pragmatist reflecting the four different stages of the Kolb model. Figure 6.7 shows the two frameworks superimposed.

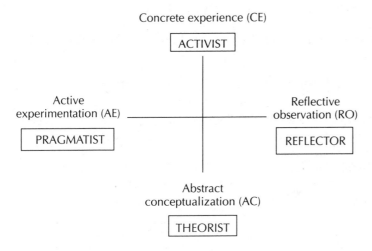

Figure 6.7 A learning styles and problem-solving framework

In summary, each of the four styles is defined as follows:

- *Activists* crave new experiences; will try anything once; revel in short-term problem-solving, action and fire-fighting.
- *Reflectors* stand back and ponder; look before they leap; consider all the angles, wonder about things.
- *Theorists* assimilate disparate facts into coherent theories; value logic and rationality: 'If its logical its good', seek to make sense of things.
- *Pragmatists* are keen to try ideas out in practice; like to move to action; are practical; 'If it works its good' and 'there is always a better way'.

How adjacent styles combine also gives information about an individual's learning and problem-solving style (see Figure 6.8).

- The *converger's* dominant learning abilities are a combination of abstract conceptualization (AC) and active experimentation (AE). Their strength lies in the practical application of ideas.
- The *diverger* has the opposite learning strength – based on actual experience (CE) and reflective observation (RO) – for them it is the combination of imaginative ability that is the greatest strength. They can see situations from many perspectives and pull these together into a more meaningful whole.
- The *assimilator's* dominant learning abilities are Abstract conceptualization (AC) and reflective observation (RO) – their greatest strength lies in the ability to create theoretical models to account for their experiences. Like the converger they are likely to be less interested in people and more interested in the practical use of theories.
- The *accommodator's* greatest strength lies in doing things and, through trial and error, learning to do them even better. Action focused and adaptive to the practical outcomes from their actions, their strengths are the opposite to those of the assimilator's.

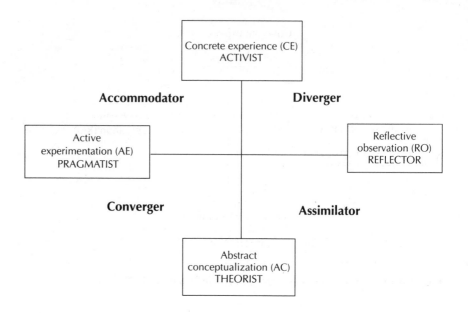

Figure 6.8 Personal learning styles

The effective learner

The successful learner is able to draw insights, in turn, from each of the different methods of learning – from taking action, from reflecting, from theorizing about what went on, and from planning new actions based on their previous experiences. Many people find this difficult to do and tend to get stuck in one or more of the four styles described. The disadvantage of this is that our learning is not as rounded or as complete as it could be and this will mean that we do not learn from our experiences as fully as we might.

There are questionnaires available which give the respondant a learning style profile. This gives an indication of how they prefer to learn and which ways of learning they tend to neglect or fail to utilize. To illustrate how this is done three brief examples follow (Figures 6.9, 6.10 and 6.11).

The profile in Figure 6.9 suggests that this individual prefers to work with ideas and their application. A converger type, they are likely to be relatively strong on the practical application of new ideas. The profile also suggests that they tend to pay little attention to reflecting about why things happen, preferring to concentrate on concrete facts rather than people's emotions.

The clear preference in Figure 6.10 is for learning from what actually happens (concrete experience) and from reflecting on those experiences (reflective observation). Here is a person who is very interested in people – a diverger – and all the activity around them, but far less interested in theories and concepts nor particularly interested in trying out new ways of doing things.

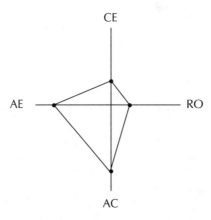

Figure 6.9 Example of a learning style profile (1)

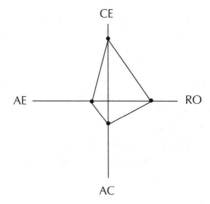

Figure 6.10 Example of a learning style profile (2)

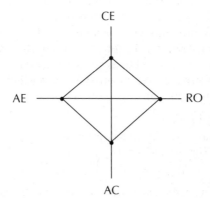

Figure 6.11 Example of a learning style profile (3)

The over-reliance on the CE and RO dimensions suggests that this person is likely to misunderstand why certain things are occurring at work and may find it difficult to adapt their actions in order to improve their decision-making and problem-solving abilities.

Figure 6.11 is a profile of a person who has an ability to understand and learn from what goes on by reviewing and thinking about events from each of these four principal perspectives. This profile is significantly different from those in the other examples where each profile showed a marked preference for some parts of the cycle and a relative neglect of others.

Most us retain a marked preference for working or thinking about issues in our own particular ways and this shows itself by a less than centrally based profile. Profiles such as that shown in Figure 6.11 appear to be far less common. The purpose of Kolb's model is not necessarily to effect major personal change so that we become uniformly centred as in the Figure 6.11 profile. One of its main uses is to remind us that there are different ways through which we receive, digest and present information, solve problems and make decisions. It is also another reminder that our personal ways of doing things are unlikely to be shared by everyone.

If, for example, you have an idea that a colleague likes to be thought of as a very practical person, then the chances of getting your ideas across to them are improved if they are presented in a very practical and realistic way. Another colleague may be more of a thinker and in that case it would be advantageous to illustrate some of the underlying theory on which you have based your propositions. Finally, another colleague may just want to 'get on with it' and here you would do well to emphasize the action components of the approach you are advocating.

This framework has several uses therefore and it can be used to gain personal insight as well as speculate about the learning and problem-solving preferances of others.

POWER, STATUS AND THE *STATUS QUO*

In making decisions it is a commonplace assumption that they are made in accordance with the logical requirements of the situation at the forefront of each person's mind. Whilst this may be so much of the time, decisions are often made which, whilst helping the job be accomplished, also help to maximize an individual's personal objectives and satisfaction.

In this connection there are four principal motives which can affect a manager's decision-making thinking:

- considerations about power
- considerations about status (personal or professional)
- avoiding failure or loss of standing
- considerations about maintaining the *status quo*.

Each of us has concerns about safeguarding our own position at work so – as far as we can – we will want decisions to be made that will not in any way threaten our standing and our influence at work. This is neither unusual nor unexpected yet much that happens in the workplace seems not to take account of these basic and very powerful considerations.

It is highly likely that a great deal of the resistance to change that is seen results from staff concerns about a possible loss of standing and influence at work.

REFERENCES AND FURTHER READING

Ackoff, R. (1978) *The Art of Problem Solving*, John Wiley & Son, Chichester.

Ackoff, R. (1986) *Management in Small Doses*, John Wiley & Sons, Chichester.

Blake, R. and Mouton, S. (1976) *Consultation*, Addison-Wesley, Reading, MA.

Honey, P. and Mumford, A. (1986) *Using your Learning Styles*, Honey, Maidenhead.

Kolb, D., Rubin, I. and McIntyre, J. (1974) *Organizational Psychology*, Prentice Hall, Englewood Cliffs.

Laski, H. (1992) in Sutherland, S. *Irrationality: The Enemy Within*, Constable, London.

7 Groups and their behaviour

This chapter looks at what goes on in groups. It introduces a number of 'Signposts' for more effective group performance; it will help you to illuminate some of the group processes in operation in your group and help you to enhance your own effectiveness in responding to them.

Whilst a significant part of your working time will be spent in the delivery of individualized care, a substantial part will be spent in a work group or team of one sort or another. By adapting and applying the ideas presented here you will become more informed, more insightful and more effective in your group relationships.

The NHS relies on groups of professionals working well enough together to be able to:

- define the work to be done
- collaborate well enough to provide the care required
- talk, listen to and help each other
- have the appropriate collection of skills required
- collaboratively sequence and release those skills to provide care.

Achieving these outcomes is easier said than done and, even if all your colleagues want to work constructively together, it can be surprisingly difficult at times.

Understanding group behaviour involves, for example, noticing and making sense of what the members of the group are doing – individually and collectively – and interpreting the types of response they make. On one level attention has to be given to the detail of what is being discussed and, on another level, it is also necessary to keep track of the overall flow and shape of how the group is functioning.

In any group situation there is a lot of activity going on simultaneously at several levels of analysis – some of it will be spoken and much of it will be left unsaid. All of it is important but trying to tune into everything is too much to attempt, so selectivity is the key.

To begin with you may gain insight into the way the group works through keeping your eye on the overall pattern and flow, and on the critical dynamics and incidents of each meeting. When you find yourself doing that without too much effort then it's time to begin to focus on the more detailed interactions too. In this way you will build up your capacity to notice, simultaneously, several different levels of group interaction.

There are two considerations of overriding importance whenever a group of people meet together, and you should look for evidence of these. They are:

- clarity of purpose of that group (i.e. *what* they are there to do)
- *how* that group decides to go about its work.

A lack of clarity of a group's purpose results in that group losing its focus and sense of direction. Effective group performance depends on a shared clarity of purpose, and adequate attention to the social dynamics that are generated when individuals come together to work in a group or team. It still surprises me just how often groups start working together without the purpose being confirmed or clarified. Perhaps this is because to do so is too simple a matter to bother with.

Whatever the reason, the consequences of not confirming what the group is there to do results in a great deal of wasted time and frustrated spirits. So this is where this chapter starts – clarifying the group's purpose.

The chapter is organized around seven Signposts towards more effective group working which are set out in Figure 7.1.

Figure 7.1 Signposts for effective group performance

SIGNPOST 1: CLARIFY THE WORK TO BE DONE

Of all the Signposts this is the most fundamental. If there is no valid purpose, no specific work that needs to done then there would seem to be no need for the group, the team or the meeting! It is vital, therefore, to determine:

- the purpose for the meeting
- what sort of contributions will be called for
- whether the meeting was called to
  - decide on something?
  - discuss possibilities?

    – build more shared understandings about a topic or issue?
    – make plans?
    – pass on information and news to those present?
- whether the meeting has some symbolic purpose
- whether it is to sanction or give approval to some work others have now completed.

It is always a sound idea to have an agenda so that everyone knows what material has to be covered, but take care to specify what is meant by the various items. It is very easy to assume that an item will mean the same to each person present but this is not the case.

If you saw 'communications' on an agenda, what would you expect to be discussed under that item? Make a note now and then refer to the end of this chapter to see other possible interpretations.

There is a lot of potential for disappointment, disagreement, dispute and frustration if several people come to a meeting expecting to talk about 'communications' only to find that their definition did not match that intended by the agenda item. So, it is important to specify the work to be done *and* also to define what is meant by the terms used. To return to the example above, a better description of the matter for discussion could be: 'Communications – to discuss the introduction of team briefing within the Directorate'.

You need to be aware too that when people meet to work together there may well be two very different agendas that have to be worked on. The first is the *formally stated work* as set out on the formal agenda; the second – often referred to as the 'hidden' agenda – refers to those matters which are not formally stated or acknowledged. For example, it might be that some of those present are working towards a particular objective but are keeping quiet about it, or an individual might openly be saying one thing whilst working to achieve something quite different – possibly even seeking to sabotage the proceedings.

This is quite common: a covert alliance may have been formed between some of those present, whereas in other instances this dynamic just emerges in a spontaneous unstated way. The hidden agenda need not always be a disruptive or negative force. The main thing to remember is that at any one time there are several agendas being worked on in any group. You need to allow for the possibility that what people are saying may not necessary be the full story. This does not necessarily mean that colleagues are being devious, merely that they have their own personal agendas which they are putting before that of the group's.

SIGNPOST 2: ATTENDING TO TASK AND PROCESS

Even when the objectives have been clarified there remain choices about *how* to achieve them. Generally we have been trained to focus on the *tasks* to be done and so understandably we tend to concentrate on 'what' has to be achieved or tackled. Far less attention is given to *how* that work is to done and this can lead to problems and complications. For example, I may be clear that my job is to take a patient from the ward to another department but *how* I do that will profoundly affect that patient's sense of being cared for.

For example, are patients to be rushed without warning from one place to another and left without explanation with the reception clerk? Alternatively the work can still be accomplished in a speedy and purposeful manner by working *with* patients rather than seeing them as goods to be transported. Taking care to hand patients over in a respectful and professional manner will ease their entry into their new surroundings and help to relax them when their treatment is given.

It is necessary to think about *what* we do and *how* we do it. This applies whether you are taking patients for their first bath after an operation, knocking on a homeowner's door for the first time when making a district call, talking to a mother about the injuries her child has received, or explaining why one of your staff cannot have time off as requested.

In any job there will be the *task aspect* (what has to be done) and the *process aspect* (how it is done). Whilst they are both important, the relative emphasis needed will depend on circumstances and on the work to be done. Figure 7.2 shows these as two complementary aspects of a job of work.

Neglect of the *how* dimension of group working can result in the decisions taken not being implemented or sustained. This could be because some critical interpersonal matter was not noticed or was not sufficiently attended to during the meeting. It could be that the manner in which the decisions were reached created unnecessary tension or frustration in those who were to be expected to implement them. *How* a group goes about its work is as important as the decisions a group subsequently makes.

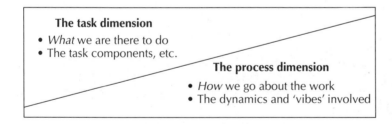

The task dimension
- *What* we are there to do
- The task components, etc.

The process dimension
- *How* we go about the work
- The dynamics and 'vibes' involved

Figure 7.2 Attending to the task and the process

Task and process behaviours

The behaviour of members in a group can similarly be classified in terms of its *task* or *process* focus. Task behaviours focus on getting the task done, on the details of the issue being tackled; examples of these are set out in Figure 7.3.

Process-focused behaviours, such as those in Figure 7.4, complement the task-focused ones and help the group to function more effectively together.

Figure 7.3 Task-focused behaviours

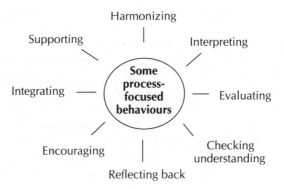

Figure 7.4 Process-focused behaviours

These behaviours help to build up relationships and maintain group cohesion by focusing on the interactions and dynamics within the group.

Some behaviours have both a task and a process function. Examples of these would be:

- evaluating
- compromising
- diagnosing
- testing for consensus
- harmonizing
- explaining.

All of the behaviours have a part to play in enabling a group, team or department to work well and productively together. Too much of a tasky focus and the quality of the working relationships is likely to diminish and – over a period – that will have an adverse effect on the quality of the decisions made. Too much of a focus on the process side can lead to too cosy and reflective a climate that getting things done just gets lost in the preoccupation with the interpersonal dynamics of the group.

A fully effective group attends to task and process considerations and is able to emphasize them as appropriate.

Self-directed behaviours

The behaviours highlighted so far contribute to the accomplishment of the group's goals. There will be occasions, however, when individual group members behave in ways which seem to be at odds with what is going on generally within the group: where the behaviour could be described more as self-directed rather than group- or goal-directed.

Whatever the reason, the purpose of such behaviour is to meet the needs of the individual over and above any other considerations. It is important to be aware that there will be times when this does happen and recognize that it will interfere with the productivity and stability of the group.

SIGNPOST 3: SPECIFY THE RULES AND PROCEDURES TO FOLLOW

A disconcerting aspect of working in any organization is not knowing what is and what is not permissible in one's interactions with colleagues. For example, is it acceptable to ask someone what to do, or how they did something? Or would that be frowned upon? Is it acceptable to make suggestions about making some changes based, for example, on good ideas you have used in a previous job? Or would you be seen as confrontational, as a Mr Know-it-all, or as being 'difficult'?

Trying to find out what is/is not acceptable behaviour can be quite a stressful activity yet we each have to do this whenever we change jobs; and each time we go about this we run the risk of being labelled in some way as difficult or a trouble-maker.

It can be very helpful to make explicit some of these things so that newcomers can quickly pick up the hidden ground rules which everyone works by. In a group one way to do this is to set out formally some 'rules of engagement' which will determine how that group will work together. These set the tone for the group's interactions with each other and make it clear what is and what is not acceptable behaviour. They build higher levels of trust and mutual understanding

Such 'rules' could cover:

- how conflict is resolved
- how resources are allocated
- how mistakes are addressed
- how success is rewarded
- how to learn from failures.

A working framework of this kind can do a great deal to settle anxiety and to create a more collective and collaborative basis for working together. It brings onto a more open and semi-formal footing many matters about working with other people in organizations that are vitally important but which often remain unstated.

 In reflecting on the groups in which you work, what are the 'rules of engagement' which shape those work relationships? They may or may not be written down; they may operate informally. There will be some rules or, at least, certain 'understandings' in operation. How would you state those?

The following are some suggestions from my experience of working with groups who wanted to do this:

- that we give each other time to talk
- we value collaboration more than attacking
- we try to understand each other's perspectives
- there should be no surprises
- we will work to support each other
- that we are all 'OK'
- we each need help from time to time.

Being able to rely on colleagues is very important for an individual's personal and professional well-being. It is particularly so for carers because of the emotional strain and the inherent anxiety of the kind of work they do – for nurses, for medical staff, for support staff, for other professional carers and for managerial and administrative staff too.

SIGNPOST 4: NOTICING WHO DOES WHAT TO WHOM

It is not necessary to have sophisticated techniques or elaborate means of recording to reach a good enough idea of what is going on in a group. The key is to gather information in an ordered and consistent manner so that you can have relevant information from which to review the group's interactions and behaviour.

There are a number of ways of collecting relevant information in an informal, unobtrusive way and three options are outlined below. Try them out in practice and see if they add to your appreciation and understanding of the group.

Method 1: Who talks to whom?

Here you simply make a note of 'who talks to whom'. Each time this happens you note it on your pad showing who initiated the communication. After the meeting, convert your notes into a diagram like Figure 7.5. Each communication is shown as a single line, between the people involved, and its direction is shown by putting an arrowhead by the person it was directed at.

It is very unlikely that you will be able to record all of the communications because of the number involved and because there will usually be several communications going on simultaneously between different group members.

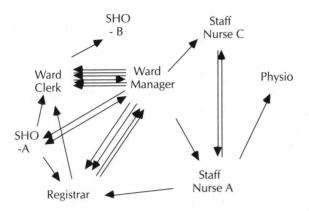

Figure 7.5 Who talks to whom

Even so you will probably be able to catch enough to give you a good enough picture of the interaction patterns within the group.

Figure 7.5 is an example of how communication patterns can be recorded. The result will usually give clues about the group's power structure and each person's influence. What would you say about a group that had Figure 7.5's pattern of interactions? Sometimes this type of analysis throws up some quite unexpected results. For example, a situation where the Ward Manager seems to have been isolated (i.e. no one initiates communication with them), or where a relatively junior member of staff seems to be at the centre of a group's work.

Method 2: Tracking who does what

The focus here is on the types of contribution which are made and by whom. You decide on the types of intervention you want to keep track of and make a list of them vertically. Then, horizontally, you put the down the members of the group.

You then wait and see what happens during the meeting. Each time one of the interventions you are tracking occurs you record it against the person concerned. A picture will soon begin to emerge of the overall types of inter-action the group generates and who does what. You then have specific, cur-rent data to work from in enabling the group to do more of some things and perhaps fewer of others.

Figure 7.6 gives an example of what this type of record looks like.

This is another uncomplicated way of collecting valuable information about how a group is working by noting what actually goes on. It can high-light who tends to use which behaviours and gives the observer an accurate idea about the tone and culture of the group.

The two methods noted above focus on specific aspects of a group's behaviour and they rely on the direct observation of the group in action for information. The third method looks at a group in a more general way, the

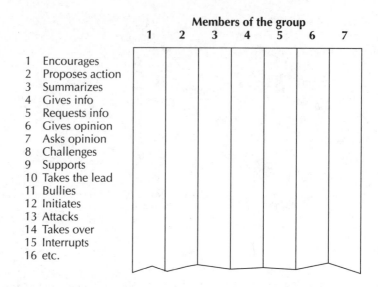

Members of the group

	1	2	3	4	5	6	7

1 Encourages
2 Proposes action
3 Summarizes
4 Gives info
5 Requests info
6 Gives opinion
7 Asks opinion
8 Challenges
9 Supports
10 Takes the lead
11 Bullies
12 Initiates
13 Attacks
14 Takes over
15 Interrupts
16 etc.

Figure 7.6 Tracking who does what

information being collected from the responses of the members to questions about the group itself outside an actual meeting.

Method 3: Overall features of the group

The purpose here is to ask individual members how they experience working in their group. This is done by asking questions about various aspects of the group's working style. For example, does the group go about its business in a way that is more democratic or autocratic?

Below are some questions that can be used to build up an overall assessment of the group using this method:

1. How would you describe the general atmosphere in the group?
   Formal .... Informal
   Competitive .... Co-operative
   Hostile .... Supportive
   Inhibited .... Permissive

   Comments ....

2. How would you assess the quantity and quality of work accomplished?
   Accomplishment: High .... Low
   Quality of production: High .... Low
   Goals: Clear .... Vague
   Methods: Clear .... Vague

   Comments ....

3. How would you describe the leadership behaviour within the group?

Attentive to group needs:	highly	scarcely
Supportive of others:	highly	scarcely
Concerned only with topic:	often	rarely
Takes sides:	often	rarely
Dominates group:	often	rarely

Comments ....

4. How would you describe the level of participation within the group?

Most people contribute	Few talk
Members involved	Members apathetic
Group is united	Group is divided

Comments ....

The individual results are then collated and the overall results can be fed back to the group as a basis for reviewing its ways of working. This questionnaire approach can be very useful in giving the group its own collective view of itself. Because it is not the view of an outsider, or of the most senior person, it is a good basis from which to reconsider what may need to alter if the group is to work more productively.

The purpose of these three methods is to highlight what actually goes on in a group to help it become more successful. With such information available more specific and careful interventions can be made to change things if this is needed.

It is very informative to start looking at group behaviour in such a multi-dimensional way. It will enhance your understanding of what may be going on and help you to consider viable change strategies. These understandings can be applied to a whole range of settings and situations: clinical situations, professional meetings, social settings, family gatherings, and so on.

SIGNPOST 5: CAPTURED BY THE GROUP?

Strange and unexpected things can happen in groups. At times it can feel as if the whole group has been taken over by the sheer emotional content of the proceedings; it can feel as if the whole thing is about to burst; or it can feel impossible to say anything even though you may have a crucial contribution to make!

The dynamics within a group can also build up to such an extent that members may find themselves propelled to contribute and agree to outcomes which they had not intended to, or which feel inappropriate. Such experiences may be evidence of group processes in action which remain out of the group's conscious awareness; where perhaps a tidal wave of emotional forces seems to carry the group along in some direction or other which – at that moment – seems right. In retrospect these experiences can leave some members feeling that the group had been almost 'taken-over' for a period.

Some members can feel intensely uncomfortable about some of the decisions made and about their personal behaviour in the group.

Some startling ideas and propositions about such processes in groups have been put forward by Wilfred Bion (1961), who was a psychiatrist and a psychoanalyst. From his clinical work he observed that, when groups form, unconscious emotional disturbances and obstacles are generated which impede group performance.

Bion noticed three patterns of group behaviour which regularly occurred and which, for a time, appeared to take over and dominated a group's behaviour. He called them 'basic assumption' behaviours. There are three of them:

• the basic assumption of *dependency*
• the basic assumption of *pairing*
• the basic assumption of *fight–flight*.

Bion used the term 'basic assumption' because it seemed to him that something happened in the group which led all the members to go along with one of the three patterns noted above. It was *as if* the members – in an unconscious and unstated way – all agreed to one or other of the basic assumptions suggested.

The basic assumption of dependency

This is where the group revolves around a chosen leader (who may or may not be the most senior person in the group) *as if* they were the only person worth listening to, and the only one who would enable the group to do its work successfully.

The basic assumption of pairing

Here group members 'unconsciously' come to pin their hopes on a collaboration between two of the group; the other group members find themselves less able to contribute and increasingly look to the 'magical' pair to resolve issues confronting the group.

The fight–flight assumption

This is where the group, rather than focusing on the issues to be tackled, becomes preoccupied with either fighting the outside world or denying the presence of any threat to them at all (effectively denying the existence of any problems or threats, and thus running away from them).

Bion suggests that, when a group is working from one of these basic assumptions, little real work is being achieved although at the time it may seem 'as if' a great deal of productive work is being done. This is because, when any one of these basic assumptions takes over, the total resources of the group are not being utilized and relations between the members come to be based on a fantasy of one of the three basic assumptions.

These ideas may sound fanciful and far fetched at first sight yet:

- Can you recall meetings where you felt it was becoming a bit strange somehow; where perhaps you felt strangely unable to get involved; where the rest of the group seemed to want everything to revolve around, be driven, and addressed by two members of the group (pairing)?
- Can you recall instances where, when faced with a challenge from outside the group (or the Trust, Directorate, etc.), the team seemed preoccupied with either denying that there was a problem at all, or hell bent on fighting those outside the group (the Trust, other Directorates) perhaps who just wanted some changes to be made (fight/flight)?
- Have you had experience of groups where so much was oriented around the selected leader of the group that all other contributions were insignificant in comparison, where almost everything rested on what the leader did (dependency)?

If so, these may have been practical examples of Bion's basic assumptions at play. The reason why it is so helpful to be in a position to spot them is that they delude the group into believing it is working productively and using its collective resources well. However, in such instances the capabilities of the group are not being utilized well because they are restricting the full contributions of all of the members of the group. Being able to spot these tendencies quickly and looking for ways and means of helping the group to break out of them becomes a priority.

SIGNPOST 6: GROUPTHINK

Irving Janis (1982) coined the word 'Groupthink' to describe a pattern of thinking which can develop in groups where all the members become so committed and convinced about a course of action that they deny or discount any contrary information or views. Janis comments how 'The more amiability and *esprit de corps* among the members of a policy-making in-group, the greater is the danger that independent critical thinking will be replaced by groupthink, which is likely to result in irrational and dehumanizing actions directed against out-groups'.

Not all groups with a strong sense of collaboration and mutual support will necessarily be prone to the 'Groupthink' phenomenon. Its distinctive feature is an over-identification with the decisions reached to such an extent that any disagreement – or dissention – becomes viewed as akin to treachery. This is not another one of Bion's basic assumptions. With the groupthink phenomena all the members are involved, issues are discussed, but it is the result of all this that – in some cases – leads to a collective view which becomes so strongly held that to question its validity or appropriateness becomes untenable.

The warning signs to watch out for are when the strong camaraderie and cohesion of the group make it difficult to voice any disagreement or to challenge the pre-dominant views being expressed; when relevant and reputable data is ridiculed or seen as irrelevant; and where there is an increasing sense that the group has *all* the answers and that the views of those outside the group do not amount to much. That they are all wallies!

From his examination of several historic fiascos Janis identified three main categories of dysfunction to look out for:

- *Type I:* an over-estimation of the group's sense of power and moral invincibility
- *Type II:* closed-mindedness, a belief in itself and a discounting of external or dissonant data
- *Type III:* pressures towards uniformity and tight cohesion.

The potential for these behaviours in groups is widespread. Janis' insights came from looking at non-clinical group behaviour and he describes how everyday group and team experiences can gather momentum and lead to inappropriate, dangerous, and foolish decision-making.

SIGNPOST 7: MODELS OF GROUP DEVELOPMENT

How a group goes about its business is affected by how long it has been constituted, how well its members know each other, and its track record of past decisions and achievements. A group's behaviour is affected by its age! As with people, the stage of development – its maturity – will be reflected in its preoccupations, the type of tensions it experiences, its history and its environment.

The history of the groups you work with will affect in some way how they go about their work, how they handle disagreement, and how they respond to the pressure to change established ways of working.

Tuckman's Four-Stage Model

From extensive research into small group behaviour Tuckman (1965) proposed a four-stage model of development. He suggested that the effectiveness of a group develops over time and that several stages in this development can be identified.

- *Stage 1 – the Forming Stage:* characterized by anxiety, confusion and uncertainty about what is required of the group and each of its members; initial politeness will be replaced by jockeying for influence and position within the group
- *Stage 2 – the Storming Stage:* characterized by increasingly open debate and challenge about roles, power and influence; working agreements begin to be sorted out and the tension of this stage begins to form the foundation for subsequent work
- *Stage 3 – the Norming Stage:* characterized by roles and working practices beginning to settle down; greater continuity and cohesion evident; members clearer about their mutual expectations and working more effectively together
- *Stage 4 – the Performing Stage:* characterized by building on the earlier stages – this is the most productive stage for the group; roles are clear;

some ways of working together have been established and there is attention to both task and process matters.

However groups may be set up, *all* groups have some period of orientation and of getting to grips with the work to be done and the personalities of group members. Tuckman's model gives an overview of the likely stages, tensions and preoccupations which will affect a group's capacity to function at different times in its development.

Tuckman's model can also predict some of ups and downs likely to arise. For instance, there will invariably be periods when people are trying to work out what their role is and also trying to protect their position. The storming stage will be 'stormy' yet this does not mean that the group's members cannot get on – it is more likely to be a facet of that group's development at that time. Equally, whilst everything may appear on the surface to be going smoothly at the inception of a group (the forming stage) remember that sooner or later there will be jockeying for position, influence and power.

MAINTAINING PERSONAL INTEGRITY AND STANDING

Two final views to consider, both of which revolve around the personal concerns of the individual as a member of a group: how individual members of a group feel about being in that group will significantly affect their contribution; and how well a group is able to work with the individuals within it will affect how well that group performs. For example to contribute or withhold information, to support team colleagues or undermine them, to be truthful or to be devious in the group revolves around how confident and secure each member feels in that group.

The model proposed by Gibb (1971) takes account of how each member develops their own sense of worth and confidence within a work group. One implication of their work is that unless a group is mature enough to enable each member to find their niche and feel able to be a contributor this will arrest the development of that group and its performance.

Gibb's Model: Characteristics of group climate

Gibb suggests that the following needs are held by every member of the group, and that if these needs are insufficiently met then the individual will not contribute to their full potential. These are:

- a need for personal acceptance
- a need to be able to communicate mutually
- a need for clear objectives and collaboration
- a need for control and shared working.

For example, those who feel accepted as a full members of the group will have more confidence and trust in other colleagues on the team, and in their ability to contribute fully. Those who do not feel accepted are far more likely to hold back and feel suspicious and mistrustful of what is going on in the group.

So far as 'communication' is concerned, members need to know that they can be open and spontaneous in contributing their ideas. Without this reassurance group members will probably maintain a polite and cautious facade, and be careful about what they say. Members need to know where they are going and what – as a group or team – they are seeking to accomplish. This will allow them to co-operate and work in a collaborative way towards outcomes they understand and see as valid. Without this they have no real focus and will lose interest, become apathetic – and probably miss the meetings!

If staff know that everything is being organized – with sufficient focus and 'control' – they will feel more willing to work together in a flexible way to achieve the outcomes wanted. If this need is not met then they will lose the cohesion and shared focus and may well resort to being difficult, to resisting – perhaps resenting – the actions proposed as they will very likely be seen as irrelevant and lacking in focus.

Group members need to:

- work together to produce better outcomes
- collaborate with each other
- have opportunities to display personal and collective competence
- avoid personal threat and loss
- feel secure and supported in what they do.

Depending on how much, or how little, the group is concerned with each of these concerns, there will be variations in the group's internal behaviour *and* how it presents itself – and will be seen – in the organization at large.

PUTTING THE 'SIGNPOSTS' TO GOOD USE

The effective group is one which is clear about its overall purpose, the work it has to do and how it goes about its responsibilities. Groups and teams give insufficient attention to reviewing *how* they function: they are usually concerned with 'getting the work done' and surviving the day-to-day pressures of work.

This lack of attention to *how* the group is working has serious consequences for its effectiveness and for the quality of the decisions made. The most serious is that a group can lose its ability to question why it is doing what it is doing; it may lose its capacity to change in response to the changing demands of the job.

The Signposts outlined in this chapter offer members of groups:

- ways of reviewing the focus and performance of the groups they work in
- a focus for making any changes that may be needed to enhance individual and group performance.

REFERENCES AND FURTHER READING

Belbin, M. (1981) *Management Teams*, Heinemann, London.
Belbin, M. (1993) *Team Roles at Work*, Butterworth Heinemann, Oxford.

Bion, W. (1961) *Experiences in Groups*, Tavistock, London.

Dyer, W. (1977) *Team Building*, Addison-Wesley, Reading, MA.

Gibb, J. (1971) The effects of human relations training, in Bergin, A. and Garfield, S. (eds) *Handbook of Psychotherapy and Behaviour Change: An Empirical Analysis*, Wiley, New York.

Harvey, J. (1988) *The Abilene Paradox*, Lexington Books, Lexington, MA.

Janis, I. (1982) *Groupthink*, 2nd edition, Houghton Mifflin Co., Boston.

Morgan, G. (1986) *Images of Organization*, Sage Publications, London.

Pines, M. (1985) *Bion and Group Psychotherapy*, Routledge, London.

Rackham, N. and Morgan, T. (1977) *Behaviour Analysis in Training*, McGraw-Hill,

Sampson, E. and Marthas, M. (1977) *Group Process for the Health Professions*, Wiley, New York.

Tuckman, B. (1965) Developmental sequence in small groups, *Psychological Bulletin*, **63** (6).

Weisbord, M. (1989) *Productive Workplaces*, Jossey-Bass, San Francisco.

Possible interpretations of 'communications' in an agenda
(see page 108):

- discussion of the reporting system
- team briefing
- introduction of new telephone answering system
- staff complaints
- problems with the Trust's automatic switchboard
- introduction of a questionnaire for patient feedback
- problems with shift handover procedure, etc.

8 Conflict at work

Mutual understanding, mutual support and mutual tolerance are three of the most significant factors which will determine whether or not a group of people will be able to work together effectively. Differences of opinion, differences of perspective, and different personal and professional priorities can frustrate genuine attempts by colleagues to work together. Managing and working with 'differences at work' is part and parcel of effective business performance and is an important component of a person's sense of well-being.

Conventional wisdom suggests than reducing differences, building and sustaining 'harmony', and defusing difficult situations will lead to enhanced work performance and better collaboration. However, whilst important, these strategies on their own primarily avoid tackling the sources of differences at work and thus fail to build enhanced levels of mutual understanding and tolerance at work. This chapter identifies some of the sources of differences in the workplace and sets out some approaches for working more productively with them.

One of the biggest challenges to be faced at work is achieving results with colleagues who see things differently. This may be due to their training, their profession, their cultural background, or it may be due to the fact that personality, beliefs and their ways of behaving are just different.

However it may show itself, each of us is different from those around us. Our background, our upbringing, our genetic heritage sets us apart from every other person in one way or another. This does not mean that we will not be prepared, able or willing to get on with others. It means that – whatever people may say – each of us is unique. Mostly this differentness will not matter too much but on some occasions we may well see things so very differently to those around us that our ability to work collaboratively with others is impaired.

This can generate difficulties because each of us is likely to seek different outcomes or want things to be done in our own preferred way. Tolerating differences at work and learning to adapt to the pressures this generates are not usually explicitly considered in the professional training of nurses, yet much of the success of carers revolves around one's personal competence in being able to accept and work with such differences in the clinic, on the ward and in the community.

Two common responses in dealing with differences at work are:

- to ignore what the other person is saying and carry on with what you were doing
- to try to get your own way and impose your view on the situation.

The hope is that, by reasserting your own perspective, you will be able to get your way and that in the end, perhaps, differences of opinion will be inconsequential and that everything will be fine. Nothing could be further from the truth. How we cope and work with differences has an enormous effect on the quality of the work delivered and on the quality of the relationships at work.

LIVING WITH DIFFERENCES

There is enormous potential for disagreement, conflict and stress at work. This may be because of the competing demands of the job itself or it could come from the combustion of different personalities required to work together in trying circumstances day after day. The potential for work-generated conflict could also be engendered by the culture of the workplace itself, or by the behaviour of individual managers.

Two prime sources of conflict are paying insufficient attention to what the other person is saying and jumping to conclusions about what others are saying without hearing them through. Even when participants are in general agreement, and want to collaborate, difficulties can arise. Working with others is not easy. Tolerance *is* a virtue!

What is very interesting is that what each person *thinks* and *believes* about a situation will determine how they makes sense of it, and this in turn will shape their mood, and their subsequent behaviour! Thought processes – and the meanings attached to any event – are profoundly personal and private to the individual. The meanings a person gives to an event, or situation, will vary from individual to individual. What may seem relatively unimportant to one person may hold great personal significance for another.

The ability to understand and relate to another person's point of view is a major attribute of an effective manager. It is a manager's ability to relate to others, over and above technical competence, which is a critical attribute in the effective management and motivation of colleagues.

An important first step in trying to understand another person's point of view is that of clarifying – and understanding – your own. If you can appreciate your own needs in a given situation then you will have a greater chance of identifying the possible needs of others involved, and of appreciating how they may be similar to, or different from, yours. In this way you are able to build up mutual regard and understandings.

1. Think of a current situation where different views are being expressed as to what the issues are, what should be done, etc. and note down your own needs as fully as you can. Clarify as fully as possible how you see the situation in question and what you feel should be done.

2. Now do the same for each of the other individuals involved in that situation. You are unlikely to do this with 100 per cent accuracy because each individual has their own very personal and individual thoughts and needs. However, you can speculate about how they are likely to see and experience the situation. You now have in front of you a note of how each of those involved see the situation, at least according to your best assessment.

Now look at the notes you have made. It may be that you assess each person as having very similar views about the situation. It is far more likely, however, that you will have identified some differences and these will reflect different needs, priorities and objectives. Some of these may be totally related to the task in hand and some of them may reflect non-task specific personal needs, such as for autonomy, for taking the lead, for being the patients' advocate, for not causing a fuss, etc.

Some of the notes will reflect hidden agendas of the people involved, some are likely to reflect the personality of the person themself, some will be about the specific work under discussion. The thing is that they will all – in some way or another – find some expression in the dynamics of the group's work. These more individual, and personal, differences generally remain unstated, yet they are often the cause of difficulties when groups of people start to work together.

One way of organizing your notes about the 'needs' held by others is shown in Figure 8.1. You can define the situation you are focusing upon in the box at the centre of the diagram and then around this set out the different types of needs which need to be considered.

This framework allows you to build up a fuller picture of 'who wants what' and you can assess how your own needs and wishes fit in with the broader array of others' needs and wants. Remember that peoples' differing wants and needs will affect the level of communality, agreement or disagreement experienced.

The 'needs' which individuals have are not simply work-related: it is unrealistic to expect anyone to distinguish and separate their 'outside work'

Figure 8.1 Assessing who is looking for what

wants and needs from their professional ones. Such non-work aspects of our-selves seep out as we go about our work and significantly influence our behaviour, preoccupations and priorities. They are absolutely relevant to who we are and what we do at work. Figure 8.1 should include the fullest range of needs possible because of the impact they have on individual perceptions, and on individual and group behaviour.

With more of an understanding of the wide range of people's needs, you can build up a more accurate representation of the overall dynamics and ten-sions in the situation. Of course this will not be totally accurate, because none of us can become totally aware of all the needs of our colleagues *et al.*, but using a framework such as that shown in Figure 8.1 will lead to a more rigorous way of looking at situations. Such a clarification of the likely goals and priorities of your colleagues will help you to work more effectively and influentially with them.

There is no one 'right' way to deal with differences at work: it depends on the specific situation and what has led up to it. What can be done though is to become as clear as possible about the differences that exist, learn to cope with them better, and build for more effective collaborative action which acknowledges and works with the differences rather than trying to pretend they do not exist.

It will usually be very difficult to know what other colleagues are thinking and feeling. Some individuals show their views quite clearly without having to spell it out for you. Others give very little intimation of what they really think of the events which unfold around them: they keep their own counsel; they keep their own 'psychological distance'; they present themselves as somewhat self-contained.

Figure 8.2 contrasts how people differ with respect to how engaged they choose to be with others (the *distance–closeness dimension*), and how they decide to relate to others (the *indirect–direct dimension*) – see Birchnell, 1993.

Distance
(remaining separate)

Likely to be more: remote private unknown discounted	*Likely to be more:* aggressive forceful 'difficult' threatening
Likely to be more: private cautious circumspect collaborative	*Likely to be more:* assertive high impact 'tough' and clear purposeful

Indirect   **Direct**

Closeness
(becoming involved)

Figure 8.2 Relating preferences and impact on others

Where a person is located on these dimensions will reflect how much personal information they tend to divulge, and their likely approach to conflict resolution and handling of differences when these emerge at work.

These two dimensions also provide clues about the impact an individual may have on others. For example, *distant and indirect* individuals may be perceived by others as remote, private and 'unknown'. The impact of this could be that their contributions generally become discounted at work: contributions which might be vitally important but which might be ignored or dismissed out of hand.

By contrast, *close and direct* individuals are likely to be experienced as assertive, high impact, and 'tough' to the degree that they will be seen to be purposeful and focused at work. One consequence of this is that such people will be listened to with care and their point of view will be taken into account. By stating clearly where they stand and what they want, they are likely to be more successful in securing their own needs.

Individuals will exercise an influence wherever they fit on the dimensions above. Some people prefer to be more 'direct and close' with colleagues than others. Whilst it does not follow that they will necessarily be more able, it is likely that their interpersonal impact will have more of an effect on those around them. It is important to remain aware however that colleagues who prefer to remain more 'distant and indirect' may at times have *the* crucial contributions to make and thus their air-time may need to be protected.

It is likely to prove more difficult to explore the views of distant and indirect individuals. Especially in conflict situations it may well be harder to find out how they experience the situation in contrast to those other colleagues who are more direct, more assertive and forthright about their position.

WHAT ARE WE DISAGREEING ABOUT?

Figure 8.3 identifies some of the areas around which differences often arise at work, one or more of which is often at the heart of many of the difficulties at work. Clarification of the root cause(s) of a disagreement increases the potential for resolving the problem. Whilst other, perhaps less definable, factors are also likely to be at play, attention to those set out in Figure 8.3 will help considerably in conflict exploration and resolution.

Differences in any or all of these areas may be present in a given situation, and their relative prominence will vary and indeed may even change during the duration of the disagreement. In some ways, the different aspects influence each other and clarification of this may also be necessary: for example, differences about objectives will probably engender differences about goals.

The separate dimensions of the framework are set out in more detail below:

Sources of difference

Facts

Disagreement occurs because of personal differences in how the problem is defined. Perhaps one or more of the parties has not had access to all the avail-

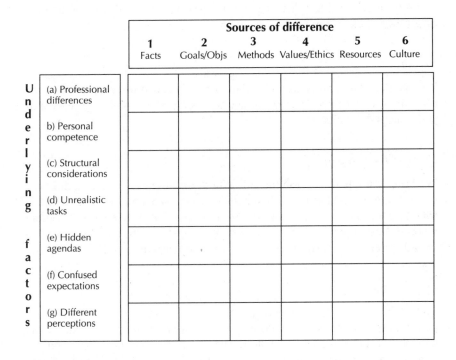

Figure 8.3 What are we disagreeing about?

able relevant information; perhaps there have been differences in how the same information has been interpreted by different individuals; perhaps there are variations in the personal stakes of involved parties.

Goals/objectives

Disagreement may arise because one party views the objective at the strategic level, another at an operational level. There may be separate professional objectives tied up in the overall goal.

Methods

Parties may disagree about the procedures to be followed, the strategies to be adopted, the development of tactical plans most likely to achieve a mutually desirable objective.

Values/Ethics

There may be differences with regard to fundamental principles governing the way in which the work is handled – issues concerning the use of power, morality at work, the rights of patients or confidentiality. Such issues may affect the choice of both goals and methods.

Resources

This is about the ability to employ the means needed to achieve the agreed objectives. (Do I have the right of access to capital equipment, offices, extra staff, the photocopier, etc?)

Cultural background

We bring with us to any job the full history and richness of the traditions of our upbringing and training. This includes where we were brought up and the traditions of our country of origin. Some sources of difference only emerge when, for example, we live in a foreign country and become aware of the very different ways of thinking and doing which are followed.

Underlying factors

These dimensions give some clues about the deeper issues involved in disagreements and conflict. The more we can discover about why disagreements happen, the more we will be able to see them for what they are – and then work to prevent them from getting in the way in future. Listed below are several underlying factors relevant to professional work in organizations.

Professional differences

As a result of our professional training and practice we become accustomed to, and rewarded by, seeing and doing things in particular ways. Professional status carries its own traditions and behavioural norms which are continually defended and reinforced

Personal competence

Individuals may not be adequately equipped to fulfil the requirements of their job. This can be addressed by reviewing current job responsibilities, by identifying unrealistic demands and by jointly identifying training needs.

Structural considerations

The organization of the department or unit may be such that certain individuals and/or professional groups are unwittingly pitted against each other as they try to perform their job effectively. The only way to sort this out is by looking at the structure itself and clarifying the exact nature of the work to be done.

Unrealistic tasks

It may be a question of trying to achieve the unachievable: ideas may have overtaken either the competence of staff in post or the technology available. There needs to be some reconciliation between goals and what can realistically be achieved.

Hidden issues/Personal agendas

Individuals probably have their own private agenda of objectives. Often work will go on smoothly so long as there is no major clash between a person's job demands and their own personal agenda. Sparks can fly (seemingly for no apparent reason) when the two agendas come into conflict however.

Confused expectations

Misperception of roles is one of the most common reasons for difficulties at work. The role of Ward Manager may be perceived differently, for example, by different individuals who each have their own expectations of her. Consequently it is not surprising therefore that the Ward Manager cannot always fulfil everyone's expectations. The way out of this dilemma is to clarify what is and what is not covered by the role of Ward Manager, and to communicate that to those involved.

Different perception/Usage of information

Each of us interprets the same information in a very personal way since we bring our own unique set of life experiences through which we filter all the information we receive. This does not often affect our ability to work well together. Sometimes, however, our personal interpretations do lead us to construe a situation very differently from others.

One of the continuing challenges when working within organizations is how to make the most constructive use of 'difference' to enhance mutual understandings and how to use differences constructively to reach more informed and better decisions.

The only way of realizing that we may have interpreted the same information very differently is if we are prepared to tell each other about this. We then have a basis for working together to find some common understanding from which to work on issues together.

RESPONDING AND TAKING ACTION

The manager is responsible for clarification and diagnosis of the causes of conflicts of interest between colleagues and some of these may involve the manager themselves. Once the issue has been diagnosed, however, the manager has to decide how to respond. From the possible responses, the manager's decision will depend on the circumstances which includes, for example, the level of tension reached and how rapid a response is required. Figure 8.4 suggests five commonly used responses, each of which have both benefits and limitations.

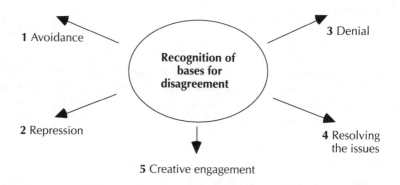

Figure 8.4 Five responses to conflict and disagreement

Avoidance of differences

The manager may aim to avoid differences and conflict by reducing the frequency of contact between those individuals involved. This may be achieved by changing shift and duty patterns, by reorganising the responsibilities of staff or by changing their place of work. This approach has its limitations in that the issue has been avoided but the underlying root cause of the problem remains.

The avoidance strategy is appropriate if:

- there is no alternative
- there is a personality clash and involved parties see positive value in the proposed changes which will make their lives better
- it is just not possible at this moment in time for the root causes of the problem to be confronted and explored directly.

Repression of differences

It is sometimes possible in the short term to prevent differences from exploding or getting out of hand by refusing to admit they exist and by emphasising loyalty, teamwork and other positive values within the group. This can make life difficult for staff concerned who are being pushed to emphasize the positive aspects of their working patterns whilst being aware that major unaddressed issues exist beneath the surface.

This is a defensive strategy which tries to hold down and repress the expression of problems and may be the favoured response, for example:

- where the manager and/or group are just unable to accept that all is not well

- where the manager finds it too much of a personal threat to accept that there are problems to be tackled
- where the culture of the organization as a whole does not allow there to be any problems!

It is likely to result in the issues being forced underground, which may 'pollute' the work of the group as a whole. It is also possible that the repressed problems will deteriorate into bigger issues.

Repressing the existence of interpersonal difficulties within the workforce can be a very dangerous strategy. At worst it can threaten the continuation of the organization. At best it will poison the climate over time and result in a duplicitous work group where everyone pretends all is well yet knows that this is not the case.

Denial of differences

With repression of differences there is an acknowledgement that there *are* problems but they are swept under the carpet in the hope that they will just go away. With denial of differences the view is that there are no problems that need attention.

This is a strategy where those involved may well be deluding themselves about the situation they are in, where perhaps it is just too personally threatening to consider that everything is not as it should be. Whilst this may help some staff handle the shock and the challenge generated by work disagreements, denial serves only to delude those involved until ultimately the situation will collapse.

The following options for handling work differences focus more on addressing and solving the issues and problems which have arisen.

Resolving the issues of difference

This is a direct approach where the manager:

- recognizes that differences exist
- is prepared for differences to be openly acknowledged
- looks for ways in which the issues of difference can be sorted out.

In effect the warring parties are presented with an ultimatum: 'Sort it out ... or I will sort it for you'. By forcing the parties involved to face up to the problems, and by giving them the opportunity to resolve whatever difficulties exist, the manager seeks to enable them to take responsibility for conflict resolution.

The creative use of differences

There is the possibility for going beyond just sorting out the differences that have arisen: differences can be transformed into creative problem-solving. The philosophy underlying this approach is that differences exist, as a feature of life, and that a consideration of all standpoints can lead to a more creative and integrative resolution which has benefits for all involved.

Differences are seen as enriching and constructive rather than as problematic and disruptive. Consequently the process of resolving differences becomes more collaborative and constructive as opposed to destructive and divisive. The creative use of differences requires a more open outlook on matters and colleagues who are able to tolerate the discussion and expression of views which may be significantly different to those they hold dear.

The benefits to such an approach can, however, be very rewarding with new and dynamic ways of collaboration being developed, and innovative approaches adopted to difficult work problems. Fundamentally this approach sets a new work culture and tone and is likely to foster increasing levels of commitment and cohesion at work.

There are both advantages and disadvantages to each of the options noted above for dealing with personal differences and conflict; as a manager it is for you to judge which is the most appropriate response at any given time. Your aim should be to convert the energy and personal intensity being expressed by interested parties into more creative and collaborative work.

It is important to recognize, however, that this will not always be possible! Sometimes whatever you try the conflict will persist and your best efforts at resolving difficulties will remain frustrated!

INTERACTIONS AT WORK

Thus far the emphasis has been on acknowledging that there is a great deal of scope for personal conflict at work and that there are various ways of responding to individuals who – for one reason or another – are in disagreement. Often though conflict at work is also associated with the relationships between different departments, or operational allegiances which those involved are committed to, within the organization itself.

Cross-functional conflict – and rivalry between departments and functions – is common within organizations. Considerable discussion about how to foster better inter-departmental relationships occupies most top level groups at one time or another. One way of addressing this recurrent phenomena is to work out the reasons why the difficulties seem to be occurring. Figure 8.5 gives one framework that can be used to begin the process of finding out.

For example, for any given situation that is causing cross-departmental or cross-functional tension, look to see where the problems seem to be originating. It could be because departments are fighting tooth and nail for a greater share of limited resources to meet their targets. Perhaps the difficulties stem from incompatible goals which have been set for various clinical areas and, although they are fighting it out, the only appropriate course of action is for the matter to be resolved further up the hierarchy, perhaps by the Trust Board.

The matrix in Figure 8.5 is a basis for setting out the presenting difficulties, noting who is involved and what the issues, conflicts and differences seem to involve. When the requisite parts of the matrix have been completed, it will be more apparent what exactly is going on and what the most critical issues seem to be about.

Who is involved

	Between individuals	Wards	Clinical areas	Directorates	Staff groups	Professions	Trust Board
Facts							
Goals/ objectives							
Methods							
Values/ ethics							
Resources							

Nature of the difficulty (row label at left of the table)

Figure 8.5 Identifying who, what and where

In turn, this can then be used to decide what courses of action are sensible, realistic and appropriate. In all cases, having more of an understanding of the needs and expectations of staff must remain of paramount importance. One of the ways of resolving conflicts at work, of enhancing the quality of care, and of building better cross-functional relationships is to define clearly what those involved are looking for and what they care about. With this information in mind the possibility for a significant positive intervention exists.

To do this means building up a clear idea of what colleagues, patients, other professionals are looking for in their work with you. One way of doing this is to note what you consider to be:

- their needs
- their expectations
- their aspirations
- their concerns
- the pressures on them in relation to their work with you.

Figure 8.6 shows a method of doing just this. When completed it will provide a snapshot of the similarities and differences between yourself and a work colleague against each of the categories specified.

Whilst it will never be possible to create complete picture of colleagues in this way, if you chart up what you know there will be sufficient information to help you work with them with greater insight and understanding. When you do this it may come as a surprise just how much information you do have at your disposal. Your awareness of the expectations and needs of others is likely to reduce interpersonal tension and the potential for conflict at work.

ASSUMPTIONS AT WORK

Many things are taken for granted at work. It is assumed that junior staff will do what is asked of them and work in an effective, thoughtful and

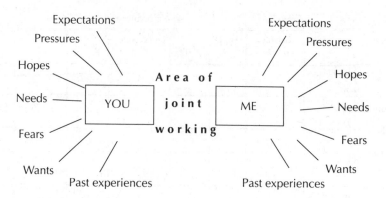

Figure 8.6 Comparing expectations and wants

considerate manner; that there will be inter-professional and inter-depart-mental co-operation and mutual regard; that individuals will work to achieve the formal responsibilities of their job, and that they will contribute to, rather than impede, the work they have been employed to do. Much of what actually happens in organizations suggests these assumptions are inaccurate.

Even though administrative work procedures are clearly set out, differences and difficulties continue to arise at work. This is especially so where there are less well-established sets of assumptions and when the nature of the work is variable – such as it is with patient care.

A useful way of looking at the behaviour of individuals at work is to view it from the four inter-linked perspectives shown in Figure 8.7. Perspective A represents what the job is about, how people should work together and what outcomes are expected. Perspective B, in contrast, acknowledges that there will be other unstated influences on what happens at work. Perspective C represents the impact of the local organization's culture which flavours how

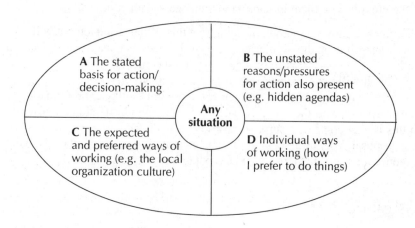

Figure 8.7 Four perspectives on work behaviour

the work is set up and how the local 'establishment' expect things to be done. Finally, perspective D embodies the influence in any situation of the individuality of those actually doing the work.

These four dimensions highlight very different influences on the work to be accomplished in any work situation. Textbooks generally tend to focus on perspective A yet, whilst this is the startpoint for consideration, it is not sufficient for understanding or predicting what actually happens in practice. Each of these four dimensions exert an influence on individual behaviour at work and, taken together, they give more depth and substance to what is going on in any work situation.

By being more aware of this interplay of forces and by being more sensitive to the complexities of how people work, you will become more effective in your work. Figure 8.7 is a reminder of the complexity of influences involved in individual (and group) decision-making.

A HIERARCHY OF DEBATE

Conflict can occur not just because of major disagreements, but because those parties involved are talking at cross purposes and fail to realize it; where essentially there is agreement between parties but because they are talking about different aspects of the same thing it seems that there are major matters to be resolved.

Conflict at work can be reduced by clarifying precisely the topic of discussion and the particular facet of the topic to be discussed. It may sound simple but this is not always done. The result is needless aggravation, tension, frustration and a waste of time for all those involved.

So, as well as trying to become clearer *why* disagreements are occurring, check that you and a colleague are not talking at cross purposes about something you essentially agree on! For example, you may both want a similar change in ward use yet one of you might be preoccupied with the *logistics* of the move or change of use, whereas the other might be preoccupied with the *resources*, or the timing of any change needed to make those changes viable and successful. Neglecting to clarify which aspect of the change each of you is momentarily concentrating upon, you may find soon find yourselves talking at cross purposes and – unnecessarily – becoming irritated and frustrated.

One way out of such confusion is to identify the different levels at which a topic can be discussed. Figure 8.8 suggests six such levels. At the top of the list is the underlying philosophy underpinning the change; at the bottom end of the hierarchy is the need to decide on the optimum sequence of steps to be taken in order to achieve the desired end result.

So this hierarchy can be used to guide discussions and remind those involved of the different types of consideration that need to be covered. Some people prefer to concentrate on the resources needed whereas others seem to be preoccupied by the logistics of it all. Both are important and both need discussion.

It may be that neither the strategy nor the philosophy involved are of interest, yet these also need some discussion because they set the wider context

1 The *philosophy*

2 The *strategy*

3 The *tactics*

4 The *resources*

5 The *timing*

6 The *sequence*

Figure 8.8 A discussion and planning hierarchy

and only by understanding these can the practical actions really be understood. So this framework has several uses. It both reduces the likelihood of miscommunication and talking at cross purposes (e.g. when person A is talking about resourcing issues, whereas person B is talking about the sequence of events, etc.) and ensures that all aspects of the matter to be discussed are considered (e.g. all the six levels are covered).

As a method of reducing the potential for conflict at work it offers a great deal and at the same time provides a basis through which colleagues can reach a better and more extensive shared understanding of the matters under consideration.

CONCLUDING COMMENTS

This chapter has emphasized the difficulties inherent in working with others and introduced several models and frameworks which help to diagnose what is going on in a situation so that action can be taken from a more informed position. Disagreements will occur; differences will exist. The question is not how to make everyone agree and become the same; the question is how to acknowledge and work with those differences and difficulties in productive and ethical ways.

In order to remain effective under the pressure and tension which is a continuing part of modern organizational life you need to know what you are after; you need to be aware of your limitations; and you need to appreciate the constraints and pressures of the wider situation of which you are part (i.e. colleagues, resources, past history, expectations, etc.). You need to be focused, organized and active in promoting and safeguarding your position.

Don't forget:

- that it is often easier to disagree than agree
- how we often look for difficulties and faults
- the impact of the organization's culture on management style
- to separate the people from the issues in a conflict
- to explore each party's interests rather than jump to solutions.

REFERENCES AND FURTHER READING

Adams, A. (1992) *Bullying at Work*, Virago Press, London.

Berbe, E. (1964) *Games People Play*, Penguin Books, Harmondsworth.

Birchnell, J. (1993) *How Humans Relate*, Psychology Press, Hove.

Fisher, R. and Ury, W. (1983) *Getting to Yes*, Penguin Books, Harmondsworth.

Fordyce, J. and Weil, R. (1983) *Managing with People*, Addison-Wesley, Reading, MA.

Hase, S. and Douglas, A. (1986) *Human Dynamics and Nursing*, Churchill Livingstone, Edinburgh.

Honey, P. (1992) *Problem People*, Institute of Personnel Management, London.

Horne, E. and Cowan, T. (1992) *Effective Communication: Some Nursing Perspectives*, Wolfe Publishing Co., London.

King, N. (1987) *The First Five Minutes*, Simon & Schuster, London.

McKenna, E. (1994) *Business Psychology and Organizational Behaviour*, Lawrence Erlbaum Associates, Hove.

O'Leary, J., Wendelgass, S. and Zimmerman, H. (1986) *Winning Strategies for Nursing Managers*, JB Lippincott, Philadelphia.

Roberts, W. (1989) *Leadership Secrets of Attila the Hun*, Bantam Books, London.

Thomas, K. (1976) Conflict and conflict management, in Dunnette, M. (ed.) *Handbook of Industrial and Organizational Psychology,* Rand McNally, Skokie, IL.

PART 3

You at Work

Part Three looks at how you 'fit in' at work. How you see yourself and what you concentrate on in getting your message across to others. Models and concepts are introduced which can help you consider your own values and behaviour and speculate on the motivations of others. This is particularly important in working with patients and clients because what is said rarely expresses fully what is meant.

Chapter 9 looks at the impact which our thoughts and beliefs have on our behaviour – and thus the subsequent behaviour of others around us – whereas Chapter 10 concerns itself with reminders about the complexity of interpersonal communications. Chapter 11 is about standing up for, and looking after, yourself at work.

The notions presented here are very much at an introductory level, so suggestions for further reading are given at the end of each chapter in case a more detailed exploration of the ideas and material introduced is required.

Thinking about yourself (thoughts and beliefs) | 9

It is important to have an awareness of organization behaviour, and of what happens in groups, if you are to be fully effective in your work, but that in itself is not enough. Self-insight, an awareness about oneself and about how one appears to others is also very important. Knowing oneself *and* an awareness of organization behaviour (OB) are vital in maintaining a sense of personal well-being. This chapter suggests ways of putting down some 'markers' about who you are and where you are heading. It builds on from the organizational dimensions covered in Part Two. There are two main sections: the first is about personal thinking patterns, the second is about the different stages of one's journey through life.

KEEPING TRACK OF YOURSELF

It is no simple matter to keep track of how each of us changes and develops over time. Reflecting on where we are in life – in our career, in our family life, with reference to our earlier ambitions, etc. – is a very valuable habit to develop however. Doing so provides reference points we can use to:

- look back on the past
- consider the present
- look to the future.

You may realize for example that you have become very skilled at doing certain things at work which perhaps, just a few years ago, may have filled you with apprehension. Acknowledging our competence can be quite a shock! You may, for example, also notice a change in how you think about yourself, your future, and your abilities. Perhaps you also see some aspects of yourself that have not developed as you had hoped and which are still important for you to develop further.

Reviewing and reflecting on what you have done and how you are doing will help you to focus on the current situation and move more purposefully to the future. Just as a Curriculum Vitae is kept up-to-date, a regular note of critical events and personal experiences will remind you of your skills and accomplishments which can otherwise be all too easily glossed over or forgotten.

A way of keeping a record of achievements, disappointments, etc. is to review what has gone on on a regular basis, perhaps on a six-monthly or annual basis. Figure 9.1 shows one way of doing this. The headings can be altered as you wish. The key though is to complete this information on a regular basis because that will give you a brief history of what has happened over the years and help you to see if there are any underlying patterns to you in life.

Another very good reason for keeping track of how you are getting on in life is that you can spot the need for changes sooner than if you don't do this on a regular basis. Decades can go by without you realizing this and the opportunity for making some of the changes to your life you may have wanted could have been lost.

Another consequence of neglecting to reflect from time to time on who you are and where you are going is that you make yourself more susceptible to accepting what *others* say about who and what you are. We are constantly told *who* or *what* we are by others (especially within families) and – if we value those people – we are more likely to accept how they see us as valid even if deep down we don't believe what they are saying.

We are also likely to take with us into the future the definitions and labels put on us by others 'as if' they are the truth! Sometimes we choose not to challenge the way others describe us because we may be worried about what they might say if we disagree with their opinion, and what we might see if we look more closely at ourselves – so it is easier (and safer) to accept what those close to us tell us about ourselves.

It may be that we fail to challenge another person's view of ourselves because we are in some way afraid of that person, so it is safer to accept what is said as accurate! Sometimes we may not feel confident enough about ourselves to express our own views, so we let others do it – after all, we might think, they have a more unbiased view of us! Either way, by not looking *for* ourselves *at* ourselves we risk surrendering a part of our 'self' to others; we put ourselves at risk by allowing others to define us in this way.

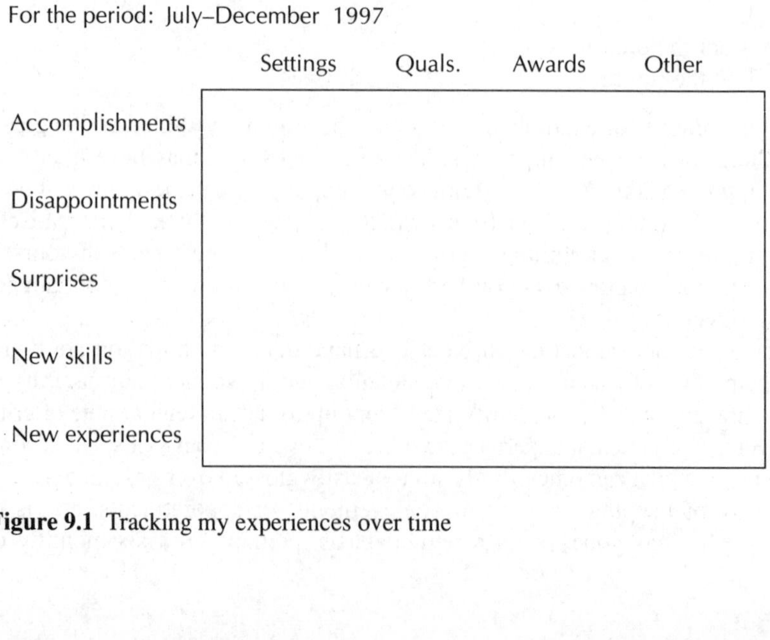

For the period: July–December 1997

	Settings	Quals.	Awards	Other
Accomplishments				
Disappointments				
Surprises				
New skills				
New experiences				

Figure 9.1 Tracking my experiences over time

If we believe others' assessments of us – without checking out the evidence for the views they are expressing – unnecessary damage can be done to our psychological and intellectual growth. Of course, others will have views and opinions about who and what we are in their eyes; but only each of us as individuals can know who we are and what we feel.

Of course, our views about ourselves will never be completely accurate because we are not unbiased, but we do each have the potential for knowing ourselves far more fully than anyone else. After all we each have our own daily conversations – with ourselves – about who we are, what we are going to do today, what we think we look like, and whether or not we think we can do whatever task is next on our agenda. The more we can know ourselves, then the more accurate and realistic these 'internal conversations' will be, and the more relaxed and less stressed we are likely to become.

The increasing availability of video cameras and VCRs in the last 15 years provides ample opportunity for people to see themselves in action, and to assess how they come across to others.

Accepting without question what others say about us can have a devastating effect on our self-image and how we then begin to live our lives. If the views others have are negative, that can damage our self-esteem and sense of well-being. If on the other hand we are held too highly in the eyes of others we may feel we to meet their unrealistic expectations of us. This could lead to a fear of failing and of letting others down.

Both of these scenarios can be quite a burden as we may find ourselves trying to live our lives to meet the expectations of others. We can help ourselves and become more confident by:

- becoming clearer about what we do and do not want
- becoming clearer about what are looking for in the future
- taking pride in ourselves
- looking at the past in a more integrated way (the good bits and the bad bits)
- deciding who we are and what we want for ourselves.

'On show'

We are 'on show' whenever we are with others. This means that those around us have knowledge of – and insights into – each of us: how we 'come over' to them, how we reach decisions, how we respond under pressure, etc.

Tapping into this information by being prepared to listen, and validating it with your own views and feelings, will give you a more complete overview of yourself. Even if you strongly disagree with some of the feedback offered it can be very useful to wonder why that person saw you so differently. Was it something to do with the circumstances they saw you in, or how they were feeling, or could it be that in some way or another you were giving inconsistent messages and they found that confusing?

A sound rule, when you receive information about yourself which does not match your own perceptions of yourself, is to wonder *why*. Why do they see you so differently? Why do you disagree with what they say? It is infinitely more constructive to respond to discrepant data in this way rather than by rejecting it out of hand as invalid.

Each of us projects how we want others to see us and we take great pains to project the desired image. One of the most influential books on this came from Goffman (1959) who, with the publication of *The Presentation of Self in Everyday Life*, opened up this field of interest to a non-academic audience. In recent years a field of study called 'impression management' has developed: it is defined as 'the process whereby people seek to control the image others have of them' (Rosenfeld *et al.*, 1995). As Rosenfeld *et al.* note 'Some of these impression management behaviours are consciously controlled while others such as eye contact and posture are often unwittingly expressed. We attempt to control our impression management behaviours because they are a primary means of influencing how we are treated by other people'.

Each of us is involved in our own 'impression management', as are Trust Boards, wards, clinical directorates, different professional groups and patients. Looking at what and how people present themselves is a very important factor to attend to at work. We can pick up a lot of information about a person from the choices they make about their own impression management and how they relate to others in the process.

ASSESSING OTHERS

When we look at others – and when they observe us – views are formed which are based on:

- what we see
- our imagination
- the meanings we give to these clues
- our past experiences.

Think about seeing a new patient for the first time. Your trained eyes notice a great deal about them and you start to build up a profile. Even as you begin to converse with them you may well find it difficult to listen attentively and not embellish what they are telling you with material that is consistent with the picture that you have already constructed of them! This happens because of the years of experience in assessing people in this way – since childhood, in fact – and because it is reassuring to define 'new' people in ways which are consistent with your past experiences and bank of information.

Whilst this type of 'short-cutting' helps in daily living, it has serious limitations since it encourages stereotyping of others on the basis of very limited and superficial information, and because it will almost certainly be inaccurate in some significant way.

The way in which we quickly form views of others – and from very limited information – can lead us to forget, dismiss or just not hear what clients, patients and colleagues tell us if it is not in line with our expectations, or what we want to hear. A way of reducing this tendency is to deliberately slow down the urge to reach conclusions about the other person as soon as possible. By allowing yourself the opportunity to listen and by keeping your mind open to hear only what you are being told gives the other person a genuine opportunity to tell you about themselves, their condition and their needs.

It is quite salutary to realize that just as you do this type of selective listening to those around you, others will be doing the same sort of thing to you. They too – initially at least – will be reaching decisions about you based on what they see, i.e. your behaviour and how you present yourself. They will base their views on very limited information too. They will be selectively listening to what you have told them and chunks of information you have given them will have been ignored, not heard or discarded as unimportant!

But what about those aspects of ourselves that are not readily visible: those parts of ourselves that we keep inside and usually to ourselves, but which are just as real – perhaps more so – than anything that can be observed externally?

Thus far the focus has been on the externals, i.e. what can be observed or deduced about ourselves from what we say or do, from what we wear, etc. What is not available to be observed or known about is our *internal world*: our values and beliefs, our attitudes and our fears. These are what influence our state of mind, and our capacity to withstand the ups and downs of daily living. The *meanings* we give to our experiences will largely determine what and who we are, and govern our capacity to overcome difficulties or be overcome by them.

What we *think*, what we *imagine* and what we *believe* are powerful and critical influences on our behaviour and our state of psychological well-being. The messages we give ourselves about our abilities, our standing and our plans for the future are all capable of changing our behaviour. In many ways what we believe about ourselves will affect what we do and how we feel.

But how does all this happen and what does this mean for you personally?

WHAT YOU THINK AFFECTS WHAT YOU DO AND HOW YOU FEEL

We are constantly being bombarded with information. In order to make sense of this information we respond to it in some way: we think about what it means for us. We decide, for example, whether we have to take any action or whether we can just ignore it. In reaching decisions, however, we are not totally aware of all the thought processes involved in deciding what to do and what we feel about a situation or a new piece of information.

Some of the thoughts we have about ourselves, or about particular situations, are unhelpful and counter-productive to our well-being. No matter how accomplished, how senior, how confident we are, there will be times when we experience self-doubt and confusion. Some of this self-doubt will be prompted by unhelpful and maybe inaccurate thoughts which undermine our ability to do well. Such thoughts affect our subsequent behaviour, mood and performance. Some examples of self doubting thoughts are 'I'm no good', or 'I don't know why I bother, the others are better than me', or 'I'm a loser and they will find me out'.

Such thoughts can flit into our thinking without us noticing what is going on. They can undermine our best efforts and be based on things said to us years and years ago but which – for whatever reason – we have just carried within us over the years. An examination of how thoughts affect an individual's mood and behaviour is a useful first step in reducing the negative impact of such automatic negative thoughts. A second step is to 'catch hold of' as many of these unhelpful internal messages as possible in order to see whether they are valid or whether they can be discarded.

When events occur we react to them and we decide how to respond. Much of our reaction is determined by the thoughts we have about the event itself and the meaning we give to what has happened. The relationship between thoughts and behaviour can be illustrated by the following 'ABC' framework, where:

- A stands for an event or an activity (the *Antecedent*)
- B stands for the way in which you have interpreted that event and the thoughts and beliefs you had about it (the *Beliefs*)
- C stands for the feelings and behaviours that occur as a result of A and B (the *Consequences*).

Figure 9.2 shows this model, which comes from the work of cognitive psychologists.

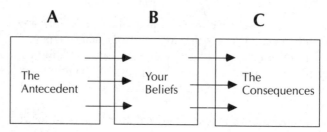

Figure 9.2 The ABC model

Most of us have not been trained to pay attention to the thoughts we have when we are deciding what to do: as often as not we 'just decide'! The cognitive-behavioural approach to psychology however draws particular attention to the critical influence which our *thinking* has on:

- the meanings we give to events
- the emotions generated
- our subsequent behaviour and mood.

The critically important message is: 'change the thinking', and then the emotions experienced, and the likely behaviour in response will also change. To do this though the first step is to *catch* the thoughts themselves and the second step is to *challenge* them to see if the thoughts are valid or spurious.

This can be done by asking some questions which test the accuracy and validity of the thoughts you may be having. For example:

- Are my thoughts *accurate*? (What evidence do I need in order to answer that question?)

- Are they *valid*?
- What *alternative explanations* could there be for what I am seeing and experiencing?
- *What can I do* about my thoughts?

By way of example, let us suppose that an individual holds the following negative belief: 'I am no good at holding my own when drawn into disagreements with senior colleagues'.

Unless this is checked for accuracy, that individual could very well shy away from any potential differences of opinion in the future even when certain of the validity of his position. This is both bad for business and destructive for that individual as a person. There are many other thoughts like this which snap into place when people try to do things. The impact of the negative thoughts – which the person may not be fully aware of – is to sabotage the person's attempts to accomplish the actions they are trying to do.

Therefore such negative beliefs need to be checked out and challenged. If they prove to be accurate then ways of addressing the problem can be sought. If they prove to be false then alternative ways of thinking about such situations in the future can be adopted. Future behaviour can then be changed where appropriate.

One of the most unhelpful aspects of negative thoughts is that they suggest that the person having them is in some way inherently bad or incapable. Rather like a condition that cannot be altered, the person is stuck with never being OK or whatever. In the example given above it may be that it *is* necessary for that individual to develop an ability to stand his ground with senior colleagues. By confronting that negative thought it is now far more likely to be seen as a training need rather some irretrievably bad personal characteristic about which nothing can be done.

In the context of the carer–patient relationship, by applying this sort of analysis to a patient's thoughts about their condition, and about hospitals, the carer may be more able to exert a positive influence on the patient's receptivity for treatment. Carers can usefully adopt this approach in their thinking about certain types of patients too. 'Thinking about thinking' is not merely an academic diversion: it offers practical insights into ways of enhancing patient care through attending more closely to the thoughts of patients and carers.

To bring about different outcomes remember to focus on the evidence, on alternative explanations and on options for action, as Figure 9.3 indicates.

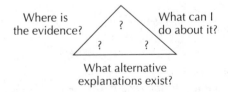

Figure 9.3 Challenging negative thoughts

THREE IMPORTANT BELIEFS

Also influential are the beliefs we hold about ourselves. How we attribute our accomplishments is significant in determining our sense of continued well-being. The work of Beck (1989), amongst others, suggests that our future behaviour and success will be influenced by the way in which we perceive our past accomplishments and whether we credit others or take personal credit for our achievements.

Beck highlighted three types of belief which appear to be particularly important in our thoughts about personal success and failure. He suggests that the way we explain to ourselves our performance (our successes and our failures) has a significant effect on our mood and behaviour and our level of optimism and self-belief. Much of Beck's work involved research on depression *and* the recommended belief patterns which follow were found to build optimism and self-belief. Since his initial work, these ideas have been used and applied more generally and with considerable success outside clinical settings.

Beck proposes that our views about ourselves, our experiences and our beliefs for our future are predictors of our psychological well-being: these beliefs concern what we do or what we believe we can do; they are about *how* and *to what* we attribute our successes and failures; and they concern our view of our own *capacity* to respond to, change and determine events rather than be determined by them.

Our sense of influence seems to revolve around the extent to which we believe we can exert some control over our lives and on the events around us. If we feel we can exercise such control then this will affect the degree to which we feel confident, self-valuing and robust in dealing with the ups and downs of life.

Beck's three types of belief form the 'cognitive triad' shown in Figure 9.4.

Figure 9.4 Beck's Cognitive Triad

Internal–External

The first set of beliefs relate to the *reason* for your successes. Do you believe that what happens is down to you (i.e. *internal*) or down to *external* circumstances or other people?

Suppose, for example, that your presentation at a meeting was very well received. Do you believe that this was down to rigorous preparation and the way the material was presented to those present (an internal belief)? Or do you believe that people were just being kind, that the material was not contentious, etc? In other words, do you believe that your success was not really down to you as presenter, but to other people being kind or because of favourable circumstances (an external belief)?

Permanent–Temporary

The second set of beliefs are about your accomplishments and whether you see them as something you can achieve over and over again (a *permanent* belief) or whether your success was a one-off (a *temporary* belief).

Using the example above, do you believe that you will *always* be able to deliver excellent presentations, irrespective of the setting or audience? Or do you put it down to good fortune and not feel confident that it will happen again because this was a lucky one-off?

Specific–Global

The third set of beliefs concerns the future applicability and generality of your accomplishments. Do you see your beliefs as influencing everything you do (*global*) or do you see them as being more restricted to particular things or situations (*specific*)? For example, do you believe that you can make successful presentations to different sized groups, in different places or to the same group again with the same themes to present?

The beliefs you hold about these matters will affect your sense of well-being and resilience in the face of adversity. Which combination(s) of beliefs would you expect to be the most productive?

Look at the options set out below and consider which would be the most positive and which would be the most unhelpful.

1. Combinations that would lead me to be more successful:
   I or E?
   P or T?
   S or G?

2. Combinations that would help me to cope with failures and disappointments
   I or E?
   P or T?
   S or G?

3. Combinations that would lead me to discount my successes and accomplishments:
   I or E?
   P or T?
   S or G?

4. Combinations that would lead me to dwell on/reinforce my failures and disappointments:
   I or E?
   P or T?
   S or G?

Suggested answers can be found at the end of this chapter.

The key message is this: your beliefs and thoughts exert a significant influence on what you do, how you do it, and how you feel. In looking after yourself and your patients, it is important to:

- be aware of the thoughts and preconceptions you have about yourself
- be prepared to test out their accuracy
- replace them with more helpful and productive ones where necessary.

LIFE STAGE FRAMEWORKS

How we think about ourselves and our accomplishments changes over time. For example, what may seem to be of overriding importance in our twenties may seem quite irrelevant in the overall scheme of things when reconsidered in our thirties.

Where we 'are' in life affects how we see ourselves. Various psychological studies suggest we all pass through 'life stages' to some extent, each of which holds particular challenges for us. Times change, and the passage of times changes us too. Our view and experience of the world is affected by our age, by the wider cultural settings we live in, by what we have achieved and what we have failed to accomplish, and through the experiences we have had.

Our ambitions and aims change as we go through life. In part this is because, as we develop in our career, we come to know more about what is involved in reaching the original goals we set ourselves and as a result we may change our minds about what we want. Or perhaps there are unexpected physical or familial considerations which come into play, causing us to change our plans. But sometimes we just start to see things differently and things that once held appeal for us now lose their lure.

Erik Erikson's life cycle

One of the most extensive and influential of the life cycle researchers is Erikson (1985) who suggested that 'every period of life has its own point, its own purpose. To find it and accept it is one of the most vital problems relating to life'.

He developed an eight-stage psycho-social model of personal development where progression from one stage to the next revolved around the resolution of dilemmas and crises specific to that stage of development. His framework in outline is shown in Figure 9.5.

Stages		Psycho-social crisis (the main challenge of this stage)	Basic strength (the primary outcome)
I	Infancy	Basic trust v. Basic mistrust	Hope
II	Early childhood	Autonomy v. Shame, doubt	Will
III	Play age	Initiative v. Guilt	Purpose
IV	School age	Industry v. Inferiority	Competence
V	Adolescence	Identity v. Identity confusion	Fidelity
VI	Young adulthood	Intimacy v. Isolation	Love
VII	Adulthood	Generativity v. Stagnation	Care
VIII	Old age	Integrity v. Despair	Wisdom

Figure 9.5 Erikson's psycho-social model of development

Erikson's model predicts that we will be challenged to define who are and what we stand for as we progress through life, that we will each have dilemmas, crises and decisions to make that will affect the course of our progression and individual development. At one level this is very reassuring because it predicts that each of us will have periods when we are faced with a number of differing life dilemmas, challenges and confusions from which we will move on as we age and develop over time.

Not only does Erikson alert us to this pattern of personal growth and development but he suggests that it is part of life, that when we do find ourselves grappling with issues and problems about our personal development that far from being unusual this is what it is all about. This developmental framework also gives the carer another way of thinking about the types of challenge which their patients may have had to contend with. Often we do not fully resolve things as we would have liked and we carry on with us some unresolved matters which may show themselves when we are most vulnerable – such as when we are ill and in hospital for example.

Other notable writers in the area include Levinson (1978), who has been attributed with the phrase 'mid-life crisis' following his studies, and Gail Sheehy (1976) with her studies of 'passages'. Both of these writers show life as a series of phases or stages of development each of which is different to the one before. They make interesting reading and can be very helpful as one way of seeing where you 'fit' within the schemes of development they have identified.

Managerial preoccupations

The changing preoccupations of a manager over time have been the subject of attention by Keichel (1987) who described the major stages of development for a professional person on a decade by decade basis as illustrated in Figure 9.6.

Figure 9.6 charts the changing preoccupations of aspiring top managers and professionals as they progress through their careers. Whilst this framework does not attempt to give a detailed explanation of the reasons why each of these concerns predominates, it does illustrate vividly the various challenges which confront professionals as they grow older.

Where would you position yourself on Figure 9.6, and how do you see your career progressing? Are you stuck with aspirations which are now no longer viable or are you leaping ahead?

The work of the life stage theorists helps to put a broader perspective on the ups and downs of life and provides a way of looking at life from a longer term perspective. This is helpful in putting current concerns and difficulties into perspective, and in realizing that others too will be experiencing similar dilemmas, problems and pressures.

In the health care sector, where the nature of the work with its high level of situational urgency and trauma can so easily take over, it can be very reassuring and calming to keep such longer-term perspectives in mind.

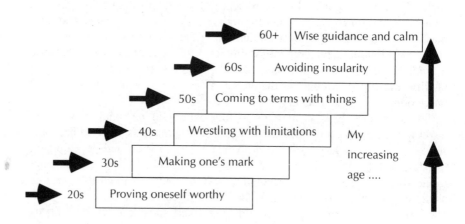

Figure 9.6 Changing preoccupations of managers

Sketching out your 'life-line'

One way of pulling together your reflections about yourself and your experiences is to draw a 'life-line'. This will help you to record on a chart your major past experiences in sequence over the course of your life.

1. Take a few moments to review what has happened to you over the years. Do this quickly and jot down what for you are the key

features, episodes, events, periods, successes, disappointments, etc. These may be specific events, particular friends at a given point in time, something dear that was lost, a holiday, an insight. Do not worry if you come up with quite a mix of things. What you need in front of you is the rich mix of data about yourself and your life as you have experienced it so far.

2. Re-order your notes into a time sequence so that you have a chronological record of when these major events in your life took place. As you are doing this you may recall additional events and important experiences to add in to your original list. If so just add them – the more the merrier!

3. Take a large sheet of paper and draw a horizontal line across it. To the left of that line enter your birth date; approximately four-fifths of the way across the line on the right-hand side enter the current date. Along the line jot down the most important items from the list you made. Enter positive events and episodes above the line; distressing or negative events below the line

4. Plot a curve that goes above and below your horizontal line that will reflect the highs and lows that you have recalled.

5. Does the curve capture what you wanted to show? You will probably want to do it a couple more times because additional thoughts are likely to occur to you as you are doing this, and because you may want to reshape the highs and lows until they feel 'right'.

Figure 9.7 is an example of a life-line which shows some ups and downs and some of the possible reasons why.

The following are some examples of keys events, the sorts of things that can deeply affect the course of a person's life.

Positive events	**Negative events**
sister born	moved house
accepted for training	loved one died
state registration	first death on ward
passed driving test	break-up of a relationship
etc.	

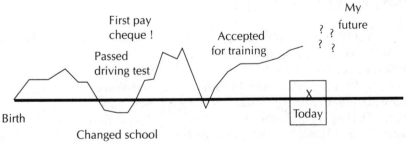

Figure 9.7 Example of a life-line

6. Now look once again at what you have depicted in your life-line and see if there are any other dimensions or episodes you want to add.

7. When you are ready, take some time to reflect on what your life-line shows you about how things have gone for you over the years. Where, for example, does that leave you now? Do you feel pleased, saddened, surprised or perhaps excited by the overall picture you have put together about yourself and what has transpired over the years?

8. Given your life-line as you see it, how do you expect the future to turn out for you? How do you anticipate things will move ahead? What key events or outcomes do you want to happen? What have you suddenly seen about the course of your life that you had not noticed before? How do you want – if at all – things to be different in the future?

One of the benefits of doing this type of self-review is that it gives an overall perspective on your life that can otherwise be missed. All sorts of things may jump out at you that you may not have considered before. It can be a most worthwhile activity. It can help you to:

- notice underlying patterns about yourself
- 'see' how you have progressed
- acknowledge the low points
- see what seems to trigger life shifts for you
- acknowledge the positives and good points
- ask questions about yourself, etc.

You could now ask yourself some questions:

- What does this tell me about myself?
- Are there any surprises?
- Are there patterns that seem to underpin what I did, what I want, and how I go about things?
- What do I want in the future?
- Who am I?

REFERENCES AND FURTHER READING

Beck, A. (1989) *Cognitive Therapy and the Emotional Disorders*, Penguin Books, Harmondsworth.

Bolles, R. (1997) *The Three Boxes of Life*, Ten Speed Press, Berkeley, CA.

Bridges, W. (1991) *Managing Transitions*, Addison-Wesley, Reading, MA.

Burns, D. (1980) *Feeling Good*, Signet Books, New York.

Burns, D. (1989) *The Feeling Good Handbook*, Plume Books, New York.

Butler, G. and Hope, T. (1995) *Manage Your Mind*, Oxford University Press, Oxford.

Erikson, E. (1985) *The Life Cycle Completed*, W.W. Norton & Co., New York.

Gellman, M. and Gage, D. (1987) *Improve Your Confidence Quotient*, Thorsons Books, Wellingborough.

Goffman, I. (1959) *The Presentation of Self in Everyday Life*, Penguin Books, Harmondsworth.

Keichel, W. (1987) Ages of a manager, *Fortune*, 11 May.

Levinson, D. *et al.* (1978) *The Seasons of a Man's Life*, Ballantine Books, New York.

Nicholson, J. (1980) *Seven Ages*, Fontana Paperbacks, Glasgow.

Roet, B. (1987) *All in the Mind?* Optima Books, London.

Rosenfeld, P., Giacalone, R. and Riordan, C. (1995) *Impression Management in Organizations*, Routledge, London.

Rowe, D. (1995) *Guide to Life*, HarperCollins, London.

Sheehy, G. (1976) *Passages*, Bantam Books, Toronto.

Spinelli, E. (1989) *The Interpreted World*, Sage Publications, London.

Suggested answers about patterns of belief (see page 149):

1. P, I, G
2. S, E, T or S, I, T
3. S, E, T
4. P, I, G

10 Social communication

One of the most basic life skills is being able to communicate so that the message you intended to communicate is the message received. It sounds relatively simple. However, successfully conveying the intended information to others is no easy matter; even listening to what others say is surprisingly difficult to do well.

This chapter looks at some of the complexities of communication and considers some ways of reducing the problems which often arise when communication fails.

WHAT DOES 'COMMUNICATION' MEAN?

'Communication' is a word used very freely, but which can be difficult to define in precise terms.

 Try writing down what the word 'communication' means to you: jot down the images and ideas that pop into your head. If you are doing this as part of a workshop or with a colleague, compare your responses and list those which are the same and those which are different. You will probably find that the word conjures up some interesting differences.

See the end of the chapter for meanings which the word 'communication' holds for me.

The point of this exercise is to illustrate how even common words can mean different things to different people. Whilst there is no right or wrong list of definitions of communication, it is surprising how differently people define it. The same is true for many others words, phrases and instructions used day-in and day-out by most of us. Some of the difficulties which arise in communicating effectively with others stem from lack of an agreed definintion of the words used – it is as simple as that.

VERBAL COMMUNICATION

Verbal communication is the use of speech to communicate information to others through the medium of words. It is the most frequently used method of communication between people, either in direct contact or indirectly through the telephone, video conferencing or videos. Although we rely heavily on verbal communication, it is not necessarily an efficient method of communicating information because of the many distortions which can arise and the 'games' that can be played with the words used.

In Figure 10.1 person A (the sender) has a message to send to person B (the receiver) with the arrow indicating the direction of the first communication. In the real world the process of communication is not so straightforward. In this example, whilst the sender may be reasonably clear about what it is that is being communicated, the receiver will not necessarily be 'on the same wavelength'. Scope for considerable mis-communication exists even in such a seemingly straightforward communication such as this.

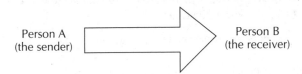

Person A (the sender) → Person B (the receiver)

Figure 10.1 A 'simple' communication

The receiver may not receive the message as it was intended and therefore is unlikely to respond in the way you would expect or they may signal a lack of understanding or some confusion. To the sender this may be surprising and disappointing especially if they believe they have communicated their message clearly to the other person.

However, there are influences which will distort the information communicated to the receiver which may have nothing to do with the sender. No matter how we try, there will always be the potential for some sort of interference to distort what is being communicated.

Figure 10.2 depicts a communication with some distorting influences impeding the clear communication from the sender.

What would *you* see as possible distorting and interferences to a communication?

Rogers and Roethlisberger (1952) investigated the 'barriers and gateways to communication'. They suggest that a 'major barrier to mutual interpersonal communication is our very natural tendency to judge, to evaluate, to approve (or disapprove) the statement of the other person or group'. The breakthrough, they suggest, comes through listening with understanding. By this they mean 'see[ing] the expressed idea and attitude from the other person's point of view, to sense how it feels to him, to achieve his frame of reference in regard to the thing he is talking about'. They note that, whilst these ways of relating may sound so simple, they are in fact complicated, difficult to follow and require considerable effort.

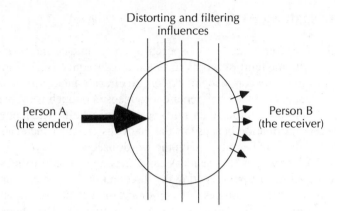

Figure 10.2 Distortions to a communication

Each of the following points will interfere with the accuracy and effective-ness of interpersonal communications:

- making judgements when others are telling you things
- interrupting
- finishing their sentences (either aloud or in your head)
- concluding what they are telling you *before* they have told you
- seeking to defend yourself and starting to put together your answers whilst they are talking
- assuming you know what they mean
- jumping to conclusions
- thinking you own thoughts instead of attending to what they are saying.

Effective, successful communication is very difficult to accomplish. It is important to listen with care *and* regard to what the other person is communi-cating; this is especially the case in health care settings which can be stress-ful and anxiety-provoking.

The cumulative effect of the distortions is to change the message so that there is a difference between the intended message and the one actually received. The result is an arc of distortion as shown in Figure 10.3.

The arc of distortion is the difference between what the sender intended to communicate and what the receiver actually received. In Figure 10.3 there will be quite a range of possible meanings picked up by the receiver (from X to Y even though the intended message was A!).

The result of all this is confusion, anxiety, conflict and lack of trust between the parties involved, and misunderstandings – even when those involved are wanting and intending to be helpful and positive towards each other.

With face-to-face communications there is the opportunity to clarify, check and test your understanding of the meaning and purpose of what is being communicated. We can look to see what non-verbal cues are being given out by the other party as they communicate with us. We can ask ques-tions, we can clarify our understandings of what they have said, and we can check to make sure we are defining the same terms in the same way.

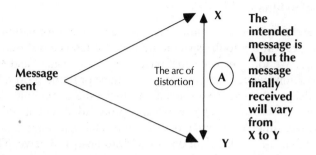

Figure 10.3 The arc of distortion

Factors that impede communication

Some of the reasons why we find it a such challenge to listen openly and freely to others are shown in Figure 10.4. These factors act as filters and get in between what was sent and what is received. Although we cannot get rid of these altogether, we can reduce the amount of distortion they cause by acknowledging they exist and by considering the possible effect they exert on interpersonal communications.

What is so surprising is that factors such as these are rarely openly talked about or taken into account when we communicate with each other. It is as if we try to deny that we all have these biases and presumptions which do influence the meanings we give to our experiences. It may be that we are taught to try to be totally neutral just too much, to the extent that we believe we can be so all the time!

The point of this discussion is to remind you that, try as we may, we will not achieve neutrality totally when relating to and communicating with others. The best each of us can do is to be alert to our own biases and prejudices (and those of others too) and take these into account in our work with colleagues, patients and the world at large.

Figure 10.4 Factors impeding communication

Communication filters

As listeners and receivers of communications we sift the information sent to us to see if we can fit it into the specific frames of reference we use to make sense of things. We look for ways that enable us to understand and relate to the communications we receive. We may then shape or round it off a little so that we can deal with it. If we are unable to make the communications we receive fit our frames of reference we are prone to discount, eliminate, reduce, trivialize, ridicule (or make personally palatable in some other manner) the communication which we do not wish to hear or receive. The psychological tools we use to sift information has been referred to as 'communication filters'. The following are some examples of such filters.

Self-image

We all have an image of how we are, whether or not we acknowledge it and irrespective of its accuracy. Our frankness about ourselves will vary and, for example, if we have too much of an idealized self-image it will be difficult for us to accept critical information about our 'self'.

This is a very potent filter because of the importance our self-image has for our self-esteem, sense of value and competence. Whilst having a positive view of oneself is desirable, too strong and idealized a view of oneself can become very unhelpful and counter-productive.

Image of others

The view we have of those communicating with us will influence the sense, the impact, and the response we give to the information communicated to us. If, for example, we value the communicator and hold them in high regard and see them as influential then we are likely to take seriously what they say. If, on the other hand, we see them as less important or influential then we are more likely to water down or even discount what they communicate to us.

Expectations

In order to make sense of what is going on, we draw on our accumulated experience and knowledge of past practice. We codify our experiences and based on what has gone before we create a range of expectations which we use as a guide for the future. These expectations act as short-cuts and help us to assess more quickly what is going on around us and what we know – from past experience – it is important for us to attend to.

Whilst this is a helpful process, there is a danger that we could allow our pre-formed expectations of what it is important to focus on to 'kick in' too quickly (in anticipation of what others are telling us) *before* we have actually heard what they have to say. In such instances our expectations get in the way of effective communication and encourage us not to attend to what is being communicated.

Our expectations can lead us to 'filter out' unexpected or unwanted messages if they do not fit what we have been trained to look for, or what we want to hear.

Stereotypes and professional images

We will categorize the sender of the information according to their role and profession, for example as 'doctor', 'nurse', 'paper-pusher', etc., and they will be dealt with by us on that basis, as if all doctors, nurses, paper-pushers *et al.* were the same. In a professionally-dominated organization such as the NHS this can have some advantages in that we can expect particular behaviours and a technical language with which to communicate with each other.

Because of the expectations from such stereotyping we come to expect shortcuts in the communications between us, we will expect for example that the other professional will understand, or 'know what we mean', when we say certain things. This may not be an accurate expectation, however, because unless we have checked out beforehand the meanings we give to commonly used terms, we cannot guarantee that each person will be using the same definitions.

Drawbacks arise too when we begin to see all doctors, nurses *et al.* as the same; where we fail to attend carefully enough to the individual before us; where we stereotype and just see 'a nurse', 'a doctor'. As a result we may discount, or conversely, over-exaggerate the importance of communications from the sender and miss the underlying messages they are giving us.

Emotional states within the organization

The effectiveness of communications are also affected by the emotional 'state' of those individuals involved and by the tension in the organization itself. In health care settings, as has been noted, anxiety, tension, uncertainty and stress are ever present. These factors make effective communication even more difficult to achieve.

Double messages

There are situations where there seems to be some discrepancy between the actual message being sent and the way it is presented. You may ask someone to come to a meeting even though, in reality, you would rather they didn't come; and you may say it in such a way that is is pretty clear to that person that he is unwelcome.

In such a case the interaction is usually concluded with a cosmetically suitable reply (from the receiver) who says he would like to attend but can't for some – genuine or otherwise – reason do so. The communication is concluded, both parties have understood what has gone on, the 'right' things have been said and the standing of both parties has been safeguarded – but the communication has not been open and straightforward. For such communications to work effectively both parties need to be sufficiently aware of the underlying message and the appropriate response that is wanted.

Double messages can confuse the receiver and they can generate disharmony and lack of trust. This is especially true when one of the parties is not aware of the underlying message being communicated or the response which is actually wanted. An example of this would be where an invitation is communicated and the other person accepts it when really they were expected to politely decline!

Other impediments to effective communications

There are other factors to bear in mind which do not have their origin in the motives, aspirations or defence filters of the parties involved but which have an effect on communication:

- *Complexity*: Complexity confuses. It is helpful to keep the message as simple as possible.
- *Consistency*: Make sure that the various constituent parts of information communicated are compatible with each other in order to avoid double messages and confusions.
- *Language*: Take care that the message is expressed in words which receivers will be able to understand and act upon.
- *Style*: There may be a particular communication pattern to be followed for particular types of messages – if so, use it. Only use what is appropriate to the situation.
- *Cultural differences*: Bear in mind that cultural differences may distort what you say – this is as important between different hospitals and departments as it is between different countries and nationalities.
- *Timing*: Think about *when* you pass on information: consider timing from the point of view of yourself and the receptivity of staff. For example, unless it cannot be avoided, giving a complex, pressured briefing at the end of a busy and traumatic shift is not the best time.
- *Capacity*: Watch and judge what receivers can take in and handle at any one time: do not overload them and check understanding at regular intervals. Make it easy for them to ask for clarification.
- *Repetition and reinforcement*: Phrasing the information in more than one way may help receivers to become clear about what it is exactly that you are communicating.
- *Emotive content*: Remember to consider the impact on both yourself and the receivers of any emotive material to be communicated. The nature of the information being transmitted will affect all the parties involved.

Environmental conditions

Many of the factors which impair effective interpersonal communication and understanding relate to the interactions between people. There are additional factors, however, which can interfere with communication and these also need to be borne in mind. These are environmental factors, such as:

- location for the meeting (choose a quiet and convenient setting)

- the number of people involved
- seating arrangements
- stopping interruptions to allow the core message to be delivered
- use aids to get over complex messages (for example, flip charts, briefing notes, etc.).

Attention to these factors will help to create a more focused, secure and ordered context for working together which, in turn, facilitates effective communication. Whilst they cannot guarantee agreement between parties, or that tension will be avoided, they will help to provide an better opportunity for people to talk with each other.

NON-VERBAL COMMUNICATION (NVC)

Whilst we usually concentrate on the spoken content of a message, we are often able to observe the sender at the same time. This makes it possible for the receiver to pick up a wide range of additional clues about what is being said in addition to the verbal messages formally communicated. Non-verbal cues and behaviours are extremely important and influential factors in communication: they provide additional insight into what is going on in social interactions. Often they make the difference in whether or not we believe what we are being told, and if we will act on that information or discard it.

The following are important non-verbal elements of social behaviour:

- stance
- facial expressions
- gaze direction and eye contact
- use of space
- proximity
- protection of own 'territory'
- gestures
- speed of movements
- physical appearance
- physical contact.

Each of the above features plays a part in signalling the belief and commitment of the sender as they deliver their messages. If what is being said matches the non-verbal communications then:

- receivers are more likely to believe what the sender is saying
- receivers are more likely to view the sender as a competent person even if they strongly disagree with the message being communicated.

If word content and non-verbal communication do not match then:

- receivers are likely to be confused and suspicious
- receivers will tend to mistrust and de-value the competence and standing of the sender.

SYMBOLIC COMMUNICATION

How a person decides to present themselves is a statement about how they see themselves and how they want others to view them. Symbols are used to convey our self-image and, whether consciously or unconsciously attended to, the following are some of the most common ways in which this is done:

- clothing and 'style' of dress
- hairstyle
- use of cosmetics
- jewellery and adornments
- use of symbolic motifs (badges, designer labels, ties, etc.)
- body tattooing and marking
- body piercing
- lifestyle artefacts (cars, type of accommodation, location of home, etc.)
- places regularly visited (for example, clubs, professional societies, etc.).

How we are 'seen' by others *is* important: 'fashion' statements devour considerable attention and who we are 'seen' with – and what we wear – occupies a lot of thought.

How, and what, we communicate is a fascinating and complicated field. Some of the messages we communicate will be deliberate and intended; others we will be unaware of or not intend. How a staff member 'comes over' is of special importance because this will influence patients and influence how they feel about their treatment and how well they feel they are being looked after by the attending professionals.

It has been said that we are what our behaviour defines us as being: that we will be described and defined in terms of the *behaviour* we exhibit and in terms of how others experience and interpret our behaviour. It is important to remember that we reach assessments about others in this way without having all the information we might need, and that the information we use to reach decisions has been filtered (unwittingly perhaps by us) through many of the communication-filters noted earlier in this chapter.

PULLING IT ALL TOGETHER: 'THE WORDS, THE MUSIC AND THE DANCE'

Thus far the verbal, the non-verbal and the symbolic aspects of interpersonal communications have been considered separately. In our day-to-day experiences they all come together as a whole; we come as a 'package' which attempts to communicate who and what we are, both to ourselves *and* to others.

The impact of any message comes from a combination of three components which are:

- what is said (the '*words*')
- how it is expressed, (the '*music*')
- use of the body when delivering the communication (the '*dance*').

There is more to effective communication than having the facts and figures carefully thought out and presenting them clearly and firmly whilst making it clear what you want. These are crucial dimensions, but how you use your body to communicate is also of considerable importance in getting the message across in a believable way. Much of what influences us comes through what we see before us. The words – the content of the communication – will not guarantee that the impact of your message is received and understood as you might want.

For maximum impact and influence the words needs to be backed up with how the message is actually expressed, and also with how the material is presented by the sender. Of these three, it is the dance – how the communicator uses their body during a communication – that has the most impact on the receivers. These are the findings of research by an American psychologist Mehrabian (1971, 1981), whose work in this area has been influential in guiding interpersonal behaviour.

To communicate effectively, and to maximize the chance of your communication being acted upon, the three key areas of communication need to be consistent and mutually supportive. In Figure 10.5 this would occur when there is a large area of overlap at the centre of the figure between the words, the music and the dance.

- The *words*: This covers the precision of the message itself; the construction of the message; the vocabulary and structure of the material to be conveyed, the actual words used.
- The *music*: This refers to the way in which the content of the message is delivered: pace, volume, force and power; phrasing and pauses.
- The *dance*: This is the way in which the communicator comes over in engaging with those receiving the message: eye contact, gestures, body movement, proximity of the sender to others, demeanour.

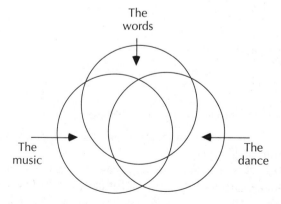

Figure 10.5 The words, the music and the dance

Reflect on your experience of what creates impact in communicating with others. Consider how would you assess the relative impact of the words, the music and the dance in influencing others. If you had to distribute 100 points – where 100 was the total impact – how many points would you give to the words, the music, and the dance?

It is likely that you assessed the effect of the words quite highly. Much of our training and education emphasizes marshalling the facts and presenting a logical argument. Paying attention to *how* you deliver your communication is something you may have been coached on in the past, but it is likely that the emphasis was still firmly centred on the message as the most important factor.

Of course to have any chance of being influential the content of the message has to make sense so the words used are crucial and they have to be understandable to the receiver. But when it comes down to it body stance, posture and movement exercise the most significant influence on the overall impact of a communication. Generally it is the dance which is likely to make the difference in the overall effectiveness of your communication from that of others.

Dance is the component least often focused upon, yet research by Mehrabian suggests that, when we are communicating, how we present ourselves affects the impact of our communication. His message is that effective communication requires more than carefully argued case. In terms of a distribution of those 100 points under 10 per cent goes against the words, around 35 per cent to the music and a huge 55 per cent to the dance!

COMMUNICATION NETWORKS

So far this chapter has briefly considered some of the ways in which we communicate, how communications can become distorted, and how to increase the impact of the messages we communicate to others. This next section moves on to consider some of the communication networks available to us.

Communication networks are the patterns or structures of communications that can be used for passing and receiving information. The structuring of communications can either be:

- formally set up, or
- evolve on an informal basis

and they can be:

- direct, or
- remote/indirect (for example as with e-mail).

It is important to match the communication with an appropriate communication channel through which to transmit the message to be given. For example, for very personal and highly charged communications a direct communication – whether formally or informally conducted – will usually be the most suitable. This is because the recipient(s) can then draw on the words and the music to help them assess the authenticity of the communication and also because they can ask at first hand for clarification of any queries they may have. You can help them to consider the message too and adjust the tone, pace and power of your communication depending on their reactions.

Conversely, communications of production line performance, of quality figures, of bed usage, etc. are more suited to an indirect communication channel, perhaps through sending a computer print-out, fax or a newsletter. You do not need to necessarily deliver that information face-to-face.

Difficulties arise when there is a mismatch between the selected communication channel and the nature of the communication. An example of this would be when an open fax is sent to advise staff of a major change affecting their well-being, or when personal and confidential information is sent via e-mail over an open communication network.

Figure 10.6 shows how different communication channels can best suit different types of communications to be relayed.

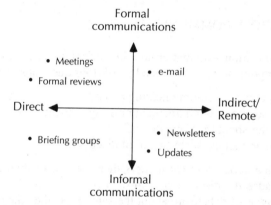

Figure 10.6 Contrasting communication channels

The flow of face-to-face communications at work can vary. Shown in Figure 10.7 are four common communication patterns of the type studied by Leavitt (1951) and his co-workers in classic studies on decision-making in small groups. He looked at the impact of different patterns of communication in work groups on cohesion, morale, speed of decision-making, leadership, resolution of difficulties, passing of information, etc.

The communication patterns in Figure 10.7 could be examples of the communication structures used where you work. The results of Leavitt's work showed that more straightforward problems were solved more quickly, with fewer mistakes and with fewer communications required in the more centralized communication network – network 4. In the case of more complex work, the better results came from communication networks which facilitated more communication between all involved on the work to be done.

Whilst these patterns may represent what actually happens in certain situations, they are unlikely to be rigidly followed in every instance and will be complemented by informal patterns of communication. Some difficulties can arise though when some of these patterns – especially patterns 1 and 2 – are rigidly enforced, because they can isolate staff and make them dependent on receiving information from others colleagues.

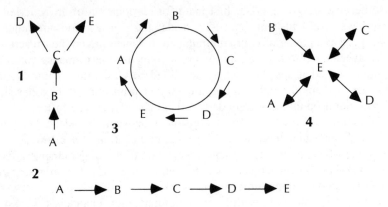

Figure 10.7 Four patterns of communication

AVOIDING CROSS-COMMUNICATIONS

In any communication – no matter how influential or successful you may be in getting your point across – you need to ask four questions:

- What is it that we are communicating about?
- What is the source of our agreement or disagreement?
- Are we talking about the same things?
- Are we focusing on the same 'level' of discussion?

If we are talking about *different* matters then the sooner that is made clear, the better because the discussions can then be refocused. If, however, it is clear that the areas of debate are about the same topic then the next step is to make sure everyone is talking about the same aspect of the topic under discussion. The framework in Figure 10.8 can be used to help this happen and to make sure that each of the different types of matters to consider (i.e. philosophy, tactics, etc.) is covered at some point in the discussions.

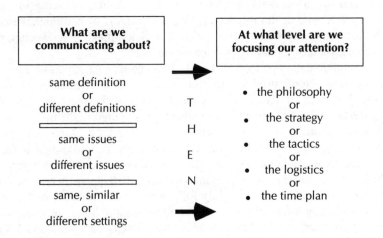

Figure 10.8 Facilitating communications

It is very easy for confusion to creep into interpersonal communications particularly when the matters under discussion are of an emotive nature and where the stakes are high. Clarity of communication is especially important when the health, care and treatment protocols of an individual are being discussed. Under pressure too it can be appealing to focus down onto the specific task that has to be done whilst forgetting to look at why that task (or treatment) is being administered.

CULTURAL DIFFERENCES

The continuing development of the EU, the increasing regularization of professional training across national borders, and the 'global market' all make it very likely that some of your current or future professional colleagues will have trained overseas. European employment legislation enables professionals to have the right to employment opportunities within member countries and working within the NHS is an attractive proposition for health care professionals from the EU and elsewhere.

This results in a rich diversity of perspectives and experiences, some of which will be new to NHS staff. To work collaboratively, and to function as an integrated care team, even more attention may need to be given to enhancing effective communication between colleagues trained abroad.

REFERENCES AND FURTHER READING

Berne, E. (1964) *Games People Play*, Penguin Books, Harmondsworth.

Bettelheim, B. and Rosenfeld, A. (1993) *The Art of the Obvious*, Thames & Hudson, London.

de Board, R. (1986) *Counselling Skills*, Gower Publishing, Aldershot.

Davis, H. and Fallowfield, L. (1991) *Counselling and Communication in Health Care*, Wiley, Chichester.

Jenkins, N. (1991) *The Business of Image*, Kogan Page, London.

King, N. (1987) *The First Five Minutes*, Simon & Schuster, London.

Leavitt, H. (1951) Some effects of certain communication patterns on group performance, *Journal of Abnormal and Social Psychology*, **46**, 38–50.

Mehrabian, A. (1971) *Tactics of Social Influence*, Prentice-Hall, Englewood Cliffs.

Mehrabian, A. (1981) *Silent Messages*, Wadsworth Books, Belmont, CA.

Nelson-Jones, R. (1993) *You Can Help*, Cassell, London.

Olins, W. (1989) *Corporate Identity*, Thames & Hudson, London.

Olins, W. (1995) *The New Guide to Identity*, Gower, Aldershot.

Rogers, C. and Roethlisberger, F. (1952) Barriers and gateways to communication, *Harvard Business Review*, XXX (4), July–August.

Suggestions for what 'communication' can mean (see page 156):

Talking	Writing	Telephone
Reading case notes	Receiving orders	Being told
Telling others	Computer technology	Listening to patients
Watching patients	Getting my way	Data processing
Passing messages	Confusion	Negotiating
Direction	Understanding	Images
Symbols	Pictures	E-mail

Looking after yourself $\boxed{11}$

This chapter is about looking after yourself. Not only does this make good sense but, unless you do so, you will not be able to do the best for your patients and your colleagues. Some thoughts about stress at work and what you can do to make things more manageable are also covered.

One of the best ways in which you can care for patients – and work effectively with colleagues – is by looking after yourself so that you can cope more ably with the stresses and the strains of nursing. It may sound indulgent to some, but it is sound common sense. You will undoubtedly be aware that some of your colleagues are clearly fatigued and are not in an optimum physical condition to give of their best yet will keep going perhaps until they go off sick rather than try to change an inappropriate work pattern.

Colleagues who are constantly tired are likely to leave, become ill, make poor decisions give bad advice and make mistakes. They may do themselves harm in some way; possibly do harm to others too. The potential for self-harm – psychological and physical – can be due to the following reasons:

- realizing their own performance is below par
- the torment of a bad clinical decision
- embarrassment at upsetting others
- a growing sense of inner-impotence
- physical over-exertion
- psychological exhaustion
- letting the side down.

Care professionals in particular need to look after themselves physically and psychologically so that they can deliver professional care to their patients. It has to be said that nurses do not always look after themselves adequately.

I recall vividly how shortly after I joined the NHS in 1972 I was invited to give a talk during a Nursing Management Study Day. I had been asked to provide a Personnel perspective and commentary on changes to the management structure of the nursing profession. I commented on the absence of guidelines and provision to safeguard the nurse from the psychological strains and rigours of their role. I said that I did not understand how nurses could provide effective care for their patients unless they themselves were sufficiently looked after.

My enduring memory is one of seeing a hall full of white starched hats slowly moving to and fro in disapproval at what I was saying! Having at that time recently joined from industry, I reflected inwardly that perhaps my NHS career was destined to be a very brief one!

In spite of that reaction many years ago – and what turned out to be a long and continuing association with the NHS – my view remains the same. Hence this chapter, which sets out some thoughts about the sources of stress that professional carers experience and some ways in which such stresses can be eased.

STRESS AT WORK

One way that you can begin to look after yourself more is by defining how you may be getting stressed and the cause of the stress. If you are unclear what might be doing you damage, you have no chance of taking action to alleviate it. If, on the other hand, you are clearer about the causes of distress then you can look to see what can be changed in order to reduce the pressures you are experiencing.

It is not that stress is in itself unhelpful or unhealthy. It is more a matter of the degree of stress experienced. Too little and too much stress are what cause the problems. Each of us has different levels of tolerance for stress which makes it hard to assess and difficult to predict when the degree of stress experienced will prove too great to bear.

The range from A to B in Figure 11.1 will vary from person to person but the general idea, that we each have limits between which we can operate optimally and outside of which we perform less well, is valid.

Whilst it may not always be possible to predict what will trigger an unhelpful stressed reaction, it is possible to identify the sources of stress. Figure 11.2 suggests four major sources of stress:

- *Stress Type 1*: Specific recent events at work – ward reorganization, changes of staff, different medical staff, death of a patient, abuse and harassment at work, etc.

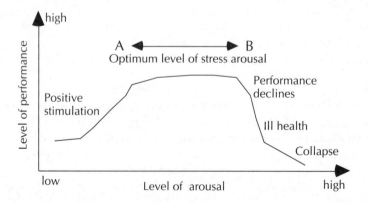

Figure 11.1 Optimum levels of stress arousal

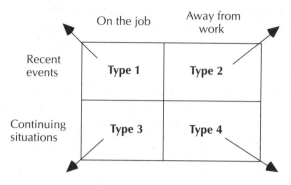

Figure 11.2 Four sources of stress

- *Stress Type 2*: Specific recent events, but outside work. These could be changes to one's pattern of social activity, marriage problems, the death of a close friend or family member, a car accident, substance abuse, a gambling loss, etc.
- *Stress Type 3*: These are different in that they arise from continuing work situations. It may be a question of not getting on with the boss who may also be difficult discuss matters with; a consultant who is difficult to work with; the realization of having made a wrong career move; work overload; victimization or bullying; lack of support from above (or below), etc.
- *Stress Type 4*: These too are continuing situations, but centred away from work. They may include marital problems; children and their needs; prolonged separation from a loved one; poor health (one's own or another), etc.

Whilst it may be very difficult to specify precisely the detailed causes for feeling stressed, it is often possible to identify what type of concern is leading to stress, and if that condition is likely to continue or if it is a 'one off'.

Figure 11. 2 summarizes the stress categories and it can be help you to decide where your own – or another's – stresses stem from.

Having identified the category of stress, you can decide whether you want to do anything about those sources of stress. You will need to decide on the criteria for choosing between those that you can work on and those that you cannot, so that you can then put to one side those which you feel you cannot address at the moment.

Once you have identified what is causing undue stress it is important to be clear what you can and what you cannot change so that you can then concentrate your attention and your efforts on those matters *you* are in a position to influence. Figure 11.2 is a bit like a radar screen that can help you to locate the type of stress that is causing you concern, you then can think about how it can be reduced.

One format for doing this is to identify stresses which:

- you can influence
- you are not in a position to address
- when you reflect on them, really do not matter so much even though they may irritate you!

In thinking about what you can do in response to the stressors you want to work on, use the headings in Figure 11.3 to summarize your assessment of your situation.

| Stressor identified | What type is it? (1, 2, 3 or 4) | Can I influence it? | | How important is it to me? |
		Yes? (then how?)	No? (then what now?)	

Figure 11.3 Summarizing the position

It is important to concentrate your energy on those areas which you can influence to the advantage of yourself and others. If there really is no way you can influence one of the stressful situations you experience, you may just have to try to stop worrying about it and accept it for the time being. You then look for opportunities to move away from those situations when viable.

If, however, the areas that cause you most stress are those that you can do least about, you may need to rethink fundamentally where you are in your job and what you are trying to do, and consider whether any major job changes – or any other changes, for that matter – might be best for you in the longer term.

Remember Swamp Theory

The notion of Swamp Theory is a way of making the very straightforward point that, when action is being planned, the more people who are involved, and the longer the time frame for that action, the less influence you will be able to exert to ensure that the action you seek is taken. If action depends on others, and there is likely to be some delay, do not be surprised if little happens. The morale is that for any change you want to happen, try to see that it is done sooner rather than later, and that as few people as are appropriate are involved.

This way of thinking is very relevant to reducing and/or coming to terms with stress at work. Try to focus on those reducing stressors which *you* have a realistic chance of easing and avoid trying to change those stressors that you can only influence remotely. Figure 11.4 shows what I mean.

Remember that if there are stressors which are causing you considerable grief, but which you cannot directly influence, then keep your focus on what you can influence, and do what you can to reduce your exposure to those stresses that you cannot directly influence.

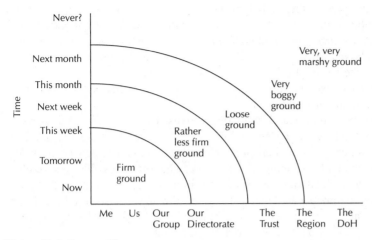

Figure 11.4 Swamp Theory

Sharing with others

The old adage that 'a problem shared is a problem halved' is debatable though it is a good idea to talk about one's concerns, when ethical and viable, with those you trust. The pressures, pace and uncertainty of some jobs – especially in nursing – can lead you to believe that you are very much on your own and induce a feeling of great loneliness. There will be situations where that is the case – both physically and emotionally – but usually there are people to whom you can turn and who should, in line with their caring responsibilities, be prepared and equipped to help and support you in your work.

A number of such people may come to mind as you read this paragraph. It might help to make a note of those you feel can most help you in particular aspects of your work, and to reflect on how often you actually use them in this way. In turn you may realize that you provide support and care for some of your colleagues as well.

Some people are good at particular types of concerns whereas others answer different needs that you may have from time to time. One way of surviving in a stressful job is to develop your own support network where you are able to draw appropriately on the guidance, experience and strength of colleagues for different types of issues. In turn you may well be part of the support network for other colleagues. Being trusted, and trusting others, is an important part of living; this applies at work just as it does elsewhere and is a great source of self-affirmation, self-regard and strength.

Who can help/support me?

One of the most interesting fields of development in management practice in recent years is peer review. The basic idea of this is that those with whom we work are uniquely placed to help us become more effective in our jobs and in thinking about our future. Joint reflection with them on current actions, past practice and future developments can be very constructive and informative over and above the responsibilities the line manager for the continuing development of their staff. Peer review offers a chance to receive and offer feedback about personal and group performance, and about the work environment and procedures.

The use of 'support and challenge groups' has also increased in recent years. This involves an agreed number of colleagues who meet regularly to help each other continue their professional development. Their purpose is to create a climate of challenge with support; where it is possible to give clear, fair and concise feedback underpinned – importantly – with mutual support. In this way members can become aware of how they are seen to be doing by colleagues and – if they believe the feedback to be valid – feel able to make some changes in what they do and how they do it.

The key to the effectiveness of such groups lies in:

- each member being genuinely willing to give and receive constructive feedback
- the discussions of the group remaining confidential to that group
- stable group membership that will allow a shared and mutually acceptable pattern of group working to develop and be sustained (see Chapter 7)
- regular scheduled meetings of the group (usually monthly).

The climate of the group is intended to be stimulating, constructive and developmental. In Figure 11.5 four different group climates are shown by combining the dimensions of 'support' and 'challenge'. If you combine a climate of high support and high challenge you are likely to create a high risk, competitive work environment. Conversely if you have a low challenge and a low support culture this is likely to result in a slow paced, apathetic and disinterested work group.

A combination of high support and low challenge gives a cosy comfy pattern that could generate an inward looking and collusive work climate. However it is with the combination of high support and high challenge that a

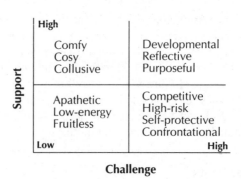

Figure 11.5 Four support and challenge group climates

more productive and developmental work climate is generated and one that will be stimulating and supportive in its work.

A mutually beneficial small group climate is more likely to be generated where members feel able to listen and learn, contribute and challenge without undue fear and trepidation. This can be achieved through creating and sustaining a high challenge and high support work group culture. The support group (or network) created is often an influential one that can cross functional barriers and continue long into the future.

Another increasingly familiar support arrangement is through setting up an internal system of mentors. The key feature here is again the confidential nature of the relationship between the mentor and their mentee. The whole purpose being to enable the mentee to reflect on their current practice and to learn from their mentor's wider experience.

In the last decade there has been more use of psychometric tests and questionnaires for assessment, recruitment and personal development purposes. Sometimes these are part of an assessment centre; at other times they are used on an individual basis, often as part another development called '360° feedback' which involves collecting information about an individual – for appraisal and development purposes – from their senior, junior and peer colleagues. Together with a self-assessment, the material is integrated by a suitably trained professional who then reviews the overall outcomes with the respondent.

Such initiatives can be very helpful in clarifying one's own preferences for doing things and for discussing personal traits and patterns of behaviour. This self knowledge can help to clarify why a person may prefer to do certain types of work more than others and explain why some aspects of a person's work may be generating undue levels of stress and strain.

Ambiguity and uncertainty

Considerable stress is caused by the unknown. When a situation is uncertain or unknown, a heightened level of discomfort is likely to be experienced. This is especially so for patients and their relatives for whom entry into a hospital is probably a rare and unwelcome event, where perhaps in the past their visits have only been to see sick or dying friends and relatives. Where they may find themselves feeling extremely vulnerable and at risk because of their unfamiliarity with being in hospital.

Figure 11.6 illustrates how the level of experienced stress builds up, when a person's understanding of what is going on is lost, and – if this is combined with unexpected and previously unexperienced events – how considerable distress will be generated.

Strategies for handling such situations and reducing the sense of experienced stress include:

- relating the unexpected events occurring now to similar past experiences
- resisting the urge to panic and think instead about what is happening – as fully as possible – and speculating why this may be happening
- clarifying the source(s) of the uncertainty being experienced.

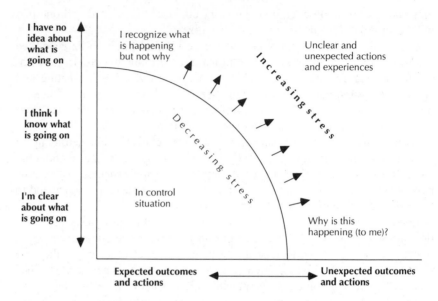

Figure 11.6 The stress of ambiguity and uncertainty

These are ways of relating what is going on now to past experiences that you do know about. Without in any way trying to pretend that the current situation is the same as a past experience, you can draw on what you do know about to reduce the uncertainty you may currently be experiencing.

Two main sources of stress are:

- ourselves and the pressures we can put on ourselves under
- the settings at home and at work in which we find ourselves with other people.

Combining these two dimensions gives a *professional–institutional* source and a *personal–interpersonal* source. Figure 11.7 highlights the four different categories of stress. These four categories are types of stress generated through the interplay of the following dimensions:

- *alpha category*: stress generated by interpersonal/professional interactions
- *beta category*: stress generated by interpersonal/institutional interactions
- *theta category*: stress generated by institutional/personal interactions
- *gamma category*: stress generated by professional/personal interactions.

Whilst this is a simple way of looking at sources of stress in organizational settings, it is quite helpful in clarifying what appear to be the main generating interactions. In turn this will help focus attention on what may need to be changed to reduce the stress-provoking reactions. Figure 11.7 directs the stressed individual where to look to identify the likely causes of tension. For example, with alpha category stress the distress would appear to be caused because of some tension between the professional demands of the job and the interactions which the stressed individual is having with professional colleagues.

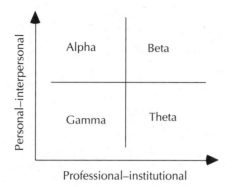

Figure 11.7 Four main sources of stress

With gamma stress the issues are very different: here the source of tension and anxiety revolves around the stressed person and the chosen profession. In this case the focus of attention would be the individual in question, to see what it that is causing distress within that person and what it means for that person to be a nurse-professional, see (Figure 11.8).

Figure 11.8 Sources of stress in organizations

More specifically Figure 11.9 itemizes some of the most frequently occurring reasons for stress at work.

MANAGING STRESS INTELLECTUALLY, EMOTIONALLY AND PHYSICALLY

When we become unduly stressed, it often seems as if there is a build-up of energy inside us. We often do not feel able to discharge this energy because the situation does not allow it, or because we do not know how to.

Effective management of stressful situations involves finding ways in which it is possible to discharge this energy, which can be either a positive or a negative force. Whilst it would be convenient to discharge our feelings immediately, this may not always be possible or appropriate, particularly with regard to other people (patients, for example) who may be involved.

Figure 11.9 Some causes of occupational stress

Tension release is very important as blocked up feelings or energies can be destructive. If you look around you at work, you may see people thumping the desk, banging the dinner trolley, smashing down the lid of the drug trolley. These can be ways in which staff have become accustomed to releasing pent-up energy without too much damage to anyone, but it would probably be more constructive in the long run to enable them to 'talk out' what they are feeling, try to pinpoint the cause and then decide whether anything can be done about it.

Stress needs to be considered and handled on three levels. At each level there are steps you can take to reduce the threat of stress:

- *on the intellectual level*:
  - Formulate realistic goals.
  - Sort out what you want to be and do.
  - Replace old ways of thinking with new ones that you want for yourself.
  - Avoid unnecessary or too frequent changes.
  - Be as honest as you can about what is going on, why it is going on and your part in it.

- *on the emotional level*:
  - Allow yourself to admit to your feelings – do not be ashamed of them.
  - Allow yourself to feel situations more fully.
  - Allow yourself to say what you want more often.
  - Be aware of your social and emotional contacts and your need for them..

- *on the physical level*:
  - Take care of your body.
  - Improve your breathing.
  - Make sure you get enough exercise.
  - Make sure your diet is adequate and balanced.
  - Consider relaxation and meditation techniques.

In order to cope with all the disturbances, influences and pressures, nurses need to be as clear and as certain as possible about what they are doing, how they are doing it and why. They also need to have confidence in themselves, but not the sort of over-confidence that refuses any review of their activities.

Organizations can de-power individuals and attempt to neutralize them in sharp contrast to the rhetoric often expressed about employees being an organization's chief asset! Organizations can seem at times determined to push out the uniqueness and individuality of the person and draw in and reward those who are more prepared to conform to the preferred norms. In spite of what may be said, it is more likely that the acquiescent employee will be favoured over the more challenging one.

A consequence of this is that people in organizations can become less certain of their own abilities, less confident in sticking out for what they think is right, and perhaps less able to handle new and difficult situations appropriately when they occur. These are vitally important characteristics for nurses to retain – the confidence to activate their professional training during an emergency, or where their experience tells them that something is going wrong and a different course of action should be considered.

Whilst in any organization there are systems, procedures and patterns of working which need to be followed, personal experience and judgement remain crucially important in judging what to do in the particular circumstances being addressed.

Some of the stressors you may have noted earlier may be generated because you feel you are being forced to function in ways that are unlike you in certain respects. If you keep tensions to yourself, and if you have no support group to turn to, then your stress level is likely to intensify, or you will find some other way of coping rather than addressing the cause of your concerns.

Managers in particular, and senior professionals too, often find it difficult to discuss difficulties and to express clearly the help they may need. People at work generally feel uneasy if asked to talk about the things they are good at, or to describe some of their achievements. Being able to value one's accomplishments and take credit for one's achievements is an important factor in maintaining personal well-being and is likely to reduce a person's sense of stress under pressure.

How people think about themselves, about their abilities and their contributions at work and at home is very important. Thinking in a realistic and positive way leads to greater self-belief, and is likely to increase a person's capacity for handling the stresses and strains of the job.

COUNSELLING IN THE WORKPLACE

One major development in the UK during the 1990s has been the growth of workplace counselling. Whilst some internal NHS counselling services have been set up, often workplace counselling is made available through an external Employee Assistance Programme (EAP). These are organizations which provide an on-call support service paid for by the employing NHS authority.

EAPs provide a wide range of services to staff who may be concerned about their personal addictions, financial and legal problems, familial difficulties, work stress, harassment, workplace bullying and intimidation, ethnic victimization, and their general mental well-being. Support can be on a face-to-face basis with a trained counsellor or – and this is the most common practice – through a 'help line' staffed by experienced and trained counsellors. Face-to-face support is made available where it is felt to be needed.

With an in-house service there will be a confidential booking service and there will be the opportunity for confidential meetings with the staff counsellor. The pressure on organizations to become more efficient, do more with fewer resources, and to work within an increasingly competitive environment have all put more strain on staff at all levels. Pressures on those in managerial positions to deliver better service levels have also contributed to workplace strain and pressure. Managers expected to perform to ever more exacting limits are under enormous pressure and may displace some of their anxiety onto their staff.

What is counselling?

This section refers to some of the different schools of counselling, since it is likely that you will be asked by staff about these at some point. It is important, therefore, that you have some idea about what is available or where they can find out a little more about what counselling is about.

It is possible that at some stage you will find yourself in a 'counselling' situation with a colleague. This could be either as the person listening or the person who wants to talk and be listened to. Remember that if a colleague wants to talk to you about their situation, your role is *not* that of a professional counsellor, but rather it is the role of a colleague listening with care – and seeking to offer support through your *counselling skills* – and not by functioning as a therapeutic counsellor. If the colleague wants some therapeutic counselling, referral to a professionally recognized counsellor is the way forward.

Counselling itself can be difficult to define with precision because of the wide range of approaches followed. The definition proposed by the Standing Conference for the Advancement of Counselling (Watts, 1977) is very useful:

> Counselling – a process through which one person helps another by purposeful conversation in an understanding atmosphere. It seeks to establish a helping relationship in which the one counselled can express his thoughts and feelings in such a way as to clarify his own situation, come to terms with some new experience, see his difficulty more objectively and so face his problem with less anxiety and tension. Its basic purpose is to assist the individual to make his own decision from among the choices available to him.

Working as a carer will often evoke deep tensions, raise questions about life's issues, and stimulate a great deal of self-reflection. One of the coping responses to this is to trivialize experienced trauma, to take things in one's stride as if they don't matter, and to generally get on with the work to be done without thinking too deeply about one's experiences at work. But there will be times when you – or a colleague – just find you need to talk about what it means to be a carer, or where an episode at work somehow triggers issues for you that you need to talk through with someone.

As a start you may want someone to listen, you may want them to use their 'counselling skills' and be there to listen with care to what is on your mind. Or it may be that you – or a colleague – really wants to discuss deeply held issues and concerns of a very personal nature. In this case a referral to a counsellor is the appropriate action to be taken.

For example, perhaps a colleague is talking to you about an upsetting and traumatic incident on the ward and you begin to feel that you are becoming too drawn in to their deeper issues and concerns, then a referral is the course of action to consider. This would need to be raised with them in a sensitive and caring way, reaffirming to them that your role is as a colleague and that your counselling skills are not the same as those of a professionally trained counsellor. Managing such situations can be very difficult but even more difficulties will follow if you find yourself inappropriately drawn into the role of untrained counsellor and psychotherapist.

There is a range of referral possibilities: to an EAP if there is one is in place; to the occupational health service; to a counsellor in private practice; to the local community psychiatric service. The British Psychological Society (BPS), the British Association for Counselling (BAC), and the UK Council for Psychotherapy (UKCP) each have registers of professionally qualified practitioners who are bound by codes of ethics and conduct and who have available names and addresses of qualified people.

Figure 11.10 notes some of the better known 'schools' of counselling. More detailed advice can be obtained from the BPS, the BAC and the UKCP.

Each of these different approaches – and there are many more I have not noted – have insights and valuable contributions to make. Some counsellors draw insights from several of the main schools of psychotherapy and follow their own integrative approach. There are some excellent introductory texts on counselling and psychotherapy which offer descriptive accounts of the main schools of practice.

Everyone can benefit from the chance to talk things through – work issues and personal issues – at some stage in their career and doing so need not

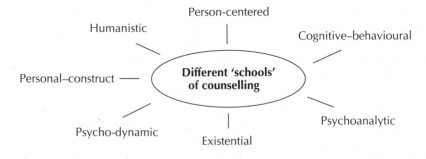

Figure 11.10 Schools of counselling

mean that that person is troubled. It may simply mean that they want an opportunity to explore and consider some issues of importance to them.

Some people view those who have counselling as weak and 'wimpish'. In fact, the contrary can be true: it takes great resolution and self-understanding to decide that it would be valuable to talk through issues with another person, and it takes even more resolution to go ahead with it. It can be the sign of a strong and able nurse, and of a person who is capable of recognizing that there are issues which need to be explored and addressed.

What sort of issue are raised?

But what sorts of issue are raised in the counselling room? Figure 11.11 identifies some issues that can arise.

Figure 11.11 Types of issue raised in therapy

ORGANIZATION–INDIVIDUAL TENSIONS

Considerable stress can be generated by the nature of the work we do and the constraints, rather than the opportunities, within the organization. It is not only the type of work but the pressure of the work that can cause problems. At times the work can be too complex, or the level of training received may be inadequate; but monotony too can give rise to extreme levels of stress.

How the individual is *treated* in the organization generates yet another set of issues and can lead them to question their self-worth and question whether they are being given adequate personal recognition. For example, where a person has a contribution to make but where they are unable to have their say or where they are not being acknowledged as a competent manager. These situations can be experienced as so frustrating and unnerving that, if prolonged or too frequent, severe internal distress can result.

TYPE A AND TYPE B

Research into the causes of heart disease has highlighted the possibility that particular types of behaviour may be significant contributory factors in a person's coronary heart disease. Rosenman and Friedman (1961, 1964) suggest that some patterns of behaviours and lifestyles render a person more prone to CHD than others.

They found that particular patterns of behaviour led some individuals – they termed them Type A - to be almost three times more likely to suffer from coronary heart disease than others whom they termed Type B.

The characteristics of Type A behaviour are:

- hyperactivity
- sense of continuing insecurity (irrespective of their achievements)
- always in a rush
- trying to do several things at the same time
- having a sense of a constant struggle
- extreme competitiveness
- aggressiveness
- haste
- impatience
- high achievement orientation.

The characteristics of Type B behaviour are:

- taking on modest and reasonably demanding commitments
- allowing 'the time it takes'
- maintaining a sense of proportion
- not putting themselves under undue pressure
- tending to be less worried about 'lost' time.

The descriptions above are at the extreme but a tendency towards either of the Type A or B characteristics can be used as a prompt to consider ways of modifying behaviour in order to reduce any of the possible risks identified by Rosenman and Friedman. Clearly there are more factors that need to be taken into account such as diet, exercise, family history, etc. but nevertheless their Type A and Type B findings have been taken up with interest in the literature on life patterns and stress management.

BULLYING AND INTIMIDATION AT WORK

Combating racial and sexual harassment has been the subject of debate and legislation for many years, but bullying at work has only emerged from the shadows of organizational life in the past few years. It is increasingly being recognized as a major problem and one which profoundly damages people's lives, and the standing and performance of the organization. Bullying and intimidation at work are difficult to tackle because of the subtlety of the measures used and the covert way in which these pressures are applied.

If bullying is talked about, the conversation often dies: people tend to clam up – try it and see. At such times one's thoughts may go back to earlier times – schooldays maybe, in the playground, within the family, in the street perhaps – places where bullying took place. The impact and trauma of bullying is long-lasting and can be deeply wounding to each of us.

Sadly such behaviour still goes on in the workplace. So what can be done about it? How can bullied and intimidated individuals be stopped from thinking that they are to blame, that it is deserved, that nothing can be done about it, or that they must be going mad?

There are major difficulties in trying to reduce workplace bullying because:

- it generally takes place without witnesses so it can be hard to prove
- it can be hard to draw the line between appropriate assertive workplace behaviour and aggressive bullying
- there are peer group pressures on the bullied to keep quiet about it
- there can be strong group processes to protect the perpetrators even though their behaviour may not be welcomed
- the organization at large will prefer to play down the incidence of bullying and may try to discredit 'whistle-blowers'.

Enduring your share of being bullied, or of being harassed in some manner, can be seen as a 'rite of passage' and, having got through it, is then seen as something which others quite naturally need to endure as well if they are to be fully 'accepted' at work. The effect of this however is to create a web of complicity and a pseudo-rationalization for bullying and intimidation at work which makes it even harder for the bullied to resist, be listened to and tell others what is going on.

The sensitive nature of the topic, the relatively secret nature of the offence itself, and the high personal risk involved by a person making such a charge mean that few cases are reported. This is clearly not a satisfactory state of affairs from any perspective, so what can be done to counter bullying at work? As with all disputes proof and evidence of bullying is needed in order to proceed with a case. Without such evidence and documented information it will be difficult to sustain any case.

If you, or a colleague, needs to take on a case of alleged bullying there are a number of stages which can be followed:

1. Collect the relevant information and substantiate it with statements from witnesses. Be as specific and detailed as you can be. Look at it from an uninvolved observer's perspective and ask youself if you have all the information you need to go to the next stage.
2. Confront the perpetrator-bully. This can be fraught with difficulties but, when supported by evidence, this is a direct and confrontive strategy that may make it very clear that you will no longer tolerate bullying/being bullied. Be prepared for counter charges or denial. Make sure you have all the information very carefully documented and supported.
3. Collate your experience with that of others. Find out if the bullying you have had reported to you (or perhaps you have experienced) is an isolated incident or if it is more widespread. If so, collect that evidence.

4. After working through these stages organize your data and highlight the next steps to be taken. Figure 11.12 suggests a format which can be used to accomplish this.

Where you take your case		1 Test your perceptions	2 Collect evidence	3 Secure witnesses	4 Substantiate evidence	5 Secure support	6 Assert your position
	Internal						
	External						

Figure 11.12 Data grid for Case X: bullying of ...

In Figure 11.12 the vertical axis suggests two possible courses of action and two sets of data that you need to consider. Begin first with the 'Internal' dimension and build up your facts for columns 1, 2, 3 and 4. Next look outside – outside the department or hospital (or both) – and look to see what is going on elsewhere. This may confirm that what is happening internally is not acceptable or it may show that similar things are happening elsewhere too. Remember though that you are building up your information about a particular case at work. Focus again on the first four columns.

If you are convinced of your case and can substantiate it, you will need to secure support (column 5) internally from other colleagues; in presenting a case of workplace bullying you do not want to be there on your own. Such support can come from colleagues who also feel bullied or intimidated and/or from other influential people.

Having secured support from others you are now in a position to formally, and with confidence, assert (column 6) your right to be treated appropriately and fairly at work.

The critical actions are to:

1. collect evidence of what is going on
2. build up information which can be confirmed by others
3. ask for advice, support and guidance from your professional body – so long as it is confidential at this stage.

If there is a confidential staff support or an occupational health service they could also be involved at some stage.

There are many reasons why an individual attempts to bully others and why one person is able to resist being bullied whereas another is not. The bully–bullied relationship is a complicated one as illustrated by Figure 11.13. The opportunity for bullying has to exist and a work context that will enable this to happen also has to exist. Then if a person is predisposed – or

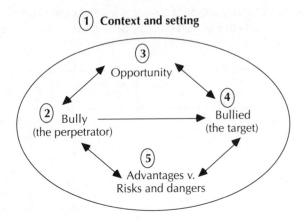

Figure 11.13 Preconditions for bullying

encouraged – to take on the role of bully they need to want to grasp that opportunity and target a person to be bullied.

Without all of these components in place the bully–bullied relationship cannot be sustained. It follows therefore that the removal of any one of these components will stop the bullying and the bullying culture. A strategy therefore for reducing bullying at work – ideally stopping it altogether – is to analyse the current situation in the light of these components and work to remove one or more of them.

How a person is perceived by others may be one of a number of factors which increase or decrease the chance of being bullied. A person's non-verbal behaviour is also likely to encourage or discourage bullying and intimidation. Two features relevant here are a person's perceived passivity, and the extent to which they are seen to direct and push for their own objectives or allow themselves to be directed by others.

These two dimensions are shown in Figure 11.14 which – when combined – suggest four different styles of behaving – W, X, Y, Z.

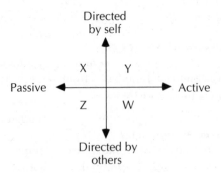

Figure 11.14 Four styles of working

I would describe these four styles as follows:

- *Style X*, directed by Self/Passive, as quiet, tolerant, will hold ground if pushed,
- *Style Y*, directed by Self/Active, as directive, independent, assertive, pushy
- *Style W*, directed by Others/Active, as a joiner, enthusiastic follower, a doer
- *Style Z*, directed by Others/Passive, as passive acquiescent follower, can be led by others.

These are not intended to be very precise or comprehensive descriptions but they illustrate how very differently a person can be viewed by combining these dimensions. Such differences may increase or reduce the likelihood of a person being bullied at work. For example, a person who is seen to be relatively self-directed and active would probably be a less likely target than a person who is seen as more retiring, passive and always prepared go along with the suggestions and ideas of others.

How you feel about yourself

Another major variable in a person's susceptibility to bullying is how they feel about themselves. Eric Berne (1964) developed an approach to understanding human behaviour which he termed 'Transactional Analysis'. One of the valuable outcomes from his work has been the setting out of four so-called 'life positions' (see Harris, 1970) which are as follows:

- *I am not OK–You are OK*: where the individual tends to accept a psychologically inferior position in relation to others. There is a defeatist attitude and a lack of confidence, and a belief that I cannot match others.
- *I am not OK–You are not OK*: where the individual believes that he is fairly worthless – but so is everyone else. Suspicious and disappointed in myself and others, I may become anxious about what I, or others, might do that would be harmful or threatening. There is a feeling of alienation from others and from the environment, with little sense of purpose in trying to do anything about this.
- *I am OK–You are not OK*: this suggests that others cannot be relied on; they are worthless. Fault will always reside in someone else and satisfaction needs to be found in myself rather than others.
- *I am OK–You are OK*: here I see myself as being competent and all right. Prepared and confident in my own ability and that of others and quite happy to take in data from others, whilst not being totally dependent upon what others say or suggest.

Relating these positions to winning and losing gives the pattern shown in Figure 11.15.

To be in a position to assert your views and to hold your ground under challenge you need to:

- feel good enough about yourself

- be able to present your case influentially
- relate positively to others.

Berne's and Harris' ideas are very helpful in enabling a person to reconfirm their value and belief in themself through adopting the I'm OK–You're OK life position.

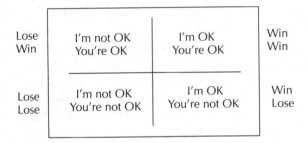

Figure 11.15 Winning and losing positions

THE GIVING AND RECEIVING OF PERSONAL FEEDBACK

It can be very difficult to assess your performance at work accurately on your own. Feedback from colleagues is essential in developing your professional practice, helping you to acknowledge issues you need to tackle, and generally to help you keep track of how you are getting on.

The process of giving and receiving feedback is most important because of its impact in reinforcing or redirecting effort. It is also a difficult task to perform because of the personal sensitivities which are inevitably involved.

Feedback given in an insensitive manner may trigger a defensive response leading to the recipient dismissing the valuable information being given. This is dangerous because we all need to know how well we are doing. Feedback has to be given in ways which will help the recipient to accept and act on what is being presented to him.

Feedback that is too kind, gratuitous, misses the point or is plainly inaccurate is no help either. Both the giver of feedback and the recipient are required to be honest and straightforward, but to be so in ways which the recipient can take-in and acknowledge.

Some useful hints for achieving this are:

- *It should be descriptive rather than evaluative.* Avoiding the use of evaluative comments reduces the danger of the recipient reacting defensively.
- *It should be specific rather than general.* There is very little that we can do if recipients are simply told that they are 'unhelpful'. It is much more useful to be told that, 'When I asked for information just now in the meeting, you had some vital material to give me, but I had to pull it out of you.' They can then be clearer about what is meant and can relate it to the behaviour exhibited.

- *It should take into account the needs of both the receiver and the giver*. Feedback can be destructive when it serves the giver's needs, but fails to consider how it can help the receiver.
- *It should be actionable*. Feedback should only draw attention to something on which recipients can take action. It is no good telling someone, 'You're too small', as there's not much they can do about it. Being constantly reminded of a shortcoming over which the individual has no control is likely to induce a sense of frustration.
- *It is more useful when asked for than when imposed*. If staff ask you to give them some information about how they are doing, then they are far more likely to use that information than if you come and give it to them without being asked.
- *Timing is important*. In general terms, feedback can be most useful if given as soon as possible after the given behaviour has occurred, depending of course on how the receiver is and whether it is logistically possible. Sometimes immediate feedback on certain situations can become part of the norms you establish for the group, ward team, etc.
- *It needs to be checked*. The giver needs to check that the receiver has understood, perhaps by asking him or her to rephrase it.
- *Validated by others*. If feedback is being given in a situation where more than the receiver and the giver are present, the opportunity to check things out with the wider group can be valuable. Not only can the feedback itself be checked, but the original actions which result in that feedback being given can also be tested out. This can pick up biases or misperceptions on the part of the feedback giver.

PULLING ALL THESE IDEAS TOGETHER

The work of a nurse is inherently anxiety-provoking; caring for those in physical and psychological distress – patients, relatives and colleagues – is no easy matter. Sickness and death are never very far away, and along with them fundamental questions about fairness and about life and death. Feelings of fear, guilt, joy, humility and shame – to mention only a few – are always near the surface, if not with you, then with someone near you, or with a relative, or a patient. In the face of these pressures and psychological strains you can do one of two things:

- begin to acknowledge and then work with the emotionality of the nursing role
- try to deflect or dismiss the emotionality of it all (perhaps as a way of coping with it) and pretend its not there or that it does not matter.

The second option could be done, for example – but only to a limited degree – by emphasizing the routines, the procedures, the tasks, etc. that need attention, in a way slowly edging the patient a little out of the central focus. Another strategy for handling the emotional dimensions can be through confidently asserting that these dynamics are being handled and that 'it is all part of a day's work' – a somewhat stoic and perhaps heroic response which may or may not be accurate, but at least it can give an impression of coping.

Perhaps the bigger challenge is to take on board the first option. To acknowledge and then to work with all the issues that are aroused as a carer. To do this means more awareness of yourself, and of your own issues, *and* looking after yourself in the process. It means having support networks and it means giving support to others too when they need it. Importantly it will help carers to undertake their nursing, caring responsibility – working with patients as people rather than as recipients of clinical conditions.

What can you do?

As a means of briefly summarizing the wide range of issues covered in this chapter, listed below are a number of steps you can take towards accepting, diagnosing and coping with stress in your job (and elsewhere). You can probably add others to this list from your reading of the chapter.

1. Be clear about the purposes of your job and your actions.
2. Value yourself more, and others for what they can do.
3. Acknowledge the difficulties inherent in your job.
4. Use conflict constructively.
5. Be prepared to both give and receive feedback and advice from others.
6. Try to develop situations where everybody can 'win' rather, than where there has to be a loser.
7. Think about which issues you can handle, and which issues you cannot. Then concentrate on what you can do.
8. Think about yourself as the same person at work and in your outside activities, rather than separating them unrealistically.
9. Try to develop a work and life strategy against which you can view what is going on.
10. Develop and/or expand a support network.

REFERENCES AND FURTHER READING

Adams, A. (1992) *Bullying at Work*, Virago, London.
Bayne, R. *et al.* (1994) *The Counsellor's Handbook*, Chapman & Hall, London.
Berne, E. (1964) *Games People Play*, Penguin, Harmondsworth.
Breakwell, G. (1997) *Coping with Aggressive Behaviour*, British Psychological Society, Leicester.
Carroll, M. (1996) *Workplace Counselling*, Sage, London.
Carroll, M. and Walton, M. (1997) *Handbook of Workplace Counselling*, Sage, London.
Clutterbuck, D. (1985) *Everyone Needs a Mentor*, Institute of Personnel and Development, London.
de Board, R. (1986) *Counselling Skills*, Gower, Aldershot.

Dexter, G. and Wash, M. (1995) *Psychiatric Nursing Skills*, Chapman & Hall, London

Harris, T. (1970) *I'm OK, You're OK*, Pan Books, London.

Hodgkinson, L. (1992) *Counselling*, Simon & Schuster, London.

Honey, P. (1992) *Problem People. ...*, IPM, Wimbledon.

Jerome, P. (1994) *Coaching Through Effective Feedback*, Kogan Page, London.

Kidman, A. (1986) *Tactics for Changing Your Life*, Kogan Page, London.

Lake, T. and Acheson, F. (1988) *Room to Listen, Room to Talk*, Bedford Square Press, London.

Lang, G. *et al.* (1990) *Personal Conversations*, Routledge, London.

MacLennan, N. (1995) *Coaching and Mentoring*, Gower, Aldershot.

Madders, J. (1988) *Stress and Relaxation*, Macdonald Optima, London.

Marshall, P. (1994) *Now I Know Why Tigers Eat Their Young*, British Psychological Society, Leicester.

Menzies, I. (1970) *The Functioning of Social Systems as a Defence Against Anxiety*, Tavistock, London.

O'Leary, J. *et al.* (1986) *Winning Strategies for Nursing Managers*, Lippincott, Philadelphia.

Parkinson, F. (1993) *Post-Trauma Stress*, Sheldon Press, London.

Proto, L. (1988) *Take Charge of Your Life*, Thorsons, Wellingborough.

Proto, L. (1989) *Who's Pulling Your Strings?* Thorsons, Wellingborough.

Reddy, M. (1987) *The Manager's Guide to Counselling at Work*, British Psychological Society, Leicester.

Rosenman, R. and Friedman, M. (1961) Association of specific behaviour pattern in women with blood and cardiovascular findings, *Circulation*, **24**, 1173–84.

Rosenman, R., Friedman, M. and Strauss, R. (1964) A predictive study of coronary heart disease, *Journal of the American Medical Association*, **189**, 15–22.

Rutter, P. (1990) *Sex in the Forbidden Zone*, HarperCollins, London.

Sauter, S. and Murphy, L. (1996) *Organizational Risk Factors for Job Stress*, American Psychological Association, Washington.

Spielberger, C. (1979) *Understanding Stress and Anxiety*, Harper & Row, London.

Walton, M. (1995) *Management On and Off the Ward*, Blackwell, Oxford.

Watts, A. (1977) *Counselling at Work*, Bedford Square Press, London.

Worden, J. (1991) *Grief Counselling and Grief Therapy*, Routledge, London.

Wykes, T. (1994) *Violence and Health Care Professionals*, Chapman & Hall, London.

Changing States

It is difficult to know precisely how the 1990s will be described in future years, but it is very likely that they will be remembered for change, for increasing pressure at work, for the threat of loss of one's job, and heightened personal insecurity in work. The information explosion, data overload, the emphasis on performance management, and the introduction of management competencies are some of the changes which are dramatically changing the face of work as we move into the next millenium.

The practical impact of the integrated global-economy-in-action, where it is less expensive to base some operations in far away countries, and where e-mail and Internet-access make communications easy and cheap, is becoming increasingly commonplace. One direct implication for carers is the possibility of remote diagnosis of a patient's condition and camera-guided remedial care, where, under guidance and camera-linked supervision treatment can be given by a carer in one location directed by a specialist from another location. Care guidelines, patient's notes, high-tech patient monitoring information can all be communicated live through the air waves accompanied by visual pictures via the Internet .

The effect of all this for carers is huge. These developments will, for a minority of staff, transform their work worlds. For the greater majority such developments will be known about but they do not directly affect them in their day-to-day work. For the profession as a whole though such changes represent a major psychological change to the nature of the patient–nurse relationship.

Part Four considers the role of the professional carer in times of change and in a period of continuing emphasis on change. There appears to be little that is exempt from the possibility of change. Whilst this has always been so, it is perhaps the pace and pressure for change in the mid and late 1990s that has elevated 'change' to a position of prominence. A consequence of this has been an increased sense of personal insecurity in work and an experienced sense of pressure – whether real or imagined – to 'perform' in order to remain in employment.

The Institute of Management's Survey of Management Morale, 'Are managers under stress?' (Charlesworth, 1996), concluded that 'symptoms of stress such as tiredness, irritability and disturbed sleep were experienced by over 80 per cent of respondents'. These figures are up on their 1993 survey and indicate very high levels of experienced stress and strain within organizations. The pressure and tension experienced by managers and supervisors is invariably transmitted further down into the organization to peers and colleagues and, in health care, there will be a knock-on effect on patients and their relatives.

Whilst most of us acknowledge that change is inevitable, it is necessary to come to terms with what this means in practice for each of us. What is very clear – yet too frequently glossed over – is that making changes in an organization is a profoundly difficult thing to accomplish successfully. This is partly because:

- change, by definition, makes it very difficult to predict and anticipate precisely what the future will be like
- the very nature of change – which is generally portrayed as a logical and rational decision-making process – discounts the personal insecurity which changes at work generate.

Effecting organizational changes successfully and making them stick is about enabling those affected to adjust, adapt and change. It is this intensely personal impact of organizational change that evokes a sense of personal disruption – and often fear, worry, and anxiety – which so often leads to resistance to the proposed organizational changes.

Part Four views carers as 'change leaders' both for themselves and for those around them, and sets out a number of 'change frameworks' which can be used to facilitate change. The challenge is how to adapt, influence and remain competent as a person and as a professional as time goes by.

Change leadership $\boxed{12}$

It may not always feel like it but nurses have considerable influence on those with whom they work. This is not a function of the job title so much as a feature of the very personal and intimate nature of the work nurses (and certain other carers) do. Psychologically and physically carers are allowed to work in areas forbidden to non-carers other than a patient's intimate circle.

In addition nurses have access to up-to-the-minute information about the condition of their patients from patient notes and from other carers. Nurses are in a privileged position to work with and guide their patients. In effect they are change leaders and guides for their patients.

The implications of this are that nurses are able to exercise considerable 'leadership' locally through working with peers, other professionals and patients. How this leadership potential is acknowledged, defined and exercised will influence the well-being, sense of purpose and accomplishment of nurses, and patients' experience of care. Earlier chapters have referred to the importance of personal self-belief and how our behaviour influences others' attitudes towards us. Consequently how the nurse as care leader presents and guides the patient will affect that patient's view of the quality of the care being received and, possibly, recovery.

This chapter is about the 'change leadership' role and the scope that exists for such a responsibility to be exercised wisely and productively in clinical work and more generally within the organization. Following clinical diagnosis and medical intervention, cures and patient care are delivered through the patterns of relationships and the interactions which take place between the patient, the designated care nurse, the wider care team and the setting.

The patient is at the hub of a network of relationships for the purpose of accurately diagnosing their condition, defining the treatment needed, and for its subsequent careful and ethical delivery.

But much depends on the quality of the care relationships that surround the patient. For example, if the members of the care team are working well together, and within an organizational setting which is experienced as supportive, this will impact positively on the delivery of care and it will be noticed by the patient. Where this is not the case the delivery of direct patient care will be affected by such non-clinical distractions.

The nurse's behaviour exercises a considerable influence on the care of the patient, and on the harmony and dynamics on the ward but there are other wider influences over which the nurse will not have total control as shown in Figure 12.1.

Neverthless the designated nurse means a great deal to patients in:

- providing continuity of patient contact
- providing access to regular updated patient information
- being the key point of referral by the wider care team
- being the access person for relatives *et al.*
- being someone the patient can trust and rely on
- playing a major part in setting the 'tone' of the ward.

The nurse is in a unique 'change leadership' position from which to influence, oversee and manage patient care, and to help facilitate any review of ward and clinic administrative practices. The nurse has the potential to take an overview and work towards changing unproductive, or dysfunctional, work situations using the wide variety of approaches and ideas set out in the earlier chapters.

Increasing pressure of work – and the need to meet work targets and deadlines – can make it difficult to think about 'change' when the priority is just getting the work done. This is where reviewing your workload can highlight options you may be able to take to alter things when you may have thought there was little you could do to change things.

Figure 12.1 Care relationships

DEMANDS AND CHOICES

Under heavy work pressure, or under pressure to do things 'the way we do it here', it is too easy to assume that there is no choice in how the work should be done. This is rarely the case as there is often some element of choice that can be made about the work. Think about your job and differentiate between:

- those parts of the job that *have* to be done in a particular way, or at a particular time, etc. (the *demands*)
- those parts of the job where there *is* some choice about how or when they are done (the *choices*).

This way of looking at work was suggested by Rosemary Stewart (1976, 1982) who looked at a manager's job in terms of its demands, its constraints and the scope for the personal choice that could be taken. This approach to looking at work can be applied to all those who have some flexibility – as with nurses – to manage their work responsibilities.

Any job can be considered as being composed of the following three elements:

- *Demands*: What any job holder must do and cannot avoid doing without attracting penalties
- *Constraints*: The factors which limit what the job holder can do, for example political decisions, legislation, rules and procedures, local guidelines, time, etc.
- *Choices*: The opportunity for choice in how aspects of the job can be organized: how it is done, what is done, when, where, etc.

Health Service managers, in all disciplines, tend to feel that the demands and constraints of their jobs leave relatively little opportunity to exercise choice. But, in spite of the increasing work pressures, there probably is scope, particularly at ward level, for nurse managers to exercise some choice and flexibility in how the work to be done can be scheduled and undertaken. Of course in an emergency you react and do what is needed, but for non emergency situations there will be some measure of choice about some aspect of the work that the nurse can exercise.

One of the factors that enhances a sense of personal well-being and resilience is the capacity to exercise some control and choice in one's working life. Where possibly building some degree of choice into work is more likely to enhance performance and effectiveness than reduce it.

Exercising responsible choice when the options are available will demonstrate to others that the work can be satisfactorily executed to the standards required and allow the nurse a degree of flexibility in how she goes about her work. Your behaviour – what you are seen to do – exerts a strong influence on those who work with and observe you. The initiation and support of change through your own behaviour is an influential strategy for influencing others.

WHY CHANGE? WHOSE PROBLEM?

The actions of the nurse are at the heart of implementing change – to care practices, to the organization and in the management of a ward or clinic. The nurse occupies an influential 'change' role too in facilitating patients' coming to terms with their medical condition and what this will mean for them in the future.

Effective change leadership occurs:

- when the need for change is clear
- where the scope for change exists
- where there are sufficient resources to enable the change to be carried through successfully
- where there is a shared commitment to change.

Those involved with facilitating change also need to be able to work with the blocks and barriers to change. Many of these will be emotionally-based and will therefore require considerable insight, sensitivity and judgement as to what the underlying issues are and how they may be worked through.

A key feature of successful change initiatives is for those who are affected by them to understand the benefits of the new ways of working for them. Clearly, if there are no perceived benefits – be they financial, status, social, psychological, etc. – then it is more likely that there will be more reluctance to change. If, however, there are some appreciable advantages to those involved in the new arrangements then those changes are likely to be more readily adopted and sustained.

There are some critical questions to be considered when thinking about any change initiative :

* What is the problem?
* Why does it matter?
* Whose problem is it?
* What if nothing is done?
* Who is involved?
* Who is the client?
* When all is said and done, why should we make any changes?

The answers to these questions will give those involved an initial understanding of what the proposed changes are about and why they matter.

A CHANGE PROCESS

As a professional nurse working in a continually changing work environment the facilitation of change is likely to be a continuing responsibility. One way of thinking about change is to keep in mind some means of guiding and ordering your thoughts about what is going on. What follows is a four-stage framework to help guide your thinking and your actions when confronted with 'change situations'.

1 Diagnostic phase

The focus here is on finding out about what is involved and what is being proposed. It means a lot of careful listening and checking out what is being said. This will lead you to be clearer about:

* what is involved
* why it seems to matter
* the primary initiators and those most affected
* the current 'state' of the department, clinic, etc.

2 Building a basis for collective change

Information and understandings from the diagnostic phase are used to build and develop shared views and understandings of what is being proposed and about any difficulties that may exist to making the changes which are planned. Arriving at shared understandings of the need for change is crucial.

3 Helping change happen

Having built a basis for action, the next step is to help, support and facilitate successful outcomes. Such support can be given in many different ways but primarily by:

- remaining focused on the need for change and reminding others of the positive outcomes that will be achieved
- addressing the doubts, worries and fears associated with making changes. This will involve considering not only the stated concerns but also those which colleagues choose not to express openly.

Generally, little progress is made if issues are not attended to, or if everyone pretends that everything is fine when it is not. What is very difficult to handle, however, is the kind of situation where problems exist and yet senior colleagues are not prepared to acknowledge this. Ultimately, if this type of 'organizational denial' persists, considerable problems are likely to arise for that organization. Whilst in the short term staff may prefer to collude with the pretence that 'all is well', all this does is to deny the existence of problems which will fester and erupt in the future.

One way of reducing the risk of this occurring is to emphasize stage two of the framework, ensuring that there are clear understandings about the reason for change, and building a firm and shared basis for it to proceed. In many respects achieving shared understandings about the need for change, and shared commitments to tackle the resistances and difficulties involved in making changes, is the key to successful organizational change.

4 Keeping it going

Here the emphasis shifts to that of securing and maintaining the benefits (physical, psychological, material, etc.) from the changes imposed and embedding them into day-to-day practice. To this end it is useful to have some measures for monitoring the new working arrangements to ensure that they are operating as intended.

Figure 12.2 shows the cyclical nature of this process.

This framework can be used as a basis for planning a change strategy, for reviewing progress on past change initiatives, and for thinking about individualized patient care.

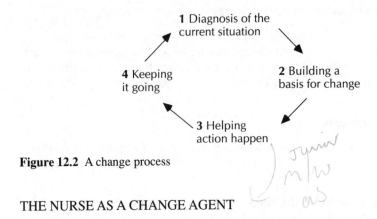

Figure 12.2 A change process

THE NURSE AS A CHANGE AGENT

The nursing role places the nurse at the centre of patient care and at the cross-over point for many of the other carers involved. The nurse's job is a 'busy' one in terms of the interactions involved, and the more senior the nurse, the more 'traffic' has to be handled. It is this high degree of exposure to what is going on that gives the nurse-manager the edge as a positive force for change. Of course, not every nurse views this aspect of the role with glee as it brings with it emotional stresses and strains.

As a 'change agent' however there are contributions which the nurse can make to facilitate the review of current practices and to encourage constructive change. A review of current practice can highlight a need for change to existing ways of working which, when first introduced, were appropriate but which now may no longer be the most appropriate.

There are several roles a nurse can occupy in facilitating a review of existing practice and in helping needed changes happen. Figure 12.3 gives some examples.

Although the formal role of the nurse may limit the scope for facilitating large scale organization change, the nurse's diagnostic and treatment skills can be applied to the nursing part of the organization.

The roles noted in Figure 12.3 are ways through which a nurse can apply

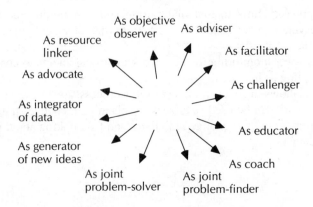

Figure 12.3 Some roles of a change agent

her training and insight to help enhance organization performance. Many may not see the role of the nurse in the way described in this chapter. It is to be hoped that over time more use will be made of the unique perspectives and skills of nurses, not only for patient care but also for the care of the organization as a whole.

EMOTIONAL COMMITMENT TO THE ORGANIZATION

Organizations are not geared exclusively to the achievement of their formally stated business goals. They are also geared to meeting the individual and collective needs of their members.

A person's emotional involvement to their organization can help to explain why at times blatantly clear instructions and directives may not be heeded, and how collective and formally agreed decisions are just not followed through. Not all the confusion that happens at work has to do with inadequate information or misunderstandings; things may not go as planned and expected because those involved do not want them to!

Staff often make a strong psychological investment in work and to their profession, and consequently they have a strong vested interest in anything which threatens what they have become committed to in their professional life.

Recent work from the Centre for Creative Leadership (1995) has emphasized the importance of work group continuity in the morale and facilitation of organizational change. The attachments which we form at work *do* matter a great deal to us: when they are threatened with disruption it is as if we as individuals are under threat too. It should come as no surprise therefore that when we feel such threat we will do what we can to resist and protect ourselves.

In a competitive working environment, such as in the UK in the 1990s, employee resistance may be pushed underground within the organization because to be openly critical of the organization, in a tight employment market, may put those employees' jobs at risk. Indeed the Institute of Management Survey (Charlesworth, 1996) found that the two most stress-inducing work issues were unreasonable deadlines and office politics. Both of these are matters which are rarely discussed openly as to do so is just too dangerous!

REFERENCES AND FURTHER READING

Argyris, C. (1990) *Overcoming Organizational Defences*, Allyn & Bacon, Boston, MA.

Block, P. (1981) *Flawless Consulting*, Learning Concepts, Austin, Texas.

Brunning, H. *et al.* (1990) *The Change Directory*, British Psychological Society, Leicester.

Casemore, R. *et al.* (1994) *What Makes Consultancy Work?* South Bank University Press, London.

Centre for Creative Leadership (1995) *Issues & Observations*, **14** (2) Greensboro, NC, USA.

Charlesworth, K. (1996) *Are Managers Under Stress? A Survey of Management Morale*, Institute of Management, London.

Covey, S. (1992) *The Seven Habits of Highly Effective People*, Simon & Schuster, London.

Fineman, S. and Gabriel, Y. (1996) *Experiencing Organizations*, Sage Publications, London.

Hochschild, A. (1983) *The Managed Heart*, University of California Press, Berkeley, CA.

Kets de Vries, M. (1989) *Prisoners of Leadership*, Wiley, New York.

King, N. (1987) *The First Five Minutes*, Simon & Schuster, London.

Lippitt, G. and Lippitt, R. (1978) *The Consulting Process in Action*, University Associates, La Jolla, USA.

McCalman, J. and Paton, R. (1992) *Change Management*, Paul Chapman Publishing, London.

McKenna, E. (1994) *Business Psychology and Organizational Behaviour*, Lawrence Erlbaum Associates Publishers, Hove.

Morgan, G. (1993) *Imaginization*, Sage Publications, London.

Schwartz, H. (1990) *Narcissistic Process and Corporate Decay*, New York University Press.

Sims, D., Fineman, S. and Gabriel, Y. (1993) *Organizing and Organizations*, Sage Publications, London.

Smale, G. (1996) *Mapping Change and Innovation*, HMSO, London.

Steele, F. (1975) *Consulting for Organizational Change*, University of Massachusetts Press, Amherst, MA.

Stewart, R. (1976) *Contrasts in Management*, McGraw-Hill, Maidenhead.

Stewart, R. (1982) *Choices for the Manager*, McGraw-Hill, London.

Zaleznik, A. (1989) *The Managerial Mystique*, Harper & Row, New York.

Change at work $\boxed{13}$

'Management of change', *'business process re-engineering'*, *'self-managed groups'*, *'empowerment'*, *JIT* ('Just in Time'), *'Kaizen'* (the philosophy of continuing improvement) and the *'learning organization'* – these are some of the labels given to a variety of change initiatives in organizations over the past ten years. The market for such approaches is vast and a large industry has developed to cater to top managers anxious to buy the approach which they hope will help their organization change, solve all their problems and enable them to become more successful.

Many of these approaches were developed for the commercial and manufacturing sector but they have been increasingly applied to the NHS during the last decade. These approaches have been used to tighten-up, re-process the workflow, and define the success and performance criteria needed. The trouble is the success rate of these approaches has been quite variable and, in spite of all the analysis and all the meticulous monitoring of work flow, etc., often the promised benefits have failed to materialize.

Perhaps some of the reasons for this are that the keys to implementing major change are about engaging the commitment of those most affected by the changes as well as reviewing work processes and procedures.

It is very possible that you have had direct experience of management consultants coming in to reorganize the work flow of the hospital or the clinic in which you work, and to assess and measure the 'best' way of doing things. Such work may well be needed but it has to be said that it is not always possible in practice to base the 'best' sequence of actions solely from a logical work flow perspective. The complexity of all the interactions within health care – the work flow, the optimum sequence of tasks, what else is going on at the same time, emergent crises, the 'emotional' tone at the time, fatigue and stress levels, etc. – all combine to make work flow management a very different proposition in a health care organization from an industrial work setting.

All too often the external consultants are given the responsibility for 'sorting it all out', while those most affected tend to be pushed to the side and are not listened to with sufficient care and respect. This puts pressure on the external consultants to show their worth and they will generally come up with the answer which can be shown to work 'if everyone does what is expected of them'. This is the let-out clause because invariably the complexity of life on the ward, etc. is not totally predictable and therefore staff will never be able always to do 'what is expected of them' because of the demands of the job.

At the same time, because of the pressure put on management consultants to sort things out, staff may not be as involved as they could be in working *with* the consultants. The end result is that a less than optimum result is obtained, and one which may have less staff commitment (and understanding) than it could have.

The question for each of us at work in the 1990s is not whether or not to adapt to changing circumstances, so much as how to become more proficient in doing this. As professionals we constantly adapt and adjust our actions in response to the patient information and behaviour. The 'management of change' has become a business in its own right rather than being seen as an integral and ever present facet of working in an organization – something which is part and parcel of everyones' job of work. The challenge for the nurse practitioner is to apply their patient change management skills to their work in the wider organization. Many of the observational and diagnostic skills which a nurse applies to the patient could also be adapted and applied to the care of the organization.

'Change' within the organization elicits similar feelings to those which are provoked by changes to an individual's personal life. Feelings of anxiety, of excitement, unease and confusion will often well up when the possibility of a change to current work practices is suggested. Yet these reactions are often denied and change at work is generally approached 'as if' such emotions do not exist, or as if they should at least be left at home and not brought in to the workplace. Perhaps this forced separation of one's feelings about change are behind why change proposals are so often resisted at work.

This chapter offers some ways of thinking about change at work and some methods for collecting information and planning for change.

THINKING ABOUT CHANGE IN ORGANIZATIONS

A need for change can be identified from within your organization or it can be imposed from outside. This makes a considerable difference to how the proposed changes are viewed, responded to and complied with. Most of us prefer to have a degree of control and influence on what is going on around us rather than being controlled and having our destiny planned for us by others. Hence, internally generated change will generally be more positively viewed by those affected than if the change is imposed from outside the group or organization.

One immediate consequence of this is that the level of resistance to externally dictated change will often be higher than if the work group itself decides that things need to be done differently. There will nevertheless be worries, doubts and some fear generated when decisions about change are made and these need to be acknowledged and worked with. Such emotional concerns should not be brushed aside when decisions about change within an organization are being considered and finalized.

Apprehension, and perhaps fear, about a new and unknown situation is to be expected and this will show itself in the personal reactions and feelings of staff. What will make or break the successful implementation of change is precisely how these very real feelings are handled and accommodated. Successful and productive change may hinge not on the logic and the methodological excellence of the procedures to be introduced but on the care and perceptiveness with which the emotional impacts of the changes have been handled.

Why is change so difficult?

It is difficult to say for certain why change is so difficult to achieve because individuals vary and tend to change from moment to moment. There are some clues, however, that can be borne in mind when thinking about this question. For a start we know that whilst certain attributes and predispositions may be shared with others, each individual is uniquely different so some recognition of individual differences needs to be given even when managing large-scale change.

By and large we want some predictability in life to balance against the ebb and flow of daily living that lies beyond our sphere of influence. We know too that we want some measure of control, and that we want to achieve something for ourselves in life and at work.

Together these factors help a person to define some personal purpose and plan to life. An important part of a person's life-plan is their work-world. It is to be expected therefore that when the stability of a person's working life comes under threat – as it can be seen to be when changes are proposed – this can undermine that person's sense of personal confidence and standing in the world. Small wonder then that change at work assumes such importance and elicits strong emotional reactions.

Securing the positive commitment of those involved is critical in any plan of action. So, if they are likely to be somewhat anxious, reserved or antagonistic to the changes planned, what can be done? What can be done to reduce the confusion and anxiety that change in organizations generates for so many people?

What follows are some suggestions for reducing the sense of disruption that may be experienced.

Reducing the sense of disruption

- *Clarify the changes to be made*:
    - Coherently and consistently state the changes to be made.
    - Explain why the *status quo* must be disrupted.
    - Specify the anticipated timetable.
    - Clarify what is and what is not negotiable.
    - Allow the opportunity to challenge and test the proposals.
    - Provide the opportunity to contribute.
    - Summarize the benefits and losses of the change.

- *Personal impacts*:
    - Acknowledge the personal disruption.

- Specify the impact on each person.
- Offer an opportunity for individual meetings.
- Listen and allow feelings to be expressed.
- Consider the group dynamics involved.
- Work with any work group changes.

- *Specify the future*:
  - Build up a picture of what it could be like.
  - Consider the possible alternatives.
  - Speculate on future career paths.
  - Acknowledge the uncertainties.

- *Details of what to do*:
  - Clarify what is to be required of each person.
  - Confirm when the changes will begin.
  - Specify who is to do what, and to whom.
  - Discuss the project plan.
  - Confirm the immediate next steps.

Some of the ambiguity and uncertainty associated with the changes can be reduced and those involved will be able to start building up a picture in their minds of the new situation and of themselves working within it.

Whilst the disruption associated with any major work change is unlikely to be completely removed by following the above suggestions, some of the emotional tension and strain can be reduced. Perhaps more than any other single action, acknowledging the concern some colleagues may be having about the impact of the changes on them – and then working constructively with this – can do a great deal to facilitate constructive organization change.

If you find yourself responsible for initiating changes in the workplace then you need to:

- explain
- involve
- understand each person's reactions
- focus on the future to be achieved
- be clear about what is/is not negotiable
- address and work with the disruption of any established work groups
- understand the politics of that organization
- be aware of the informal leadership structure and manage it.

Conversely if you are affected by changes at work you need to:

- know what is being proposed
- understand how it will affect you
- be able to give your views
- feel able to get upset and react
- know what is/is not negotiable
- know what the next steps are
- know what the likely timetable will be
- be able to talk to a senior colleague about it all.

Making changes at work, if they are to have a good chance of succeeding, is *not* about the imposition of fully shaped plans for the future from remote senior staff. It is important, if at all possible, to allow scope for those affected to become actively engaged and help in shaping the final outcomes and decisions about the changes to be made.

Change is not a neutral matter and often there will be some who will – or will feel themselves to be – disadvantaged by the change. This will need to be acknowledged and resolved. The successful implementation of organization change is facilitated when the expression of the issues and anxieties of those affected by the changes is encouraged, heeded and addressed. A denial of problems or difficulties will only push the concerns of staff underground and make them even harder to deal with and resolve at a later stage.

How we think about the change influences our responses

One of the most significant determinants of how the planned changes will work out in practice is how those affected *think* about the changes and how they are being implemented. If they think the changes are needed and that they have had an opportunity to make a genuine contribution and shape things, then this is likely to increase the chance of positive outcomes. If, on the other hand, they believe the changes are unnecessary, that they remain unclear about what is to happen and are denied the opportunity to contribute, then the changes are less likely to be successful.

There is a heavy responsibility placed on those charged with guiding and promoting change. The points noted above enlarge, transform even, the change-maker's role from that of telling others what is required to that of explaining and then harnessing emotional commitment towards helping the changes happen.

According to the Institute of Management Survey (Charlesworth, 1996) 'unreasonable deadlines and office politics were identified as the two most stressful work issues by about half of respondents' – stressful, primarily because those experiencing the tension were unable to do much to alleviate their discomfort without putting themselves at risk! 'Office politics' are a common feature of working life.

Underlying these causes of workplace stress is the threat of retaliation – real or imagined – that a staff member risks if they challenge or disagree too strongly with what is being asked of them. 'Organizational power' – what it is, who has it, and how it is applied within an organization – is an important consideration in how staff manage their reactions to workplace change. There are few in any workplace who do not take into account the hierarchical standing of who they are talking to about problems and difficulties at work. Most people will tailor what they say – and how they say it – according to who it is they are speaking to.

The way in which changes are introduced will be affected by:

- the traditions of that organization
- the culture that has developed
- the type of change being made

- the time pressure for the changes to be made
- the confidence and competence of those responsible
- the recent history and track record of the department involved
- the level of trust in that organization
- external business pressures.

These factors are not about the details of the actual changes themselves but about *how* the changes are taken forward. *How* changes are introduced, explained and sustained significantly influences how successful they will be in practice. An example of this would be how the changes to the NHS during the 1990s have been implemented – and experienced – differently across the Service. Both the successes and the failures of these changes, at local level, have been widely reported in the Health Service press. Some of these outcomes will have been due to the manner in which the changes to be made were explained and introduced rather than the details of the specific changes *per se*.

THE EMOTIONALITY OF CHANGE

Change can be imposed. The price for this though may be the sabotaging or, ultimately, a failure of the changes implemented. As noted above, how those affected by the change feel about it will have an effect on how successfully the changes are implemented. In order to remain in employment, to keep on the 'good side' of the boss, or to enhance career prospects nurses *et al.* will often hide their feelings and emotions about the imposed changes.

Managing emotions and behaviour to make ourselves acceptable to the situation is common practice at work (and socially too). It is not hard to recall instances where what colleagues said, and how they said it, contrasted markedly with what they subsequently said in private about the matters being discussed in the formal meeting.

Most of us are skilled in hiding our feelings or, at the very least, in presenting enough of what others expect from us in order to be seen as 'OK'. Whilst too much of a discrepancy between our feelings about an imposed situation will ultimately generate distress and heighten anxiety, many people at work are able to tolerate some measure of *person : organization dissonance* without untoward adverse effects. Problems have started to emerge though in places where staff are required to present a constantly positive and friendly face to customers (examples could be staff in restaurants, or pleasure parks, etc.).

A change is likely to be more successful if those affected – and those responsible for its introduction – feel it to be worthwhile rather than being forced to believe it is appropriate. Two contrasting patterns of thought about any change are:

- *Change Pattern A*:
  - It is worth it.
  - I have a future.
  - I am OK.
  - I can exercise influence.

- *Change Pattern B*:
  - It is unnecessary.
  - There is nothing left for me.
  - I am not OK.
  - There is nothing I can do.

Change pattern A is the one which gives the change a chance of being successfully implemented, and remaining sustainable in the long term. On the other hand, change pattern B is likely to make any meaningful change far harder to achieve, and may ultimately impede the desired benefits.

Each of these change patterns describes some of the emotional reactions of those affected. These reactions may also, of course, describe how some of those who are responsible for implementing the changes may be thinking. In such a case successful organization change will be even harder to achieve if those responsible for promoting the change hold a change pattern B perspective.

For any change some work may need to be done to clarify what the prevailing views are about the planned changes. If most of those affected think in line with change pattern B, this suggests that considerable work will need to be done to:

- convert those involved from pattern B to pattern A thinking, or to
- reconsider the proposed changes in the light of the predominant pattern B thinking.

It seems that many proposed changes are introduced and pushed ahead even if it becomes clear that most of the people on whom the success of the changes depend hold pattern B thinking. This is not a very sound change strategy and, unless staff begin to believe in and see the benefits of the changes being introduced, is likely to fail.

One reason why changes are still pushed ahead even when there is evidence that they will fail is that those committed to the change disregard and discount the information they are receiving because they do not want to hear it.

It will be a rare situation though where everyone affected by a proposed change to working practices and routines feels positive about, and welcomes, them. It is far more likely that there will be some who are very pleased, some who are OK about it all, and a few who are strongly against the change. With such a range of reactions it is prudent to:

- reinforce those who value the changes to be made
- clarify the bases of resistance
- encourage those who are resistant to reconsider what is being proposed to see if their reservations can in some way be allayed.

There are several ways in which this type of assessment, and the whole business in planning for change at work, can be undertaken.

METHODS TO HELP YOU PLAN FOR CHANGE

The change equation

There are three important prerequisites for change:

- a dissatisfaction with the current situation
- a view of what the more desirable future is like
- action steps for beginning the process of change.

Whilst these may be held by just one key and influential person, little progress will be possible until they are *shared* by group of people wanting to change the current situation.

These simple points have been put together into a format called the *change equation*, which sets out an approach for planning and implementing changes. The change equation suggests that three conditions need to be present if a proposed change is to have a chance of success:

- sufficient unease with the current situation for those within it to recognize the need for a change (*shared dissatisfaction*)
- sufficient clarity about the desired future and how it will be better (*shared view of the desired future*)
- clarity about the detailed steps needed to make a start (*shared view about the next steps*).

These three together give a greater chance of your ideas and plans for change to move ahead. If any one of these three is missing then there will be problems. For example, think of the confusion if:

- there is dissatisfaction with the present but no shared view of what should replace it
- it is known what is wanted but not which steps to take
- the desired future state can be envisaged but most people are satisfied and complacent and do not want to make any changes.

Seeking to initiate change with either of the three scenarios noted above is likely to be a fruitless and disruptive venture leading to failure. For a change to have a chance of success, there needs to be dissatisfaction with the present, a view of the desired future, and a plan of action which details the steps to be taken. In addition, each of these components needs to be *shared* within the group.

There are costs involved in making changes: these may be financial, disruption to business, emotional and psychological costs. It may be that when all these factors are fully considered a decision is taken to 'stay as we are'. The change equation as shown in Figure 13.1 indicates that unless the benefits of the changes proposed are assessed against the costs involved then a clear decision about whether or not to make changes cannot readily be made.

The change equation is a practical and user-friendly framework that can be used to shape and guide change plans and proposals. As an exercise it can be usefully applied to one or more of the following, as well as to workplace matters:

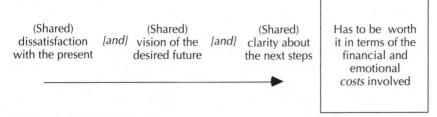

Figure 13.1 The change equation

- deciding where to go on holiday
- deciding what house to move to
- deciding to change the car.

Lewin's force field analysis

Another practical and enduring approach to planning for change is *force field analysis* which gives:

- a way of diagnosing a situation
- a means of planning for change
- a way of implementing a change strategy and programme.

It suggests that any situation can be looked at as if it were the result of a balance between conflicting forces and pressures. According to this approach, there will be one set of influences and pressures *pushing for a change* and a different set *pushing to keep things as they are*, the result of this interplay of influences having resulted in the current position. So, whilst we may look at a situation as given and quite stable, this is in fact an illusion. In effect any situation is really a state of 'dynamic equilibrium' between these two sets of forces.

In reality therefore, any situation is far more unstable than it appears to be, or is presented as being. The force field analysis approach suggests that change will occur when the interplay of the various forces and influences at play in that situation alter. You change the net effect of the influences involved and the situation will realign itself into a new 'dynamic equilibrium'!

This approach raises a radically different way of trying to change any situation. Rather than – as is often the case – trying to force others to change their view, the notion of the force field suggests that if you are able to reduce some of their reasons for resisting the change then a change would be more likely to occur.

One of the key skills involved here is a diagnostic one of looking to see what the resistances are, of trying to understand why colleagues may be that way, and seeing what can be done to ease their fears (or reduce some of the resisting forces). For example, it may emerge that considerable anxiety is provoked by the proposals for change and at the heart of these are:

- fears about personal competence in the new situation
- fear of failure

- worries about job security and tenure
- distrust of management (or nurses, doctors, psychologists, GPs *et al.*), etc.

All of these are quite reasonable but the way to reduce them is probably through explaining more fully what is involved, talking about job security, etc., rather than by increasing the pressure on people to accept the changes being proposed.

The example in Figure 13.2 comes from a colleague who was concerned about a possible conflict between her desire to do a good job and her responsibilities as a wife and mother. This emerged during a seminar and the senior health professional found it to be a valuable and practical exercise. The approach identified a number of actions she could take – with regard to both the driving and the restraining forces – which would help ease her situation.

Concentrating on the restraining forces, she established that:

- her husband could take over some of the burden of running the family if he accepted her wish to continue as a professional carer
- the other staff could be more involved, thus reducing her workload and the pressure on her – and probably building up staff morale
- talking about the 'forces' with other colleagues and within the family would help to review the overall situation.

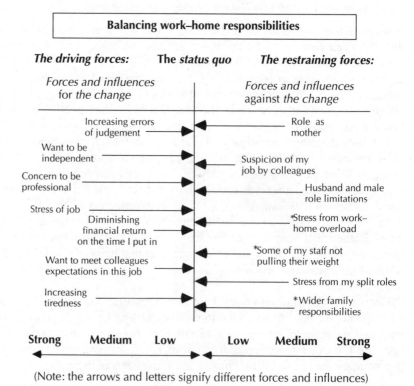

(Note: the arrows and letters signify different forces and influences)

Figure 13.2 An example of a force field analysis

The important thing about these, and other points which she raised in discussion, is that she looked at the underlying influences and forces, as well as the obvious ones in building up a more comprehensive assessment of her situation. She found that there were a number of ways in which it might be possible for her to reduce the restraining forces (ones which were blocking the changes she wanted to happen) and thus help the change to occur. When some of the restraining forces are reduced, this model predicts that the overall position will alter and a new *status quo* will become established.

In Figure 13.2 the asterisked restraining forces are those where she decided it was possible to make a change in the short term and over time changes to these would subsequently have an effect on some of the other forces too.

In this case, the carer decided to make a start by concentrating on the three asterisked restraining forces. By encouraging her staff to take more of the workload which was legitimately theirs her work overload would reduce; through more contact with colleagues they were likely to become less suspicious about her job and role, and in turn the stress from her 'split roles' would decline, and so on.

One of the benefits of a force field analysis is that the interconnections between different influences and forces are more easily seen, and this can help you decide which influences should be worked on first.

To use this approach, first build up a force field analysis around the issue you wish to change. Include all the forces which you think affect the situation and do this in as open and creative a way as possible, making sure you include those influences and forces which may at first seem 'silly' or ill-founded. The key to getting the most from a force field analysis is to make it as complete as you possibly can.

Then revise your first attempt. This time put similar influences and forces together so that you make your diagram easier to handle and work with. Then look to see if there are any common themes which you can cluster several items under and decide how strong each of the forces are. This way you may decide that an initial strategy is to reduce some of the strong resistant forces but to try to remove completely a couple of the weaker ones.

A force field analysis gives you a complementary change strategy to one of just pushing harder and harder for what you want to happen. One of the unwanted outcomes from pushing too strongly for a change is that the people you want to change can become even more intransigent and difficult to budge. The more you try to push the more they dig in to their position of opposition. Stalemate!

The real delight of Lewin's approach is that a change can also be brought about by reducing some of the resisting forces, not solely by increasing the pressure for change. So 'change' is not just about pushing harder for something to happen, it is about:

- understanding more fully the situation you are working on and
- seeing if some of the resistances and blocks to action can be reduced or even eliminated. This can then lead to a rebalancing of that situation and the chance of a change taking place.

The gap model

One of the most frequently used methods for charting a programme of change is the *gap model*. Essentially it asks two key questions. The first is 'Where do we want to be?', and the second is 'Where are we now?' If there is a difference – a gap – between the two, this then forms the basis for a programme of change.

What that programme of change will consist of is determined by the various gaps identified. For example, there may be a gap between the level of service currently provided at the point of care delivery and the standard of service desired, or there could be a 'gap' in the speed with which bloods are returned from the lab from the response rate that is needed. Once the desired future position has been defined, the current levels of performance are assessed against the future position, and the detailed changes to be made to reach the desired future position are specified as shown in Figure 13.3.

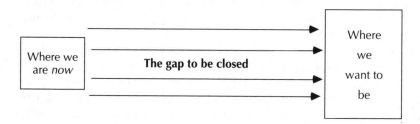

Figure 13.3 An outline gap analysis

1. *Where we are now*: Assess this in terms of the criteria that are important to your situation and which are relevant to the changes you want to make (for example, services provided, performance to budget, financial limits, Patient's Charter standards, staff flexibility, response rates, care levels, staff turnover, etc.).
2. *Define the desired future*: Build up as complete a picture as you can to give everyone the clearest perceptions possible (using the same dimensions as in 1 above) of what standards need to be achieved.
3. *Defining the gap*: Compare 1 and 2 above and specify as precisely as possible the major differences between the current and the desired future position. The differences identified then give a clear indication of the scope and detail of the changes that need to be completed to move to the desired future position. This can be formally summarized into a 'change agenda' and because of the detail and precision taken to specify the changes to be made it can also be used as a basis for monitoring progress.

An associated technique which is commonly used to complement a gap analysis is the SWOT analysis (strengths, weaknesses, opportunities and threats). Used in combination with a gap assessment a SWOT analysis will provide information about the overall ability of the organization to reach the desired future position and it can highlight where some of the changes needed may be particularly difficult to accomplish.

A strengths, weaknesses, opportunities and threats assessment can be undertaken for each ward, clinic, clinical directorate or hospital, Trust or NHSE department. Usually they are shown in the format shown in Figure 13.4. This format sums up in one 'go' the overall picture.

Strengths • • • • •	Weaknesses • • • •
Opportunities • • •	Threats • •

Figure 13.4 A SWOT format

Often when change is being discussed it is very easy to forget the strengths about the department. A SWOT analysis is very helpful in reminding those involved of the good things about the ward (clinic, directorate or Trust) upon which to build in the period ahead. A SWOT analysis can also reinforce some of the characteristics of the organization that must not change, something that can be overlooked in the pressure to perform.

One of the most influential management books of the last two decades was *In Search of Excellence* by Peters and Waterman (1982). Interestingly many of the organizations they highlighted as exemplars of organizational excellence are far less successful now, and some have gone out of business! What can so often happen is that organizations lose their way as they become successful. They forget what made them successful in the first place and they can become so self-satisfied that they fail to keep track of what is happening in their marketplace and start to fail.

The critical mass

When any change is proposed the support of a few key people will be vital to any chance that change initiative will have of being successfully implemented. In most organizations there are just a few people who exercise considerable influence on the opinions of others. The support of as many of these people as possible is a necessary and critical prerequisite for success. For any change these colleagues need to be identified.

The first step is to make a list of who it is that you see to be influential in helping or impeding implementation of the specific changes desired. Then for each person decide whether or not they will:

- support
- help
- allow

- hinder
- block

what you are trying to do.

Or it may be they are uninterested. Deciding which of these categories each person falls into will help clarify how difficult or straightforward the planned change is likely to be. For example, if none of these key people fall into the 'block' category then the proposed changes are going to be far easier to move forward than if two or three of this group are in the 'hinder' or 'block' category. If that is the case work will need to be done to find out why they are reticent about the proposed changes and what can be done to reassure them so that they will not impede the work to be done.

Building up an assessment of the *critical mass* for the specific changes you want to implement is an important task and should not be neglected in the planning for any change initiative. A very good way of doing this is for each member of the change team to do their own list of critical mass and to assess independently which category they fit into. Then these views are shared together and a plan to tackle any difficulties identified can be agreed.

PEOPLE, SECURITY, DEVELOPMENT AND TASKS

The process and dynamics of change can be so controversial because they deeply affect a person's sense of stability and confidence in the future. One of the advantages of a 'no-change' strategy at work is the degree of certainty this can provide, as well as the opportunity to become proficient in undertaking work which, by and large, is predictable.

Change by definition means that this level of predictability – and the level of proficiency attained – becomes threatened as soon as the possibility of a change at work is contemplated. Change poses a threat to a person's sense of security and has implications for:

- *People and tasks*: the extent to which the impact will be on changes in the nature of the work to be done or to the type of carers needed for the future
- *Security and development*: the degree to which the changes will be experienced as reducing the security of the existing arrangements or provide significant developmental opportunities for the future.

Some changes will affect each of these four dimensions whereas others will primarily impact on only one or two of them. Figure 13.5 suggests what might characterize each of the four quadrants.

The relative weighting of these four dimensions – people, security, development and tasks (PSDT) – will affect the tone, pattern and intensity of the changes being made. For example, whilst there will always be some element of personal anxiety and uncertainty generated by change at work, this will be heightened when the changes are mostly to do with the people domain. In turn, if the changes are principally concerned with routine procedural changes (perhaps security and tasks) then the emotional and personal anxiety component will be reduced.

Figure 13.5 Personal implications of change at work

You can use this framework to determine where you see the major impact of the changes falling. You can also use it to highlight any potential mismatches in the way the changes are being introduced. For example, if the changes are mostly to do with people then a lot of attention and effort must be given to exploring the personal implications of the changes on those staff most affected. However, if you see that this is not being done, with most of the attention being given to the detailed (tasks) job specifications, for example, attention could be drawn to this mismatch and the necessary change in emphasis could then be made.

FINAL THOUGHTS

Personal change and organizational change involve complex processes and it is difficult to predict what the final outcome of any change initiative will be because of the very many influences and factors which are involved. What is known is that change is a deeply emotional matter and even seemingly straightforward and needed changes can unleash intense emotional reactions from those affected by the proposals being made.

It is acknowledging, understanding and working with these forces that makes the 'management of change' somewhat of a misnomer because it could be argued that it is not possible to ever totally manage change as such. Perhaps the best we can do is to acknowledge the complexity of change processes and pay more attention to why change is so difficult to achieve.

REFERENCES AND FURTHER READING

Bor, R. and Miller, R. (1991) *Internal Consultation in Health Care Settings*, Karnac Books, London.

Brunning, H., Cole, C. and Huffington, C. (1990) *The Change Directory*, British Psychological Society, Leicester.

Carter, R. *et al.* (1984) *Systems, Management and Change*, Harper & Row, London.

Charlesworth, K. (1996) *Are Managers Under Stress? A Survey of Management Morale*, Institute of Management, London.

Collins, J. and Porras, J. (1966) *Built to Last*, Century Ltd, London.

Covey, S. (1992) *The Seven Habits of Highly Effective People*, Simon & Schuster, London

Fineman, S. (1993) *Emotion in Organizations*, Sage, London.

Harrison, R. (1995) *Consultant's Journey,* McGraw-Hill, Maidenhead.

Harrison, R. (1995) *The Collected Papers of Roger Harrison*, McGraw-Hill, Maidenhead.

Levinson, H. (1972) *Organizational Diagnosis*, Jossey-Bass, San Francisco.

McCalman, J. and Paton, R. (1992) *Change Management*, Paul Chapman, London.

Mitrani, A. *et al.* (1992) *Competency Based Human Resource Management*, Kogan Page, London.

Ohmae, K. (1990) *The Borderless World*, Collins, London.

Peters, T. and Waterman, R. (1982) *In Search of Excellence*, Harper & Row, New York.

Smale, G. (1996) *Mapping Change and Innovation*, HMSO, London.

Spurgeon, P. and Barwell, F. (1991) *Implementing Change in the NHS*, Chapman & Hall, London.

Trompenaars, F. (1993) *Riding the Waves of Culture*, Nicolas Brealey, London.

Watson, T. (1994) *In Search of Management*, Routledge, London.

Looking to the future $\boxed{14}$

Working as a professional within the NHS of the 1990s is a very different experience to that of earlier times in its evolution. There have been changes for the better and there are no doubt regrets about the loss of some features which characterized it as an employer in the past.

What is clear though is that the legislation of the 1990s has transformed the overall structure of the Service and the nature of the relationships between its constituent parts – principally the operational relationship between the Purchasers and the Providers. However the relationship between the NHSE, and with patients and the community at large has also altered radically.

Patient expectations, patient knowledge about their conditions and what is available to them has also significantly changed the once sacrosanct relationship between patient and carer. The Patient's Charter, league tables, tight funding limits, internal competition, and more knowledgeable consumers keeps the NHS in the spotlight and increases the pressure on the Service to perform – with perfection – at all levels and in all circumstances however difficult.

Whilst an unrealistic expectation this continues, by and large, to remain an expectation held by many. The impact of internal competition for resources and for client populations to provide services for, combined with a high level of scrutiny from the public *et al.*, increases the pressure to perform within the Service. This is the scenario for health care and it is one that puts a premium on carers becoming more able to understand the non-clinical pressures of their work, and ways through which they can become more robust as a people in coping well with the changes at work noted above.

To do this carers need to know about the features set out in Figure 14.1.

Knowing about these matters will enable the carer to cope better in the future by being more aware of what is happening around them as they go about their clinical responsibilities. A failure to consider each of these main areas can lead the carer to become confused, more anxious and self-protective about some of the pressures that will be encountered on a regular basis.

Part One, for example, touched on the history of health care in the UK and on some important features of organizational life, such as how the internal culture of your organization can exert a profound influence on how things are done, and how it is very difficult to alter the *status quo* at work too. The style of the Chief Executive, the Chairperson, the key clinicians

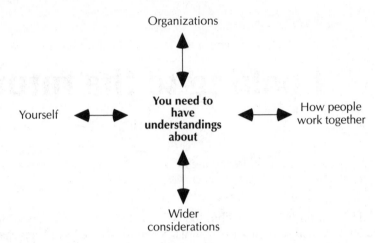

Figure 14.1 Coping in the future

also exerts tremendous influence on what goes on within the Trust, in the clinic, and so on.

Attending to the internal dynamics between the key influential figures – including yourself – is yet another dimension that can and does affect the personal and the collective well-being of people at work. When you work inside an organization there are pressures put on you to conform to the local ways of doing things, and in return benefits such as security, mutual support, group cohesion, prospects, professional status and protection are offered. Being part of any organization differentiates you, and your colleagues, from those who are not part of that 'community'; this places expectations on you and imposes restrictions on what you can and cannot do.

Also fundamental changes to your work and standing can be initiated from outside your organization which can challenge and change the whole structure of care provision. In turn this can affect what, and how, you want to function as a professional.

To remain effective it is necessary to keep these constraints in mind and decide – whilst remaining ethical, caring and pragmatic – how to work within them, and where appropriate, help them to be reviewed and where necessary to be changed.

This book has looked at some of the ways in which carers' wider world of work in the NHS has changed in the mid-1990s and the implications this has had for the practising nurse delivering care. Delivering direct patient care, exercising management, providing leadership, and managing the resources of any health care organization can no longer be looked at only on a local basis.

This book places management and leadership ideas into the context of the changing dynamics of the NHS at local level, and as an integral aspects of all carers. Ideas about leadership and management should help everyday practice in some way whether this be working with a patient or their relatives; in relating to colleagues; in the making of a difficult choice between fundamentally different business options and in coping with the pressures and strains of it all.

This book has been organized around the four main domains set out in Figure 14.1. By working through the ideas and perspectives introduced in this book about each of these areas, you will be more alert to the types of issues which may arise and more aware of the stresses and pressures which may be experienced. Importantly you will be more able to cope and work through such day-to-day pressures.

When issues arise it will be easier to:

- identify where they seem to be coming from
- be able to make more sense of them as part of the broader perspective on the organization and its workings
- put them into a broader perspective (i.e. broader than a ward issue)
- deal with them in a more informed manner
- think which aspects of the broader picture need to change and in what way – build up a shared change agenda
- contribute to facilitating change.

Without a broader view of your organization, and of the impact of the changes at local level within the NHS, it is harder to cope with experienced pressures because there is no wider context within which they can be positioned. The absence of a wider context also can lead a carer to feel increasingly that the job is getting them down no matter what they do, that they are slowly being pulled apart, and that it is their fault (and not part of a wider picture). Of course, issues and problems at work can result from a person's poor performance in some respect but this will not always be the case. Each of us needs to keep in mind the broader perspective within which we do our work.

Whilst each of us will be prone to see things from a parochial perspective – and thus miss the bigger picture and opportunities to influence and change things – this book invites you to keep the broader context *and* the local situation in mind at the same time.

Index